SCALE MODELS

SCALE MODELS

Houses of the 20th Century

Edited by
Friedrich Kurrent

Verlag Anton Pustet
Salzburg · München

Birkhäuser – Publishers for Architecture
Basel · Boston · Berlin

Translation from German into English: Gail Schamberger, Salzburg
Copy-Editing: Claudia Mazanek, Vienna
Layout: Franz Wimmer
Collaboration: Christian Hartranft, Thomas Wilnhammer
Printing: Salzburger Druckerei

A CIP catalogue record for this book is available from the Library of Congress, Washington D.C., USA.

Deutsche Bibliothek Cataloging-in-Publication Data

Scale models : houses of the 20ᵗʰ century / ed. by Friedrich Kurrent.
Transl. from German into English: Gail Schamberger. - Basel ;
Boston ; Berlin : Birkhäuser, 1999
    Einheitssacht.: Raummodelle ‹eng.›
    ISBN 3-7643-6102-6 (Basel ...)
    ISBN 0-8176-6102-6 (Boston)

Printed on acid-free paper produced from chlorine-free pulp. TCF ∞

Printed in Austria

ISBN 3-7643-6102-6
ISBN 0-8176-6102-6

9 8 7 6 5 4 3 2 1

Contents

Houses

Hans Luckhardt (1890–1954)
Wassili Luckhardt (1889–1972)

André Lurçat (1894–1970)

Ernst May (1886–1970)

Richard Meier (1934)

Konstantin Melnikov (1890–1974)

Ludwig Mies van der Rohe (1886–1969)

Richard Neutra (1892–1970)

Robert Örley (1876–1945)

Jacobus Johannes Pieter Oud (1890–1963)

Jože Plečnik (1872–1957)

Ernst Anton Plischke (1903–1992)

Gerrit Rietveld (1888–1964)

Appendix

Anonymous buildings

Religious buildings

Dominikus Zimmermann (1685–1766)

Cosmas Damian Asam (1686–1739)

Johann Michael Fischer (1692–1766)

Jože Plečnik (1872–1957)

This documentation shows some 200 scale models, primarily of 20th-century houses designed by distinguished architects, together with a few anonymous houses and religious buildings.

The scale models were constructed – over a period of more than twenty years and with the help of assistants and the woodwork supervisor – by students of architecture at the Department of Interior Design and Religious Building in the Technical University in Munich, which I have directed from 1973. They are built to the scale 1 : 33 $^1/_3$ (religious buildings 1 : 50) and can be taken apart and reassembled, to convey more readily the ideas of movement, succession of rooms and distribution of light, and to facilitate comprehension of the three-dimensional construction. The examples used are not only existing buildings, but also unrealised projects which, through being rendered in three dimensions, afford for the first time a vivid impression of the design.

In the teaching of architecture, these exercises were intended principally to train the capacity to visualise in three dimensions – which I consider the architect's prime qualification. To this extent, the purpose was not so much the development of a "naturalistic" model, but the learning process that arises from working out the interior correlation and the exterior form of a building.

Scale models have already been shown at exhibitions of the work of Adolf Loos, Jože Plečnik, Rudolph Schindler, Lois Welzenbacher, Josef Frank, Theodor Fischer and Hans Döllgast, in Munich and other places, as well as some years ago a small selection in the Kreibig Museum in Munich.

Munich, spring 1999   Friedrich Kurrent

Thanks to the following persons, institutions and companies for their co-operation on both the catalogue and the exhibition: Professor W. A. Herrmann, President of the Technical University, Munich; the Berberich Foundation of the Technical University, Munich; Communications department of the Bavarian Hypotheken und Wechsel-Bank AG; Dietmar Preisler, Munich; "Südhausbau", Paul Ottmann, Munich; Lindner, Arnstorf; Bartenbach Lighting Studio, Aldrans/Tirol; Alanod, Ennepetal; Osram, Munich; Walter Schreiber Transport, Munich; "Aktionsforum Praterinsel" represented by Cornelia Faist and Ruth Scala; Mona Leitner of the Anton Pustet Verlag, Salzburg – Munich.

Houses

Alvar Aalto
1898–1976

Summerhouse in Muuratsalo
Finland
1953

Scale model 1 : 33 ¹/₃
Klaus Chrubasik

This experimental house by the Finnish architect Alvar Aalto is situated in a remote spot, surrounded by high trees, on the banks of one of the many small inland lakes in central Finland. Originally, the house was accessible only by boat. One wing of the L-shaped house contains the low-ceilinged bedrooms, the other the large, galleried, high-ceilinged living-room and study, with the kitchen, bathroom and entrance in the intersecting area. The high end walls extend, each with a large aperture, to form a rectangle, enclosing a courtyard or open-air room of some 9 × 9 m. The interior courtyard walls are divided into some fifty squares and rectangles faced with a wide variety of bricks and ceramic tiles, so that the light effects can be observed through the changing seasons.
F. W.

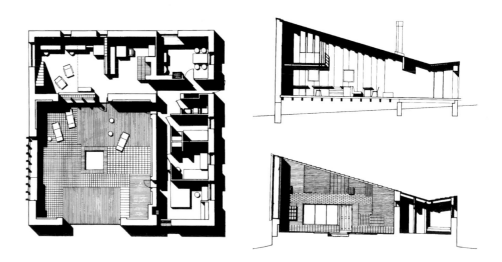

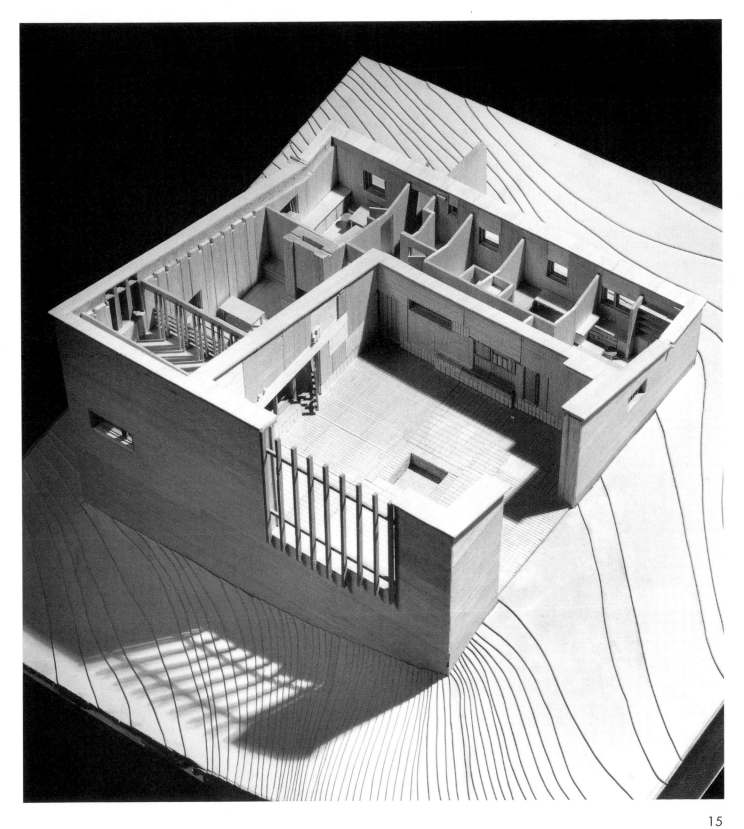

Gunnar Asplund
1885–1940

**Summerhouse
for the architect Stennäs
Stockholm
1937**

Scale model 1 : 33 ¹/₃
Peter Krieger
Viktoria Weberling

Asplund's small summerhouse was one of his last buildings. He had started work on his masterpiece, the crematorium in the forest cemetery in Stockholm, the extension buildings for the Göteborg town hall had just been completed, and his earlier buildings in Stockholm, such as the Skandia cinema and the municipal library, had already become classics. The summerhouse has a modest exterior, in the spirit of traditional Swedish architecture, but the interior is subtly diversified. The long, narrow ground plan contains a line of rooms on four successive levels, leading from the kitchen on the north side through the bedrooms, to the large living-room on the south side with a view over the sea. The slight angle at which the living-room is set gives the dining-area light from the south and a sea view, as well as allowing direct access from the covered west-facing terrace to the living-room. F. W.

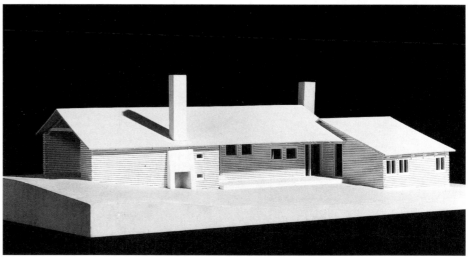

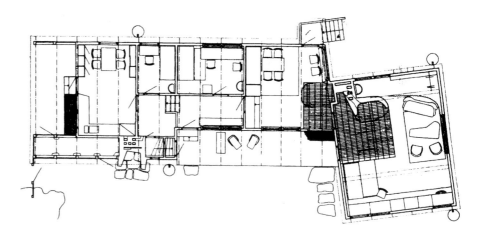

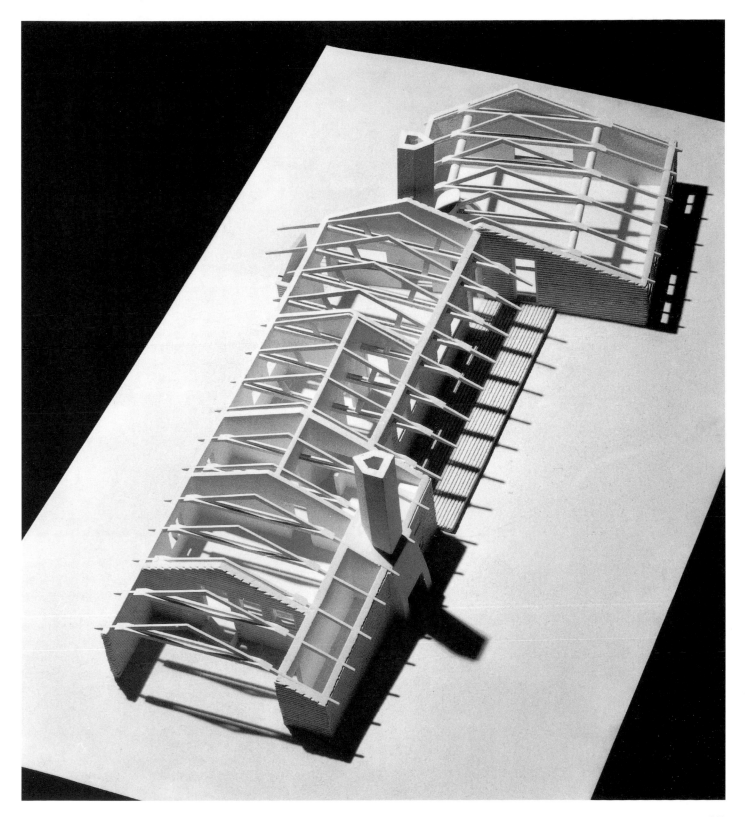

Anton Brenner
1898–1957

Vienna Werkbund housing estate Engelbrechtweg 9/11
1932

Scale model 1 : 33 ¹/₃
Rainer Brunke
Helmut Huber

For this estate, Anton Brenner designed single-storey houses with a living-area of 63 m².

The living-room and bedrooms are grouped in an L-shape around a courtyard, which serves as an "open-air room" in the shelter of the overall cubic form. The entrance hall, kitchen, bathroom and access to the cellar are all on the north side.

Anton Brenner sees the future in the single-storey estate house, where the owner can find privacy and refuge from the increasingly hectic bustle of life; so he harks back to the ancient Roman atrium house, which combines the advantages of a flat – everything on one level – with those of an economical terrace house close to nature.

"Similarly to this idea, in my design the living-room and bedrooms are grouped round a courtyard, offering – with flower borders, pergola and paddling-pool – a complete open-air living-room which, curtained off from the open garden, allows the family to shower and sunbathe in peace. According to the orientation, the living-room and bedrooms are on the sunny side, facing the garden, the side and utility rooms to the north, facing the street." (Anton Brenner, Das ebenerdige Siedlungshaus)
S. M.

Le Corbusier
1887–1965

**Schwob villa
La Chaux-de-Fonds
1916**

*Scale model 1 : 33 ¹/₃
Anke Herrmann
Petra Wiedemann*

The house for the watch manufacturer Hans Bieri is the last building – his final early work, so to speak – that the architect Charles-Édouard Jeanneret erected in his home town before abandoning it for Paris and calling himself Le Corbusier.

During the preceding years, the following houses had been built in the same town: Fallet (1905), Stotzer (1908), Jacquemet (1908), Jeanneret-Perret (1912), and the Scala Cinema.

On a ground plan of 11 × 11 m, Jeanneret erected a ferroconcrete skeleton construction covered in brick, a solid concrete ledge round the roof area, and two symmetrically-set apse-like extensions.

The central split-level living-room has a large south-facing window. The building as a whole has a sculptural effect and the proportions are convincing. "Le Corbusier's villa is more than a house, it is an architecture." It was restored in 1957/58 by the Milan architect Angelo Mangiarotti.

F. W.

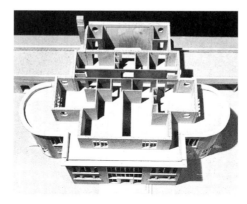

Le Corbusier
1887–1965

Citrohan house project
1920

Scale model 1 : 33 $^1/_3$
Hans Konrad
Martina Täube

The designs for the so-called Citrohan house are the starting-point for Le Corbusier's research and experimental work on the subject of industrially produced residential units. The reference in the name to the French car manufacturer Citroën shows on the one hand Le Corbusier's enthusiasm for technology, and on the other his desire for the mass-production of this type of house.

The ideal living-quarters should be achieved on the basis of new forms and constructions, by dividing the space as functionally as possible ("It is a crime to built toilets with a floor area of four square metres."), by keeping the building costs within the reach of every worker, by using standard forms, industrial prefabrication and standardisation of constructional elements.

According to Le Corbusier and Pierre Jeanneret, they found the idea for the arrangement of the rooms in this Citrohan type when they visited a small Paris restaurant called "Le Zinc": "[...] in the background is the kitchen; a gallery divides the height of the restaurant, and the whole thing is open towards the street. [...] a large opening at each end; two lateral load-bearing walls with a flat roof – a box, in fact, that can very well serve as a house."
F. W.

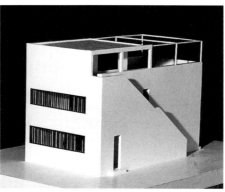

Le Corbusier
1887–1965

Mass-produced house project for workers
1920

Scale model 1 : 33 ⅓
Andreas Deilmann
Anette Kreye

The house is designed as a free-standing one-room type suitable for mass production. It consists of a small cube with sparing but clever use of windows.
The floor area is 7 × 7 m, the height 4.5 m. The placing of the gallery makes the room seem larger, since the diagonal is about 10 m.
The roof surfaces slope inwards, and are drained through the support in the exact centre of the room.
F. W.

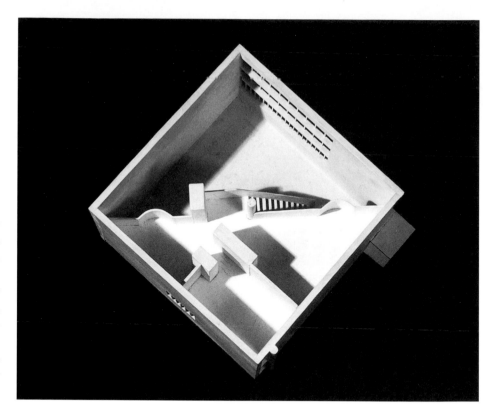

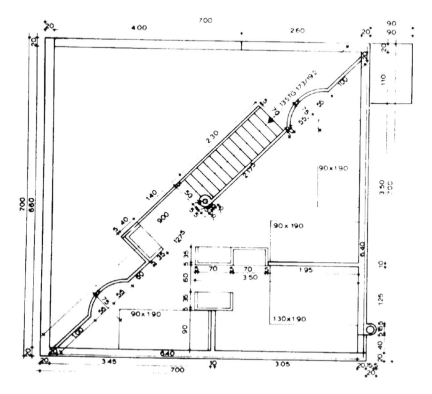

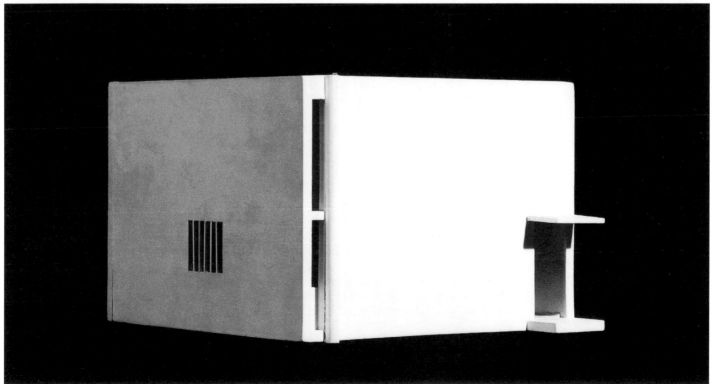

Le Corbusier
1887–1965

Citrohan house project (variant with terrace for the "Salon d'Automne" in Paris) 1922

Scale model 1 : 33 $^1/_3$
Inge Dinauer
Carola Dornstädter

The Citrohan type was further developed for the 1922 "Salon d'Automne", with a view to a systematic standardisation of the structural elements.

The load-bearing construction was planned in concrete, to be poured directly on the site and erected by crane. The walls are to be formed with double shuttering, and the windows designed like factory windows, with practical sliding sections.

The ground floor is reserved for utility rooms and garage space, and is contrasted with the other storeys by the surrounding pillars. The spacious two-storey living-quarters, with a terrace in front, begin on the first floor; the kitchen and dining-area are on two levels in the rear, and a bedroom with a gallery above.

On the fourth level are the children's rooms, with a sun-terrace in front.

The internal height of all four levels is 2.12 m. This gives the split-level living-room – with a ceiling construction 30 cm thick – an internal height of 4.6 m.

F. W.

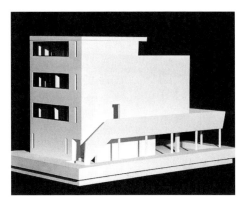

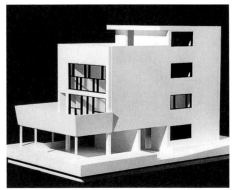

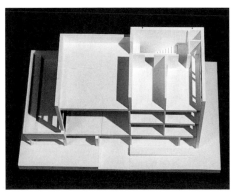

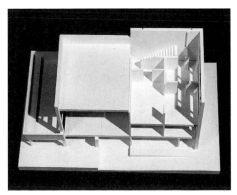

Le Corbusier
1887–1965

Auteuil house project
1922

Scale model 1 : 33 ¹/₃
Stefan Franz
Georg Stöttner

This project is the first study for the pair of semi-detached houses for La Roche and Albert Jeanneret.

The principles developed in the Citrohan type are applied here in a modified form with generous dimensions.

On the ground floor, besides garages and a integrated flatlet, is an entrance hall from which a half-newelled staircase leads up to the main level on the first floor. An open ramp leads through the split-level living-room to the gallery level with the library, and behind it the bedrooms. The fourth level is the flat roof – partly covered, partly open sun-terrace.

In contrast to the Citrohan projects, which are designed as free-standing, the Auteuil project is designed as a terraced house, so that the light enters the rooms through the long sides of the building.
F. W.

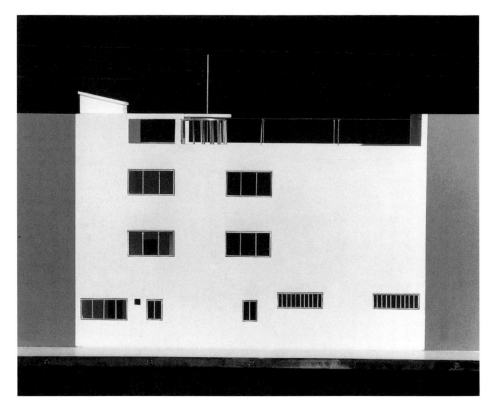

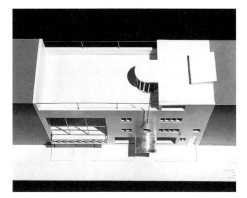

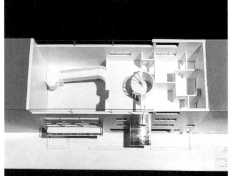

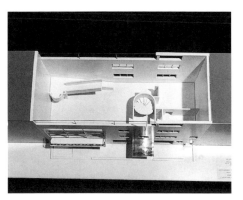

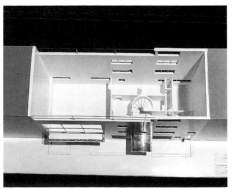

Le Corbusier
1887–1965

"House for an artist" project
1922

Scale model 1 : 33 $^1/_3$
Thomas Kiermeyer
Thomas Rasche

The project is designed as a free-standing house with living-quarters and a studio for an artist, and should be surrounded by a garden with fruit-trees.
A single straight outside staircase leads directly into the living- and sleeping-quarters.
The studio proper is at the top, with a partly vaulted ceiling opening to form a north light, giving the room extra light. The vaulted roof of the studio and the offset semicylindrical interior staircase give the house its volumetrically unmistakable character.
F. W.

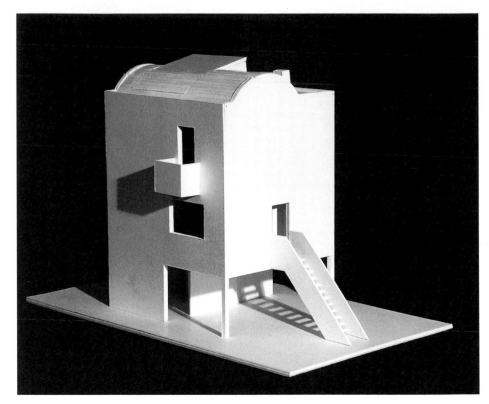

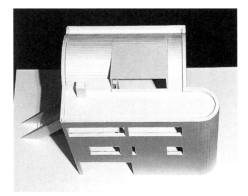
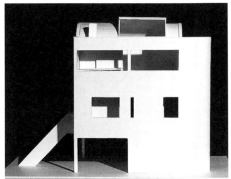

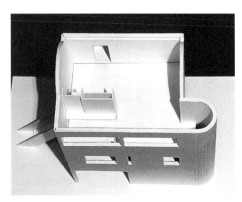
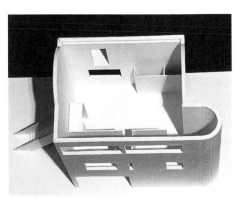

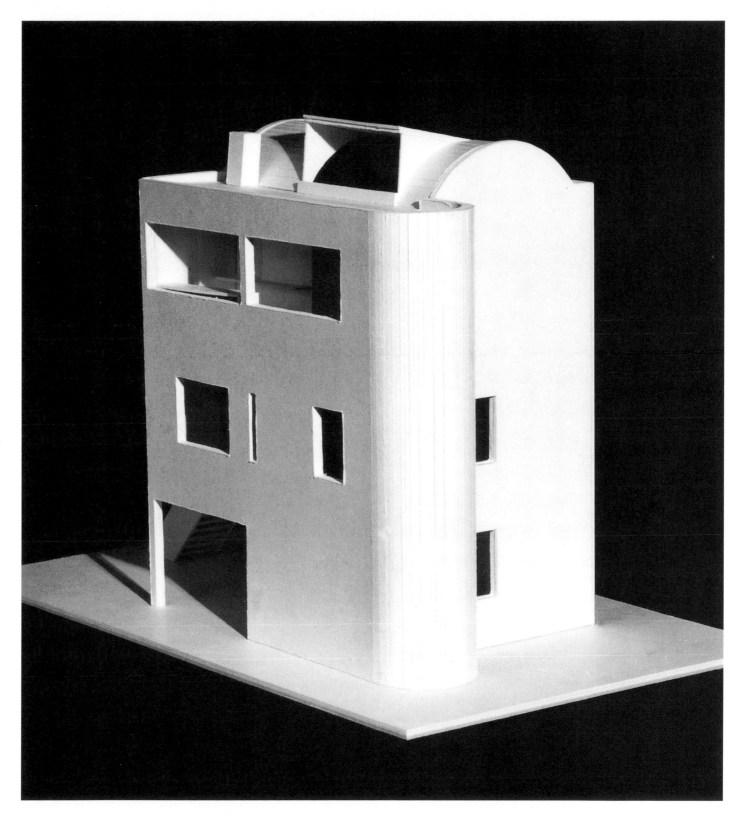

Le Corbusier
1887–1965

**Ozenfant house
Paris
1922**

*Scale model 1 : 33 ¹/₃
Wolfgang Häusler*

Through the architect Auguste Perret, with whom he had worked in his early years, Le Corbusier made the acquaintance of the Parisian painter Amédée Ozenfant, who advocated a trend in painting which he called Purism. This friendship was in many ways stimulating for Le Corbusier, who himself began to paint in 1918, at the age of 31.

The Ozenfant house stands on an irregularly-shaped site at the corner of Avenue Reille / Place de Montsouris. The upper storey is dominated by the large studio with a glassed corner and two north lights. The living-area is on the lower floor.

The ground floor with a garage and a small integrated flatlet is designed rather like a basement, in strong contrast to the brighter upper floors.
F. W.

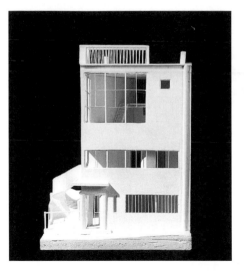

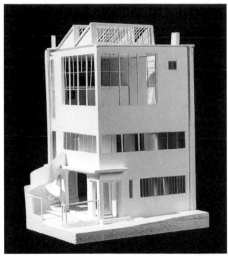

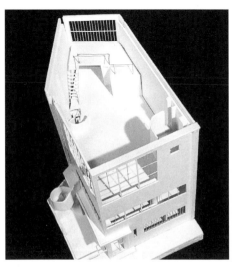

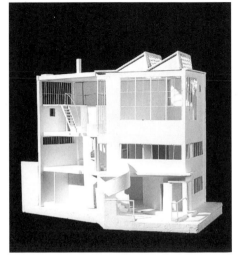

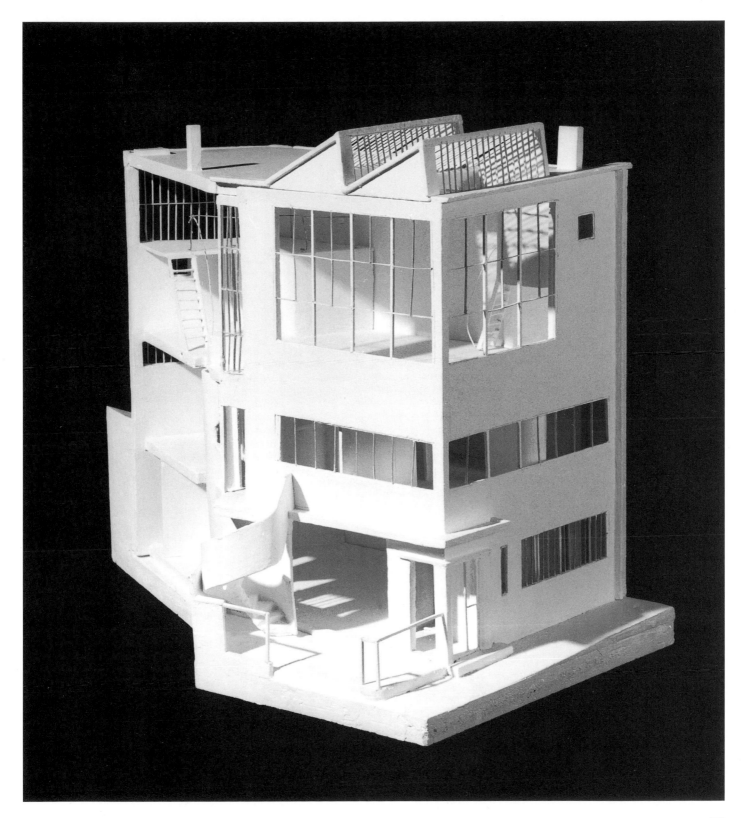

Le Corbusier
1887–1965

Besnus villa
Vaucresson
1922

Scale model 1 : 33 ¹/₃
Norbert Reinfuß
Christine Sailer

"It was with this house in Vaucresson that Le Corbusier's real involvement with architecture began," he writes retrospectively in his autobiography. The characteristic staircase is attached laterally, as an independent element bordered with glass. Only very few parts, such as the small bay window of the library or the projecting balcony which also serves as a roof over the entrance, stand out as sculptural elements from the strictly cubic building.

The principle of the "open floor plan" is also applied here; the bathroom is placed in the middle of the bedroom.

The atypical feature of the house – one of his earliest realisations – is the absence of a split-level living-area.

F. W.

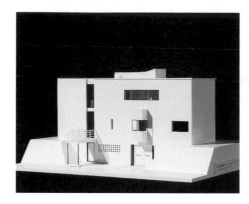
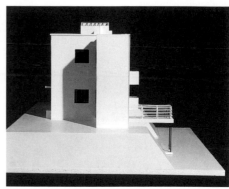
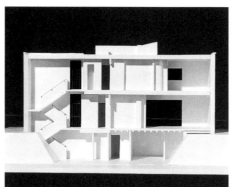
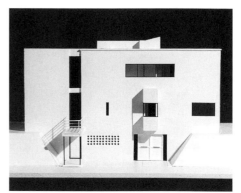
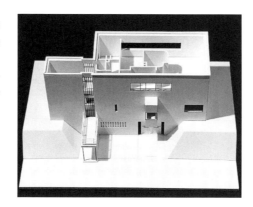
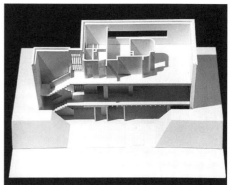
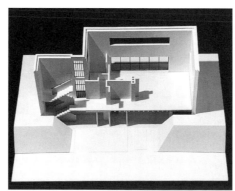
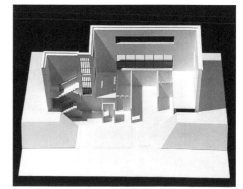

Le Corbusier
1887–1965

**Weekend house project
Rambouillet
1922**

*Scale model 1 : 33 ¹/₃
Gerhard Bolkart
Ulrik Hinze*

A model of this weekend house project was exhibited at the 1924 "Salon d'Automne" in Paris together with the models of Le Corbusier's Vaucresson house and the house in Auteuil.
The models are designed to demonstrate the aesthetic value of ferroconcrete in architecture.
F. W.

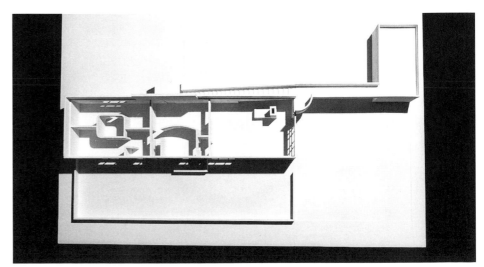

Le Corbusier
1887–1965

La Roche/Jeanneret house
Paris
1923

Scale model 1 : 33 ¹/₃
Gerd Otter
Stefanie Reithwieser
Jürgen Thum

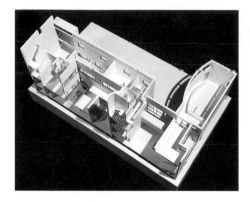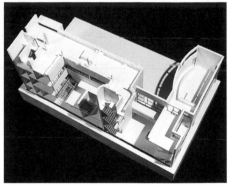

This building complex actually consists of two houses – one for the musician Albert Jeanneret, Le Corbusier's brother, and one with a gallery at right angles to the main building for Raoul La Roche.
The living-area is linked with the picture gallery and the library by a spacious three-storey hall with stairways, galleries, roof-lights and windows.
The site was extremely difficult to build on; existing trees had to be allowed for and specific room heights observed. "It took quite some cunning to catch the sun in this house." (Le Corbusier)
Today, the building houses the "Fondation Le Corbusier".
F. W.

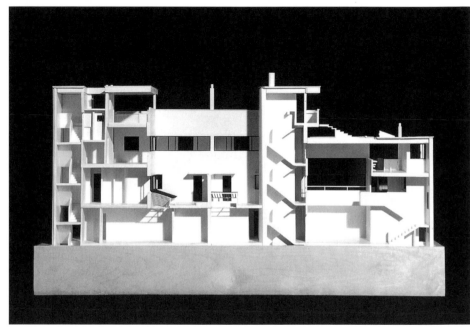

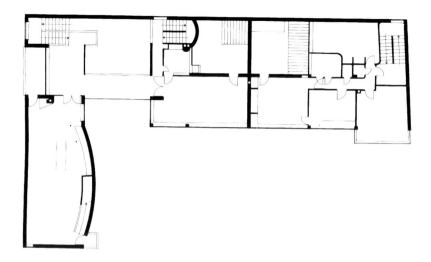

Le Corbusier
1887–1965

House for his mother
Vevey on Lake Geneva
1923

Scale model 1 : 33 ¹/₃
Barbara Wendorff

The small single-storey house was built by Le Corbusier from 1923/24 for his parents. His father, a nature-lover, died only one year after it was finished, but his mother, a piano teacher, lived here until 1960, when she died aged 100.

The house is 4 m wide and 16 m long, with an 11 m-long window facing the lake. Four metres in front of it is the lake, four metres behind it the road. There is a surrounding wall – almost like a monastery – with viewpoints overlooking the lake and the countryside.

The arrangement of the rooms is functional in the extreme, while making the most of the space available.

F. W.

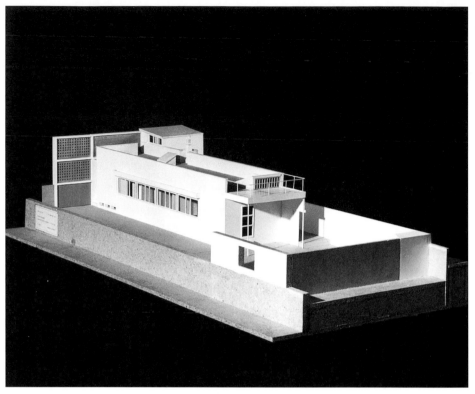

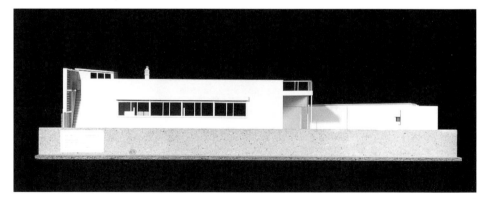

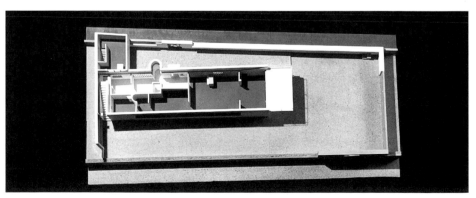

Le Corbusier
1887–1965

Project for student accomodation
1925

Scale model 1 : 33 $^1/_3$
Karin Luginger

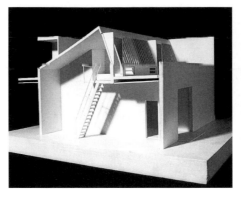

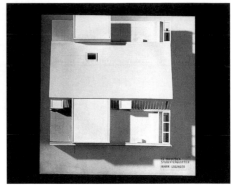

The model shows one living-unit of the student residence. 56 such units (7 × 8 m) are organised into a block, and distributed in a carpet-like structure between sports grounds and community facilities. Each unit has a vestibule, a kitchen, WC, living-room and its own roof garden. A large, high side window provides light for the entire unit.
F. W.

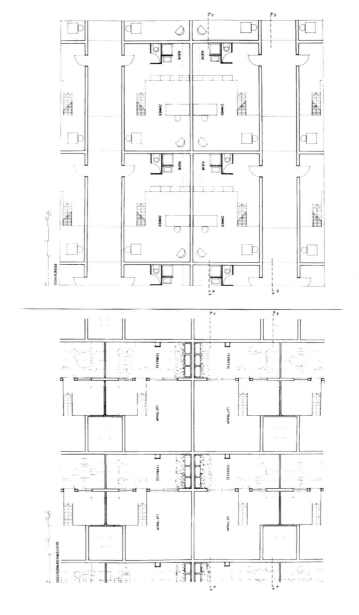

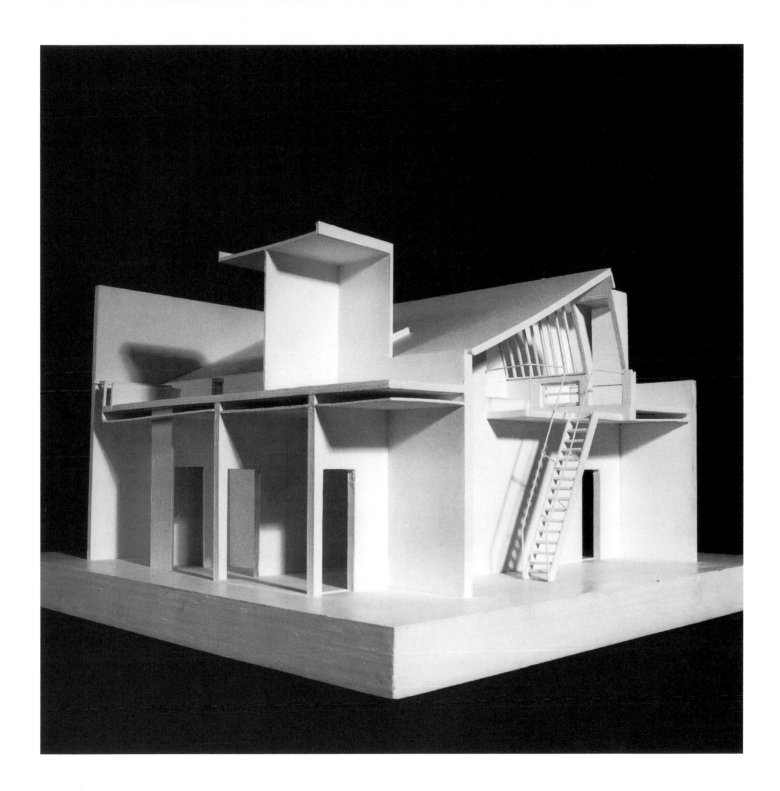

Le Corbusier
1887–1965

**Meyer house project
Paris
1925**

*Scale model 1 : 33 $^1/_3$
Richard Breitenhuber
Christian Conrad
Claudia Zeilhofer*

The model shows the second variant of the project for the Meyer villa.

The house is constructed on a ground area of about 17×17 m. The entrance, on the street side, faces north; the garden is on the south side. The east (or west) wall is designed for fire protection. With its interior arrangement of rooms, the project demonstrates the advantages of the "open floor plan". Curved walls and staircases provide a certain tension in combination with right-angled elements. The supporting concrete structure allows complete freedom in dividing the storeys.

A spacious ramp on the east wall leads from the vestibule on the ground floor via the library and the salon on the first floor to the bedrooms on the second floor, ending on the roof terrace with garden and swimming-pool.

The split-level living-area is placed, as is Le Corbusier's custom, on the first and second floors.

F. W.

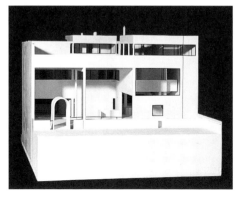

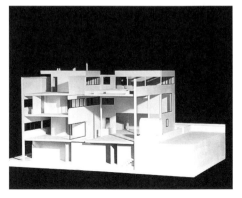

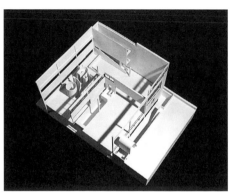

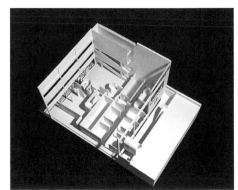

Le Corbusier
1887–1965

"Esprit Nouveau" pavillon
1925

Scale model 1 : 33 ¹/₃
Lothar Elster
Engelbert Gottsmann

The "Esprit Nouveau" pavilion was built
for the 1925 Exposition Internationale des
Arts Décoratifs et Industriels Modernes in
Paris. It consists of two parts. Le Corbusier's plans for urban development were
displayed in the rotunda – some 60 m²
or 80 m² panoramic pictures of the "Plan
Voisin" (1925) of Paris, and "Une ville
contemporaine" (a contemporary city
for 3 million inhabitants, designed in
1922).

The orthogonal part of the pavilion
contained a fully-furnished unit of his
"immeubles-villas", with living-area and
roof garden. The idea for this came to
him, he said, when he visited the
Charterhouse of Ema, near Florence.
F. W.

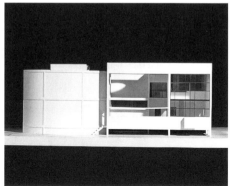

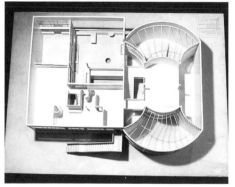
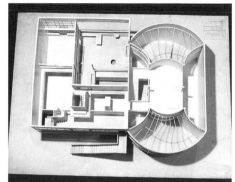

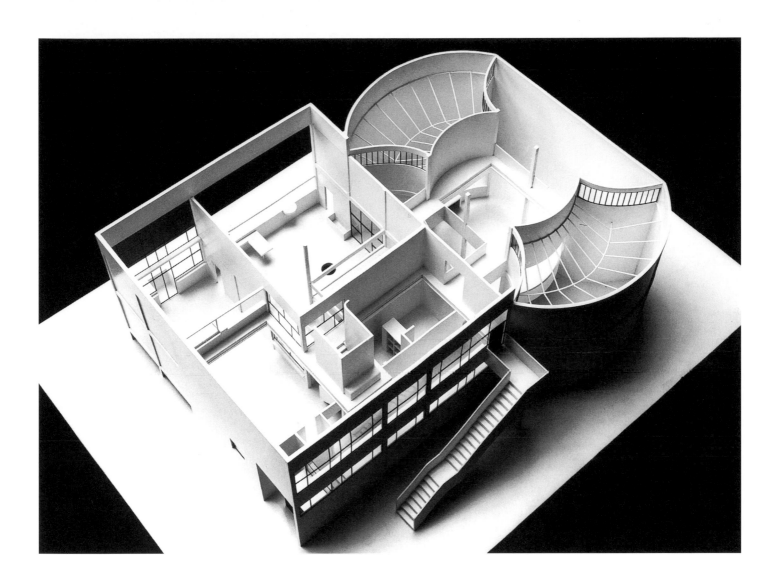

Le Corbusier
1887–1965

Workers' city at Pessac
1925
(two-storey type)

Scale model 1 : 33 $^1/_3$
Urs Engelmayr
Tasja Tesche

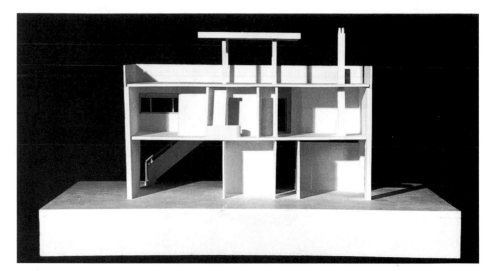

The garden city of Pessac (near Bordeaux), consisting of 51 houses, was built in less than a year.

This housing development, planned as a garden city by Le Corbusier and Pierre Jeanneret, was intended to serve as a laboratory for the two architects.

"I expect you to formulate clearly the problem of the floor plan, and to draw up a standard floor plan": this was the task allotted to them by their client, the Bordeaux industrialist Henri Frugès.

Thus all the house types were realised in a system of units, open to variation and adaptable to facing in any direction, with a floor plan based on a 5 m-long concrete girder.

Despite the standardisation of individual elements, Le Corbusier aimed to achieve the greatest possible variety for the entire housing estate. Terraced houses and free-standing two- or three-storey buildings with external staircases and roof terraces were the formal architectural elements.

From the start, however, the garden city proved ill-starred and was the object of vehement protest.

F. W.

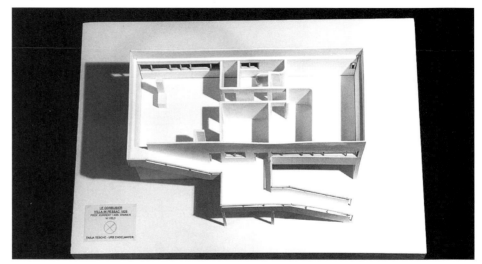

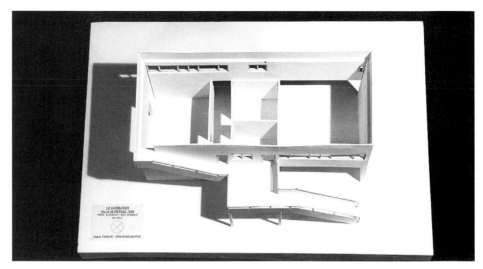

Le Corbusier
1887–1965

Workers' city at Pessac
1925
(three-storey type)

Scale model 1 : 33 ¹/₃
Christian Stalla
Robert Wagner

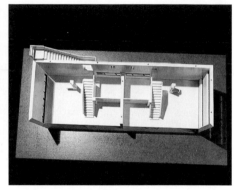

The model shows the three-storey double house for the Pessac housing estate with the room divisions as follows: on the ground floor a covered entrance, a small store-room and a garage; on the first floor the living-room with kitchen and another small room; on the second floor the bedrooms, and on the roof the partly covered garden.
F. W.

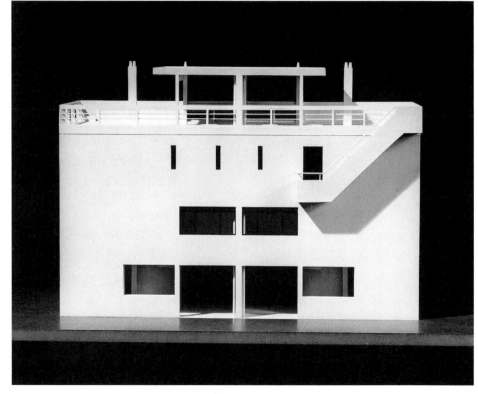

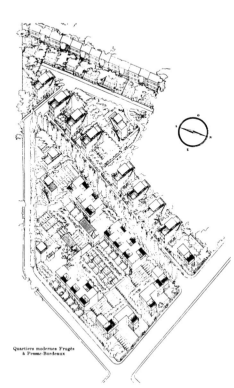

Quartiers modernes Frugès
à Pessac-Bordeaux

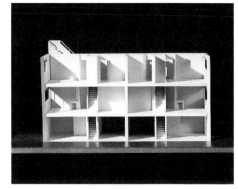

50

Le Corbusier
1887–1965

**Ternisien house
Paris-Boulogne
1926**

*Scale model 1 : 33 ¹/₃
Hedwig Ranke
Manfred Steuerwald*

The Ternisien house was intended for an artist couple – a musician and a painter. It was designed for a small triangular site, around a large tree. The Czech architect Vladimir Karfik, who worked with Le Corbusier on the plans for this house, said: "A conventional architect would have placed the house not at the point, but at the broad end of the triangle."

The tree marks the entrance and combines with it to form a small forecourt between the right-angled split-level studio and the living-area, which runs to a point. The shape of the lower section of the building is partly dictated by the shape of the site.

The roofs are intended for walking on, and designed partly as terraces.

The house later changed hands, and essential parts of the building were demolished during the years 1932–36.
F. W.

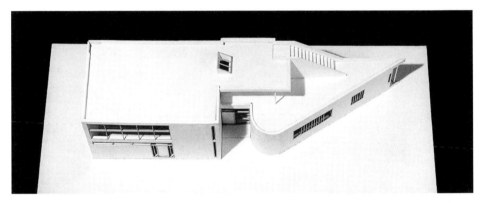

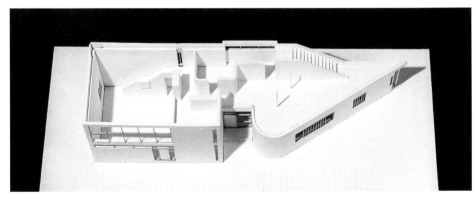

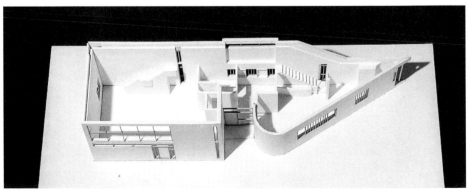

52

Le Corbusier
1887–1965

Cook villa
Boulogne-sur-Seine
1926

Scale model 1 : 33 ¹/₃
Sabine Güldner
Till Kaltwasser
Andreas Keller

This house was built for a progressive American journalist named Cook, in Boulogne-sur-Seine.

It is part of a built-up area, and therefore had to conform to specific guidelines.

In this house, all the principles of Le Corbusier's new architecture are applied:

The house on pillars

The house is raised off the ground, and the garden is continued under it. Only a small entrance hall appears on the ground floor

The open floor plan

The constructional system of supports allows the dividing walls to be placed without reference to structure.

In the Cook house, all the bedrooms are on the first floor. The living-area with kitchen and dining-area is on the second floor, a staircase leading from the split-level living-room to the third floor with the library, and the *roof garden* – another important element for Le Corbusier – with a view over the Bois de Boulogne. The *freedom of exterior planning* makes it possible to develop the arrangement of the windows in accordance with the interior.

F. W.

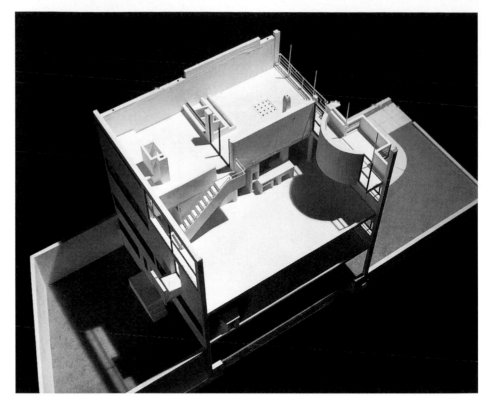

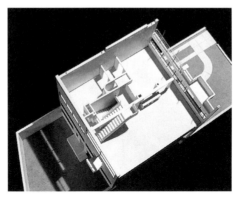

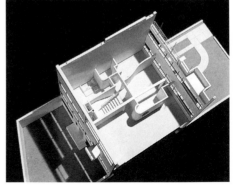

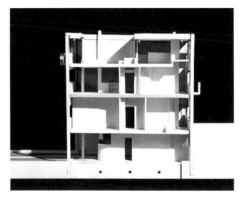

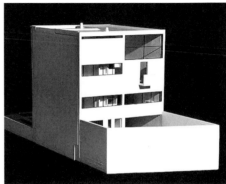

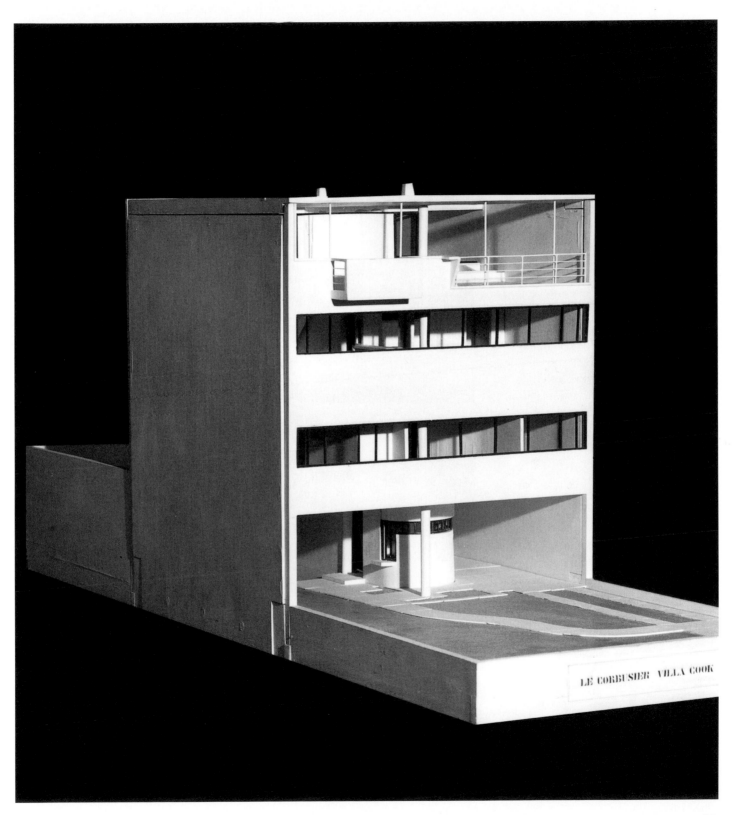

LE CORBUSIER VILLA COOK

Le Corbusier
1887–1965

Guiette house
Antwerp
1926

Scale model 1 : 33 $^1/_3$
Ralf Becht
Matthias Schwarz

This cubic house with studio is planned over four storeys on a ground area of 7 × 14 m, in a proportion of 1:2.

A characteristic feature is the long single staircase, reminiscent of Jacob's Ladder, leading laterally through the entire house.

Contrary to Le Corbusier's demands, the ground floor is occupied by a living-room, and thus not kept free for a garden. On the first floor are the bedrooms; on the second floor begins the studio area, which has a split-level main room with a gallery leading to the roof garden.

F. W.

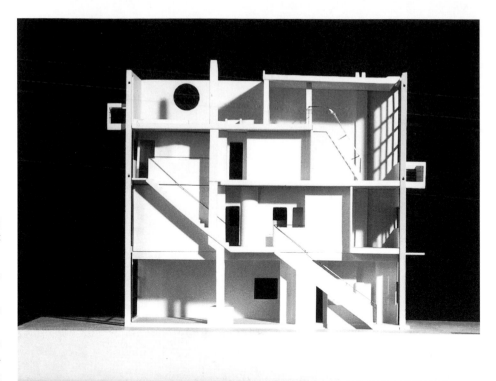

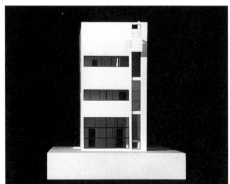

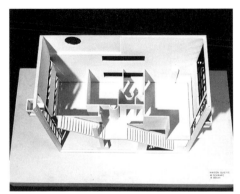

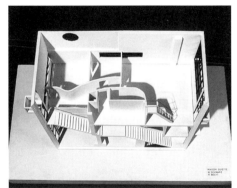

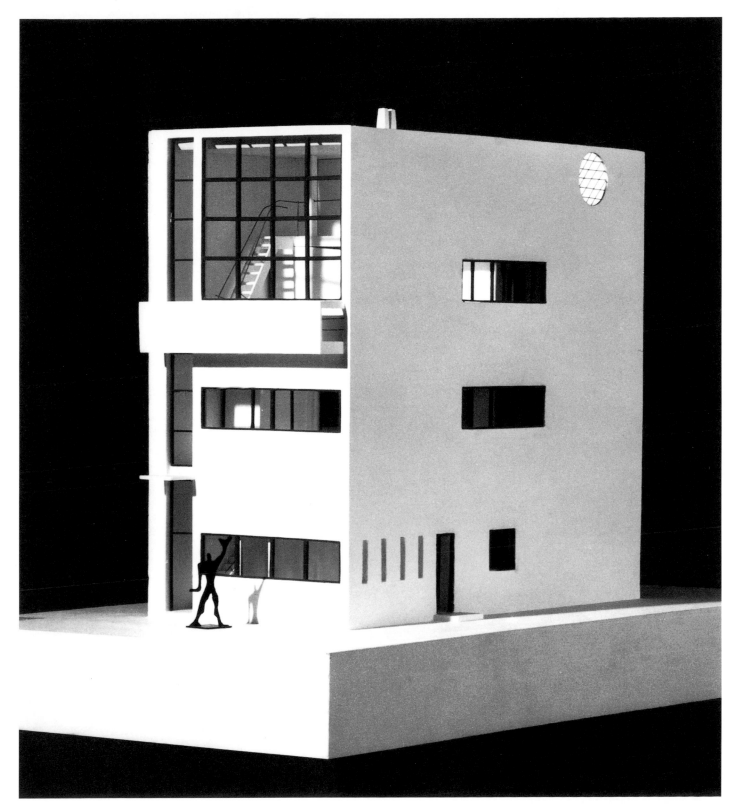

Le Corbusier
1887–1965

"Minimum house" project
1926
(three-storey type)

Scale model 1 : 33 ¹/₃
Thomas Diez

This free-standing house is constructed on three levels on a ground area of 5.5 × 8.25 m.

The ground floor is reserved for utility rooms, and the exterior staircase leads to the living-area on the first floor, from which an internal single staircase gives access to the two bedrooms on the second floor.

F. W.

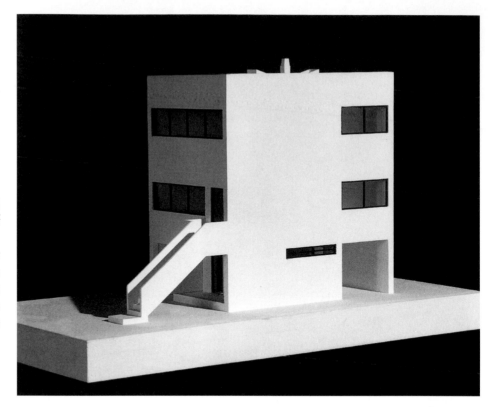

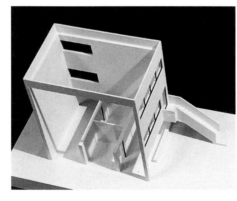
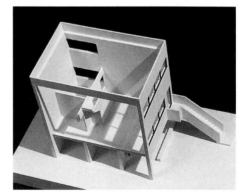

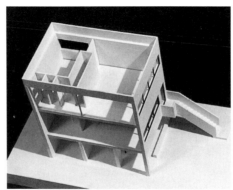
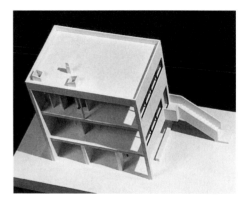

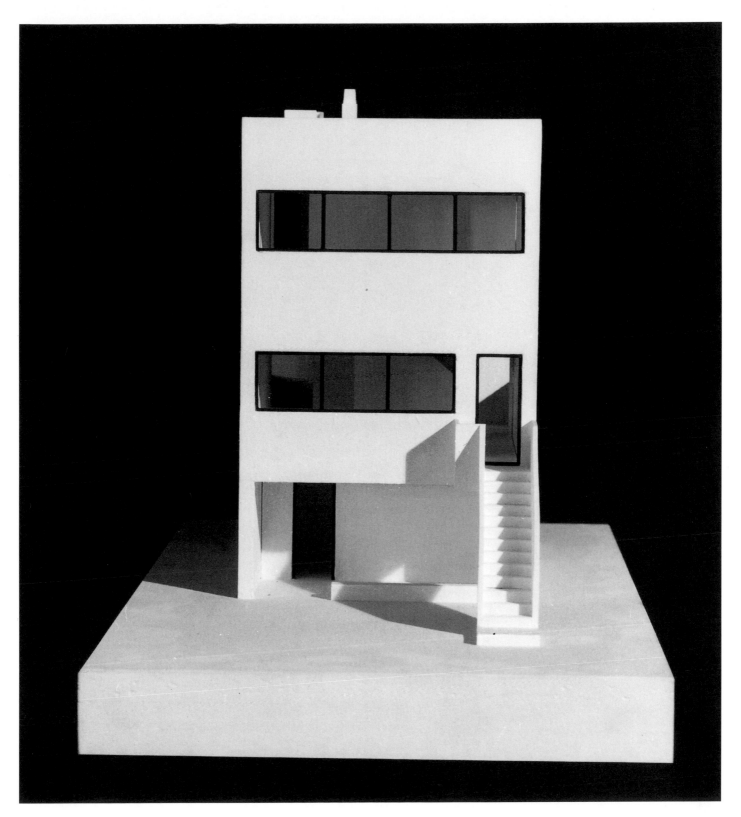

Le Corbusier
1887–1965

"Minimum house" project
1926
(two-storey type, double house)

Scale model 1 : 33 $^1/_3$
Peter Augustin

The two-storey "minimum house" is a pair of semi-detached houses on a ground area of 5.5 × 13.5 m, with the characteristic exterior staircases leading via a small porch directly into the living-rooms.

The living-area, of some 30 m², is on the first floor; the ground floor is intended for utility rooms.

The ends of the house face east-west.
F. W.

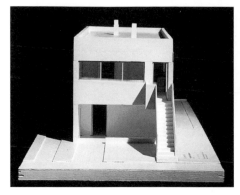
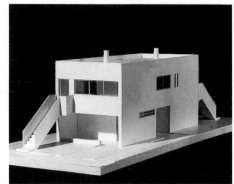
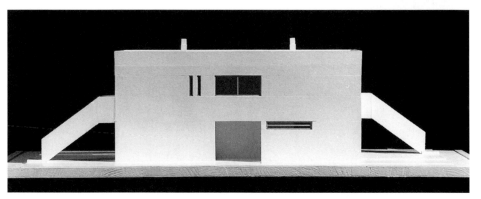
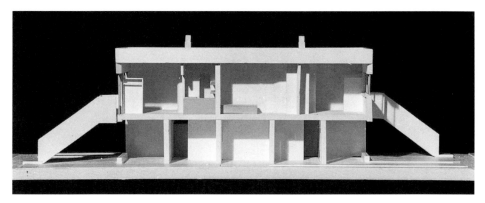
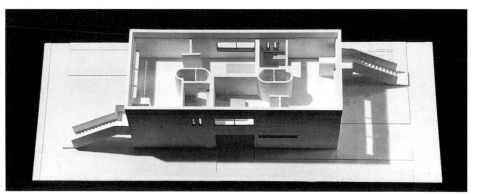

Le Corbusier
1887–1965

**Plainex house
Paris
1926**

*Scale model 1 : 33 ¹/₃
Romana Lachermayer
Wolfgang Eichner*

This house contains three studios and
one apartment, on five levels. On the
ground floor, accessible from the street,
there is a central garage, on each side
of which is a split-level studio with a
gallery. Each of these is equipped with a
bedroom, kitchen and bathroom.

The apartment is reached by a free-
standing double staircase with semicircular landings, accessible from the
garden side, and gives access via a
small bridge to a terrace.

On the fourth floor is the third and
largest studio, with a saw-tooth roof
giving extra light from above. A further
free-standing staircase leads from the
large studio to the fifth level – the open
roof terrace.

F. W.

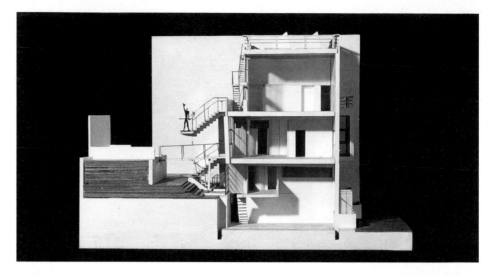

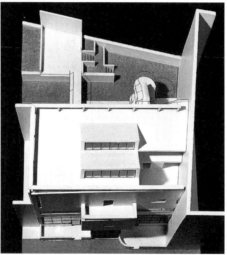

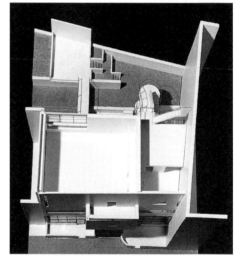

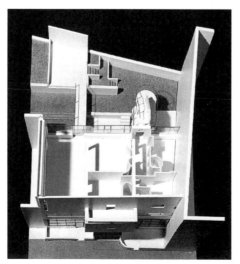

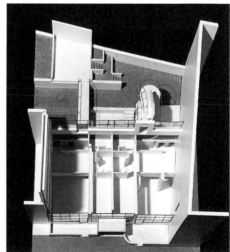

Le Corbusier
1887–1965

Stein villa
Garches
1927

Scale model 1 : 33 ¹/₃
Sabine Gressel
Alfred Maier
Andrea Schulte-Täumer

The Stein villa – one of the most marvellous houses of the period, according to Julius Posener – was built some way outside Paris, near the western suburb of Garches.

The clients, Michael and Sarah Stein, were great art-lovers and collectors, so the house was required not only to fulfil a high standard of living, but also to provide fitting accommodation for their collection of modern painting and sculpture.

The most striking feature of the house is its spaciousness, achieved by light distribution and balanced proportions, with ample stairs and passageways. Both the ground plan and the exterior of the building show great harmony of design.

"The entire house conforms to rigorous measurements which led to the modification, to about one centimetre, of the sides of the various sections. The science of mathematics contributes reassuring facts here, and one can leave one's own work with the assurance of having achieved precision." (Le Corbusier)

When Henri Matisse went to tea at the Stein villa one day, Le Corbusier asked him: "What do you think of this house?" Matisse, bewildered and delighted, replied: "I am quite confused!"

F. W.

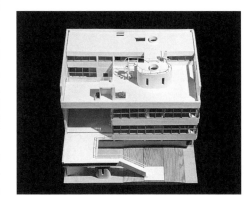

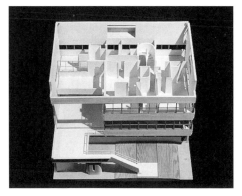

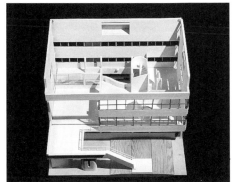

Le Corbusier
1887–1965

Detached house for the Weissenhof housing estate Stuttgart
1927

Scale model 1 : 33 ⅓
Matthias Jakob

"The two houses in the Weissenhof housing estate in Stuttgart were built in 1927. Hitler denounced them as testaments to Bolshevism and ordered their demolition. They survived, however, and to Le Corbusier's surprise and delight were placed under preservation order by the State Department for the preservation of historic monuments." (Le Corbusier)

The conception is that of the Citrohan house, developed seven years previously, with the split-level living-room and the lateral single staircase.

The structural framework is of ferro-concrete, filled out with pumice concrete hollow blocks. The distance between the pillars – 2.5 m along the length, 5 m along the breadth of the house – results from the use of standard horizontal sliding windows of 2.5 × 1.1 m, which, arranged singly or in groups, provide the main source of light for the rooms.

Externally, the house is a simple cube; the internal arrangement, on the other hand, is based on a completely open floor plan.

F. W.

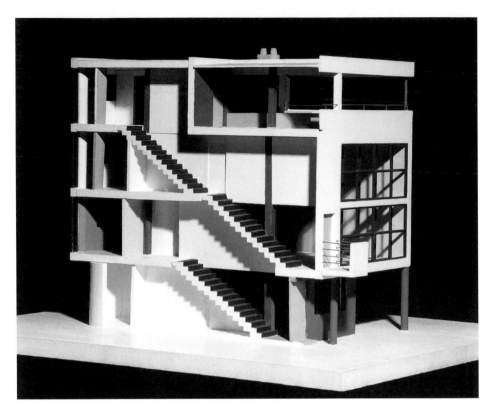

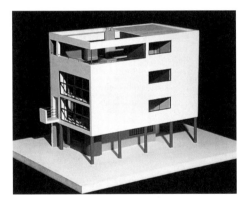

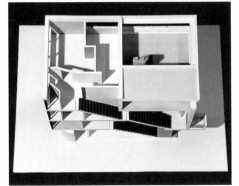

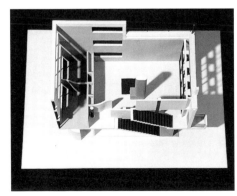

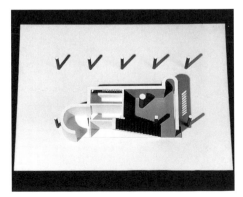

Le Corbusier
1887–1965

Double house for tho Weissenhof housing estate Stuttgart 1927

Scale model 1 : 33 ¹/₃
Panagiotis Michos
Athina Afendouli

The double house demonstrates clearly Le Corbusier's five requirements for a new architecture:
the *pillars*, i. e. separation of load-bearing and non-load-bearing elements;
the use of the *flat roof* for living purposes (summer living-area, terrace, garden);
an *open floor plan*;
the use of *strip windows*;
freedom of exterior planning.
In order to save space, this house experiments with transformable rooms; by the use of sliding walls and movable beds, the day living-area is divided at night into sleeping-compartments, which are linked by a narrow lateral corridor to the permanent offices such as kitchen, bathroom and WC.
Thus there is an interplay between the "fixed" rooms behind the staircase – such as the breakfast room, study or library, and the living- and sleeping-areas which are subject to constant alteration in size.
F. W.

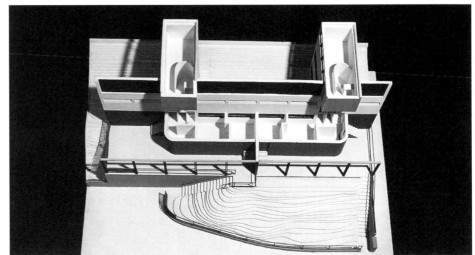

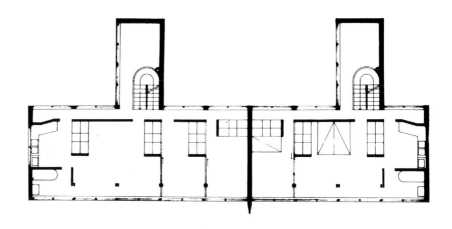

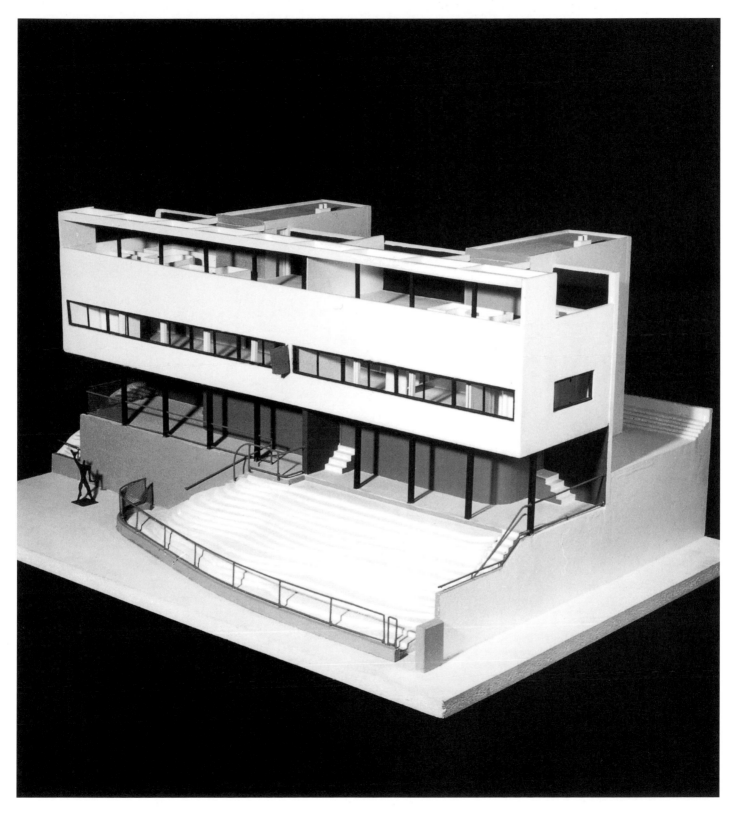

Le Corbusier
1887–1965

Baizeau villa project
Carthage
1928

Scale model 1 : 33 ¹/₃
Dan Jakob Heerde
Werner Stolle

The first project for the Baizeau villa in Carthage, a suburb of Tunis, was designed to be built free-standing on level ground near the sea, taking into account the demands of the Mediterranean climate.

Apart from questions of spatial function, the main aim was to offer protection from the sun and to guarantee a constant stream of air through the house.

The solution lies in the dynamic structure of the house. Two storeys, each 4.5 m in height, are juxtaposed, but staggered by half their height. The roof has the effect of a sunshade for the terraces beneath it. The intersections of the two major elements form open intermediate galleries, so that air is in constant vertical motion throughout the house.

This also gives a feeling of spaciousness between the individual levels.

F. W.

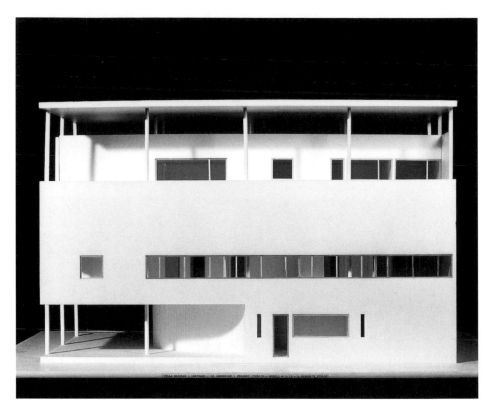

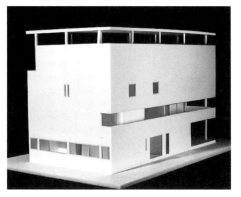

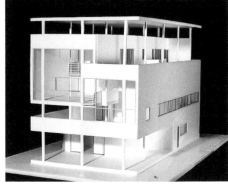

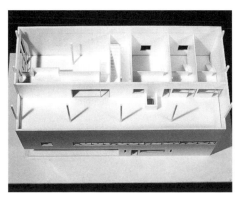

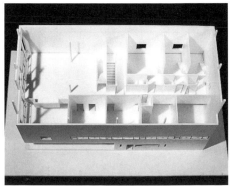

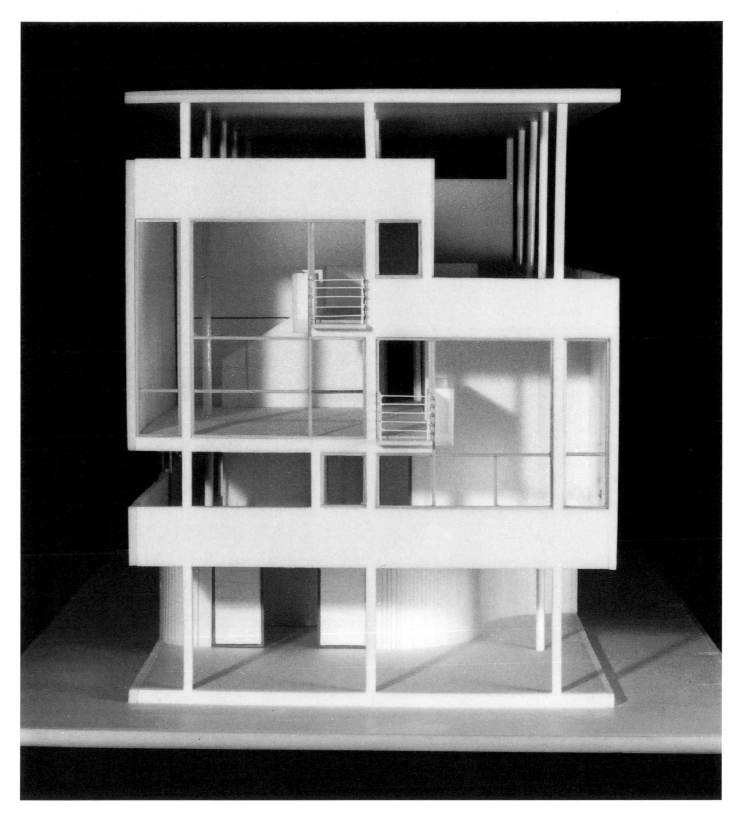

Le Corbusier
1887–1965

**Baizeau villa
Carthage
1928**

*Scale model 1 : 33 ¹/₃
Susanne Treuheit
Anke Wündisch*

The realisation of the second design for the Baizeau villa differs in essential features from the first project.

The ground plan is reduced from the original four supporting axes to three, within a framework of 5 × 6 m. The vertical intersection has been abandoned, so that the split-level rooms with gallery have completely disappeared.

Although the division of rooms follows the "open floor plan", the individual storeys are simply placed one on top of the other.

F. W.

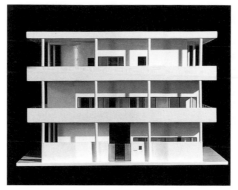

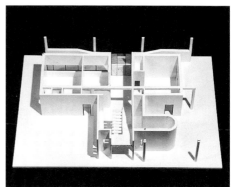
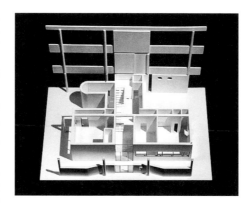
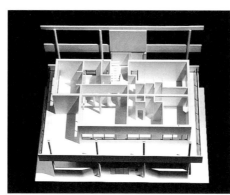
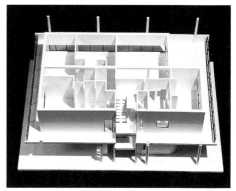
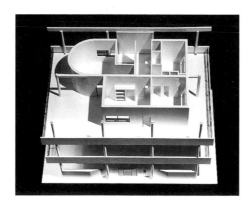
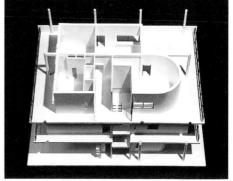

Le Corbusier 1887–1965

Savoye villa
Paris-Poissy
1928

Scale model 1 : 33 ¹/₃
Irene Rammensee
Rolf Richard Rammensee

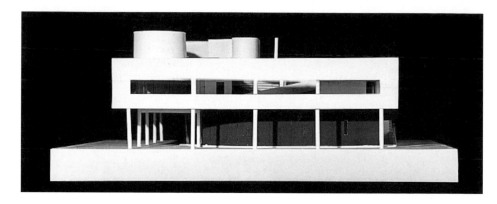

The commission to design a weekend house for the progressive Savoye couple three kilometres away from Paris allowed Le Corbusier great latitude to express his ideas on architecture in an "ideal project".

When talking of this house, he often used the epithet "promenade architecturale" to describe a new kind of architectonic experience:

"One goes up a ramp, ascending imperceptibly, which gives a completely different feeling from going up the steps of a staircase. It becomes accessible by degrees. As one walks along, one can see how the architectural arrangement unfolds. [...] a real 'promenade architecturale', which continuously opens up changing, unexpected and sometimes astonishing views." (Le Corbusier, Complete Works, 1921–34)

The first floor, which houses the living-quarters – about 19 × 21.5 m in area and strongly horizontal in line – seems almost to hover, like an UFO just landed from a distant star, on the ground-level supports, which are placed 4.75 m apart.

F. W.

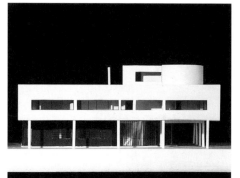

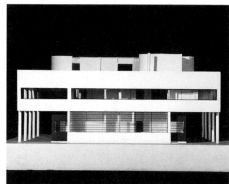

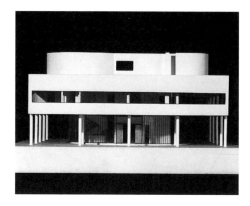

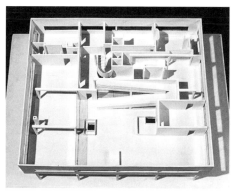

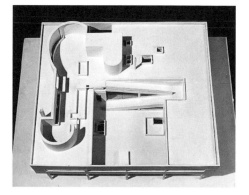

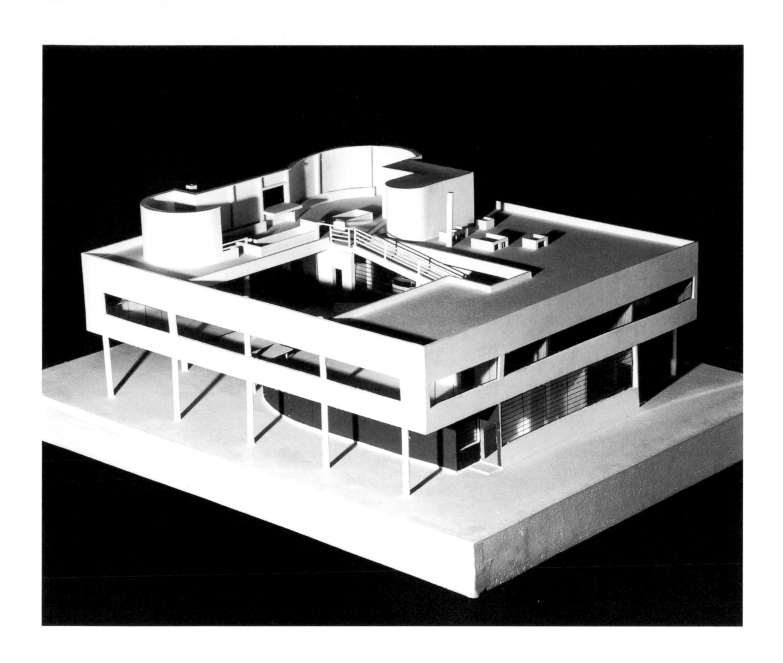

Le Corbusier
1887–1965

Lodge for the Savoye villa
Paris-Poissy
1928

Scale model 1 : 33 ¹/₃
Karin Melcher
Sabine Rietschle

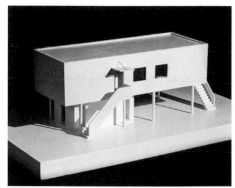
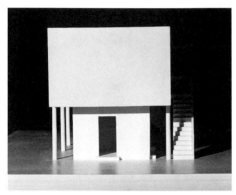

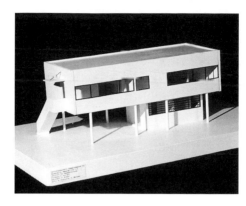
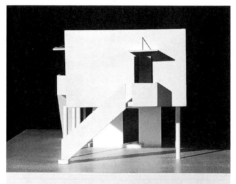

Between the original idea and the actual building of the lodge, there are four designs which, although similar, differ in the size of the building and its position in relation to the wall surrounding the estate.

The first design, a kind of semi-detached pair, contains two identical dovetailed apartments on the upper storey, reached by external lateral staircases. The building was to stand parallel to the surrounding wall.

The second design (shown here as a model) is the more interesting. The whole building now stands at right angles to the wall, the chauffeur's flat being accessible via an external staircase at the end of the house, the gardener's flat from the side. On the ground floor, a passageway leads underneath one half of the building; under the other is a free-standing cube containing the domestic offices.

The third phase began by reducing the size of one of the flats, and in the version which was finally built, the chauffeur's flat was omitted entirely, so that the lodge was in the end realised simply as a gardener's cottage.
F. W.

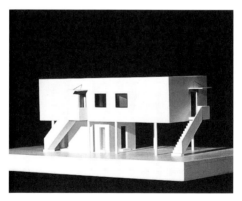

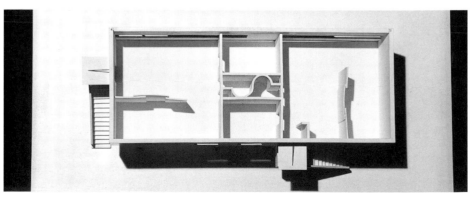

Le Corbusier
1887–1965

Canneel house project
Brussels
1929

Scale model 1 : 33 ¹/₃
Clemens Frosch
Tobias Fusban
Andreas Gaiser

This narrow, compact four-storey build-ing was planned with the following inter-ior:
The garden is laid out under the house, with only the entrance to the staircase and the garage on the ground floor. On the first floor are the servants' rooms and a large bedroom with a bathroom. A small bridge leads directly from the bedroom to an open-air swimming-pool over the garage roof.
The main living-area is on the top two levels. A split-level living-room links kitchen and dining-room on the third floor with the library on the fourth floor, leading to the roof garden.
An unusual feature is the vertical com-munication within the house. Into the gently curving main staircase is inserted a second, independent, servants' stair-case linking ground-floor entrance, servants' quarters and kitchen level.
F. W.

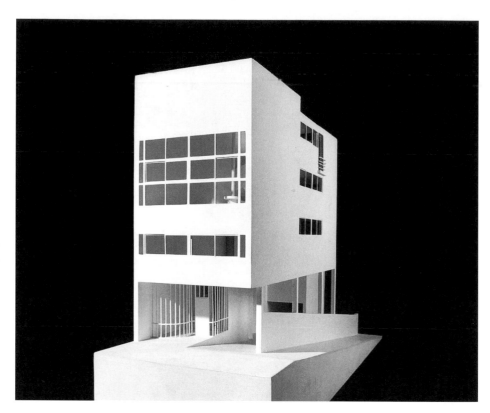

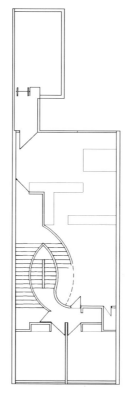

Le Corbusier
1887–1965

**Mandrot house
Le Pradet
1930**

*Scale model 1 : 33 ¹/₃
Stefan Greger*

This composite building stands in a commanding position on a plain amongst the foothills near Toulon. Thus the whole design is related to the landscape.

Various cubic elements are grouped around a raised terrace in such a way as to provide different views and points of reference to the surrounding countryside. Staircases and small bridges of different lengths link the building and the raised courtyard with its surroundings.

The external appearance of the buildings is characterised by the structure of the walls, which are made of local natural stone.

F. W.

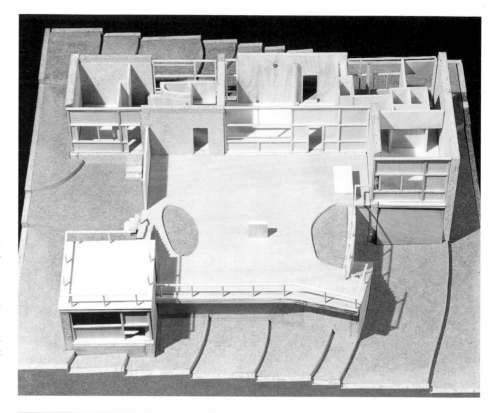

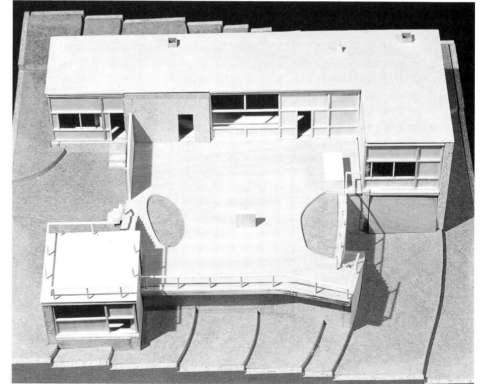

Le Corbusier
1887–1965

Errazuris house
Chile
1930

Scale model 1 : 33 ¹/₃
Kerstin Mahnel
Richard Schleich

The house stands on the Pacific coast, on a west-facing slope. The main building, 8 × 20 m in area, is designed parallel to the contour lines; beside it, separated by a small courtyard, is a low building containing domestic offices.

Entering the house from the closed-in east side facing the mountains, one comes to a room positioned lengthways, from which a spacious ramp leads up to a gallery and bedroom.

The side facing the valley has large openings affording a view over the sea. This house was built of local materials – round timbers, walls mainly of undressed stone.

The pent roofs, sloping up to north and south, lend the house its unmistakable sculptural character.

F. W.

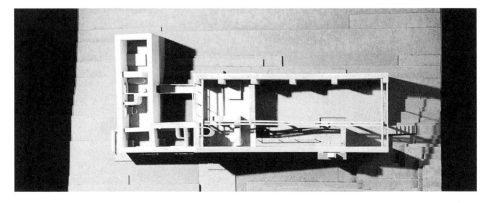

Le Corbusier
1887–1965

Maison aux Mathes
France
1935

Scale model 1 : 33 ¹/₃
Bob Strotz

This house was planned in three independent stages and built by the
village craftsmen, at the lowest possible
cost and without the supervision of the
architect.

The walls – of local undressed stone and
45 cm thick – which constitute the basic
structure of the building were completed
in a single building phase.

The second phase consisted of carpentry
work, plumbing, and roofing with Eternit
corrugated sheets.

The woodwork – windows, doors, dividing walls and cupboards – was
adapted to standard-size elements and
accessories. The building was completed with glass, plywood and Eternit.
F. W.

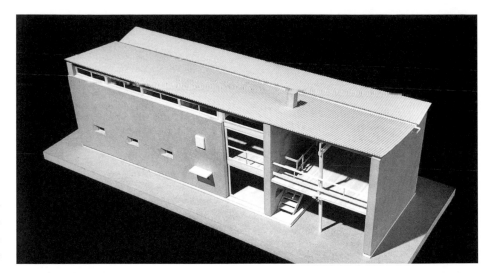

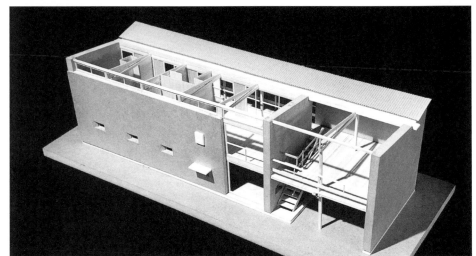

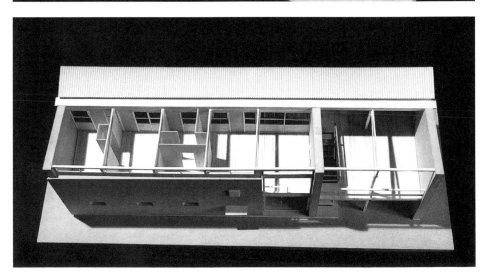

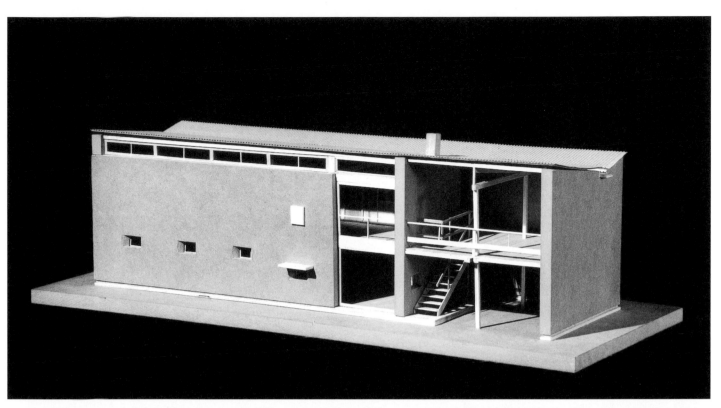

VILLA AUX MATHES LE CORBUSIER 1935

BOB STROTZ WS 1995 / 1996

Le Corbusier
1887–1965

"Unitó d'habitation"
Marseille
1945
Basic unit

Scale model 1 : 33 ¹/₃
Waltraud Vogler
Ulrich Michaelis

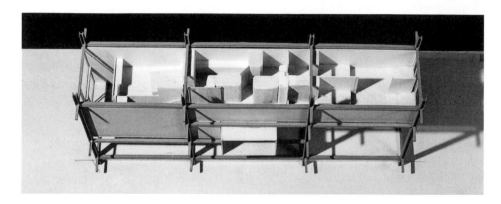

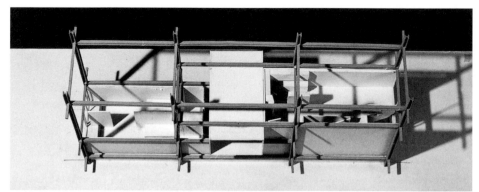

The model shows the basic elements of Le Corbusier's "unité d'habitation": the staggered living-units, the composite structure with concrete sunshades and the internal access road.

The "unités" are basically high-rise blocks, with different sizes of apartments and community services. The best-known and also most controversial "unité", in Marseille, is 165 m long, 24 m wide and 56 m high. The building stands on stilts, so that the ground is kept free for pedestrian traffic.

There are more than 300 apartments, of 23 different types. The standard apartments are duplex and have a living-room 4.8 m in height, with a magnificent view. Access to the apartments is by internal "streets", vertical communication is effected by lifts. On the seventh and eighth floors, there is a street with shops catering for all everyday requirements, as well as bars and restaurants.

On the top floor, the seventeenth, there is a kindergarten and a nursery. The spacious roof garden is reserved for the resident community.

F. W.

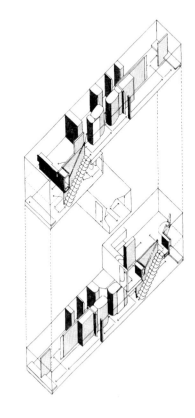

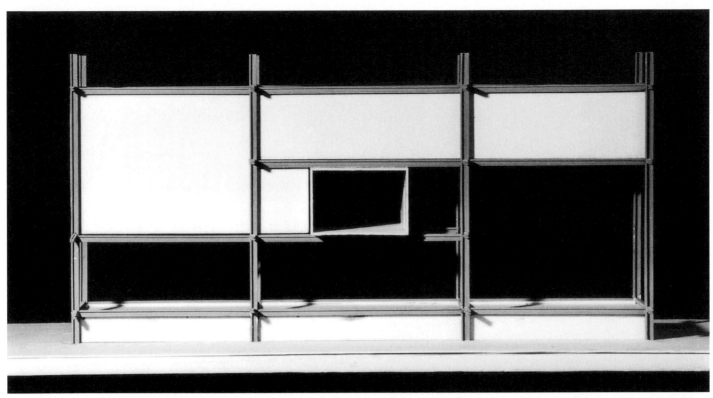

Le Corbusier
1887–1965

"Rob et Roq" project
1949

Scale model 1 : 33 $^1/_3$
Tilman Probst

The "Rob et Roq" studies are concerned with building on a relatively steep slope on the Côte d'Azur. The long, narrow type shown in the model was designed as a closely-ranged group, harmonising the architecture with the landscape. The intention was that each house should have a share in the magnificent view over the countryside.

The structural development followed the design devised by Le Corbusier: 226 × 226 × 226. The principle of this method, developed from the "Modulor" concept, consists in one basic living-unit, which allows a variety of applications, and which can be constructed from a single angle-iron section, assembled to form supports and girders.

Not until years later was the "Maison de l'Homme" pavilion in Zurich realised, using this method.

F. W.

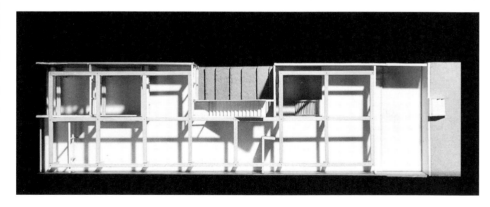

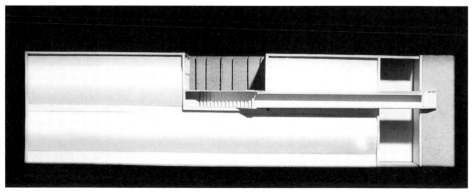

Le Corbusier
1887–1965

Dr. Currutchet house
La Plata, Buenos Aires
1949

Scale model 1 : 33 1/3
Karl Frey
Karl H. Höllerer
Alfons Lengdobler

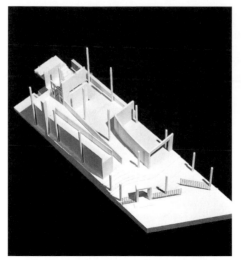

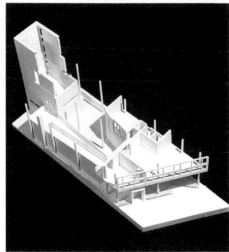

The house with doctor's practice has the characteristic façades with concrete sunshades. It stands on a small site, enclosed on three sides by fire walls. Only the fourth, slanting side looks on to a boulevard with a park; this view was the determining factor in the design.

On a strict structural framework, an open floor plan is developed, resulting in a house with great spatial variety.

A ramp leads to the doctor's practice on the first floor which, like the terrace of the living-area above, overlooks the boulevard.

The apartment itself is disposed on the upper floors, to the rear of the site. Open spaces and courtyards of various sizes make it light and airy.

F. W.

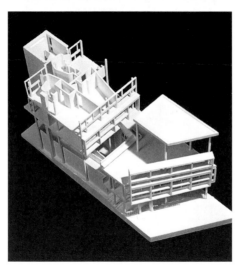

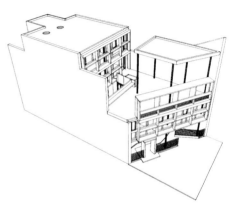

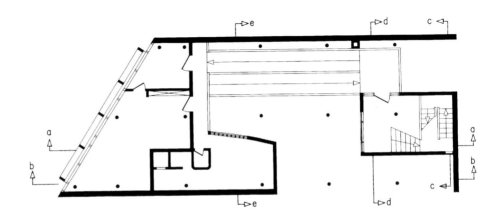

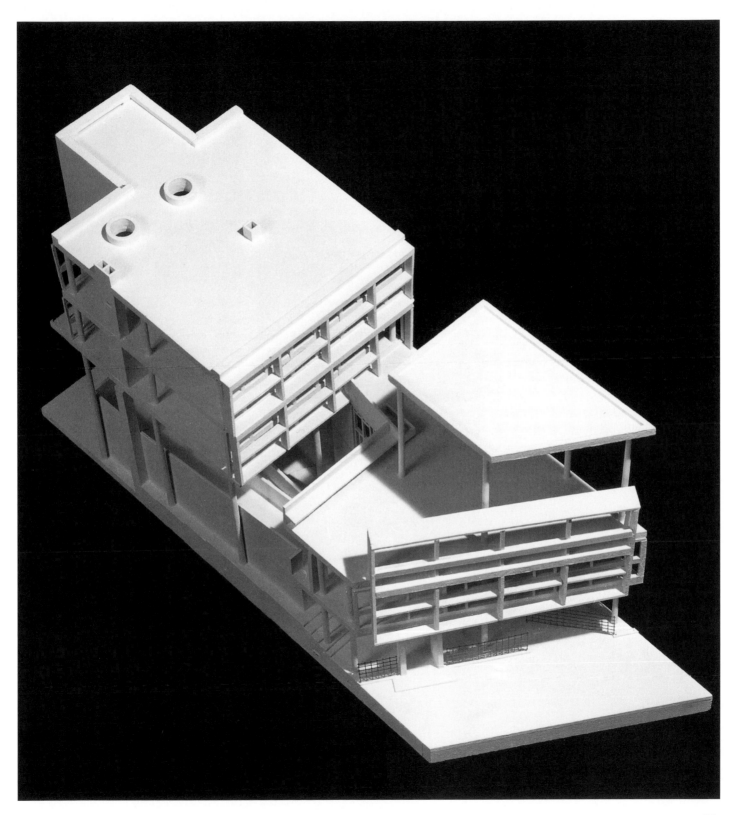

Le Corbusier
1887–1965

Shodhan villa
Ahmadabad, India
1956

Scale model 1 : 33 $^1/_3$
Attila Eris
Antonia Sacha
Christian Vorleiter

Under a sun-roof and shielded by concrete sunshades on the façades, there evolves over five storeys an architectural landscape of rooms linked with open terraces, reached by spacious ramps and staircases.

From a spatial and volumetric point of view, this luxury villa is an architectural mega-event, conceivable only in the hot climate of India.

Brightly-coloured wall panels enhance the contrast with the rough concrete of the main structure.

F. W.

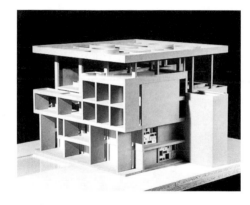

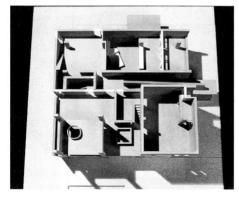

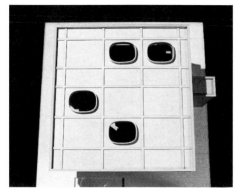

Le Corbusier
1887–1965

"Maison de l'Homme" pavilion
Zurich
1963

Scale model 1 : 33 ¹/₃
Andreas Rieger
Ulrich Lausen

The first sketches for this exhibition pavilion date back to 1961, but it was not until after Le Corbusier's death that it was actually built, on the initiative of Heidi Weber.

Basically, the architect combines two ideas which, although they often appear in his projects, were never realised in this form: firstly, the free-standing roof (welded from 5 mm thick metal sheets) like an umbrella protecting the building from sun and rain; secondly, a complex of rooms independent of the roof, simply placed under it.

The gallery, constructed purely of steel, was realised in Le Corbusier's patent system "Le brevet 226 × 226 × 226": angle irons with sides 3 mm thick, in sets of four, form cross-supports and thus the basic structural element of the framework, the spaces then being fitted with coloured enamel panels.

The building consists of one two-storey and five single-storey rooms. A concrete ramp leads up to the roof.

"It is the first time I have seen a building assembled from prefabricated elements of a type that possesses truly sculptural qualities." (José Luis Sert)

F. W.

94

Hans Döllgast
1891–1974

Fritz Döllgast house
Augsburg
1935

Scale model 1 : 33 ¹/₃
Attila Eris
Antonia Sacha
Christian Vorleiter

Döllgast built this simple house (ground area 7.2 × 12 m) in what were then the outskirts of Augsburg, for his brother Fritz and wife. The structure is a clearcut, smoothly plastered cuboid with a gable roof hardly overlapping at the eaves and verges. The only features in relief are the balcony and the canopy over the entrance, on the two gable sides. Windows with glazing bars and folding shutters, wrought-iron grilles, sundial and a trellis mitigate the severity of the building and give the house a friendly ambience.

The interior planning is simple and functional: living-room, dining-room, kitchen and WC on the ground floor, three rooms, box-room, bathroom and WC on the upper floor. All the interior walls, including the load-bearing ones, are only 12 cm thick.

Fritz Döllgast and his wife Jossy, both artists, lived in this house until they died. Furniture designed by Hans Döllgast, watercolours by his brother and tapestries by his sister-in-law lent a unique atmosphere to the simple rooms.

F. P.

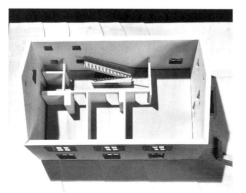

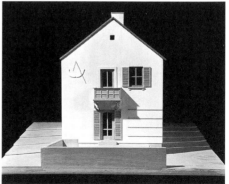

Hans Döllgast
1891–1974

**Terrace houses
for the leather factory
Grafing
1948/49**

*Scale model 1 : 33 ¹/₃
Gerald Hardler
Hanne Kääb
Markus Kress*

"When everything grinds to a halt, manna still falls through a slit in heaven, in this case on to an unused foundation [...] a handful of terrace houses, not half as much as the Fugger estate in Augsburg. That was in Grafing, for a manufacturer called Glass (Viennese leather goods). Partner Köhler, Dinkel. Herr Tessenow would have liked it, too." (Hans Döllgast, journal retour, vol. 1)
Of the planned refugee estate for workers in the leather factory, only this single row was built. As might be expected, considering the distressed circumstances in the early post-war years, the individual units in the main section are kept to a minimum (two rooms), and only the two three-roomed flats in the end building are of slightly more generous proportions. There are no cellars or box-rooms; instead, wooden sheds were built at right angles to the end of the terrace, rounding off the long row.
F. P.

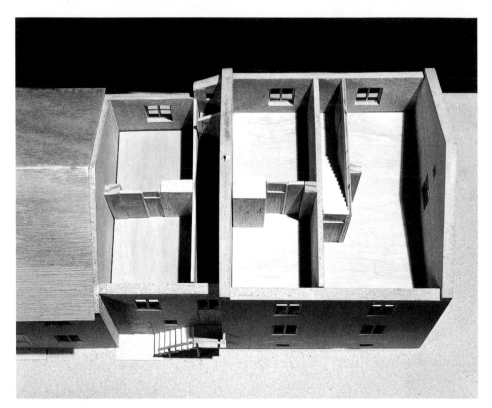

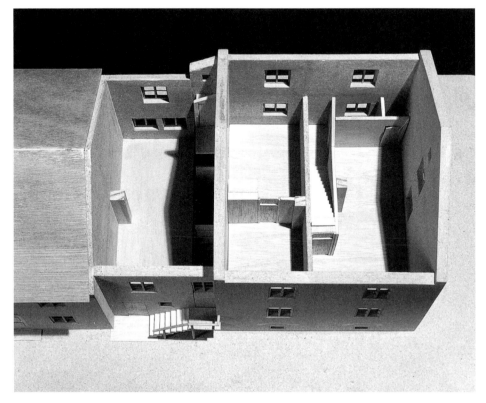

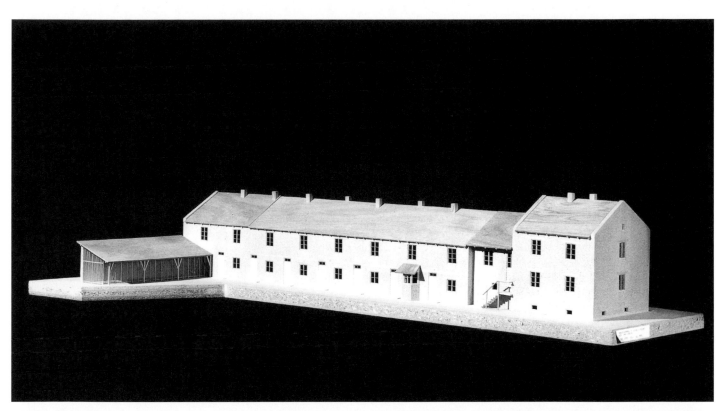

Hans Döllgast
1891–1974

Studio building
Gabelsbergerstrasse, Munich
1948

Scale model 1 : 33 ¹/₃
Ursula Müller
Doris Lackerbauer
Patrik Zeilhofer

The preliminary design for this un-realised project shows a building situated at the rear of a house and accessible only from the courtyard. The narrow sides of the rectangular structure adjoin the two courtyard walls, so that a further courtyard is formed at the rear.

The house is divided by two pent roofs sloping up towards the rear (north), parallel but at different levels. Under the higher of these is the studio, lit by a large north-facing window, and ac-cessible through a large two-winged wooden door.

Under the lower roof on the north side, at the door to the rear yard, are WC and washroom; above these is a gallery, accessible by a wooden staircase from the studio; over the door is a roof sloping down from the west wall of the courtyard. At the front, with a south window, is a study/bedroom the full height of the building, accessible from the studio by a step. The building consists of unplastered walls, visible concrete lintels, wooden doors and windows; the central purlin over the studio is supported by a truss.
W. G.

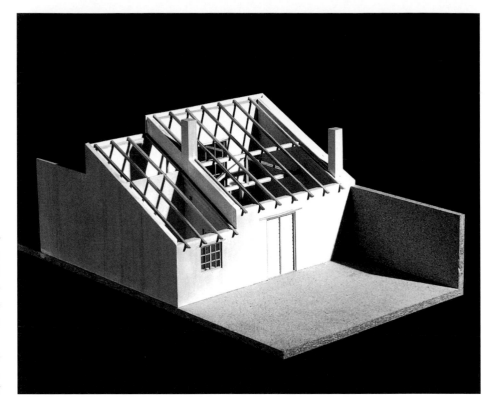

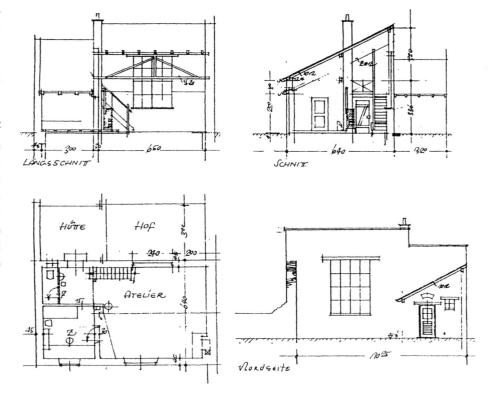

Hans Döllgast
1891–1974

House project
Kaulbachstrasse 51, Munich
1950

Scale model 1 : 33 ¹/₃
Karlheinz Raupach

This model shows the last of a series of projects starting in 1948, for a garden plot behind the row of houses in the Kaulbachstrasse. Directly on the northern boundary is the rear building of a printing-works, with a windowless fire wall which this house was to adjoin.

The structure is a cube of $8 \times 8 \times 8$ m, its almost flat gable roof surmounted by a roof terrace.

The ground plan is practically identical for all three storeys. On the ground floor are a studio with separate entrance, a laundry-room and WC. The first floor, distinguished by French balconies as the bel étage, contains living-room and kitchen, the second floor bedroom and bathroom.

Both in the structural form and in the diversity of the three façades, this is one of Döllgast's most original and individual projects. It is not known who commissioned it. Years of preparation and the complete congruity of dimension with the later house in the Nederlinger-strasse suggest that Döllgast was planning here for himself.

F. P.

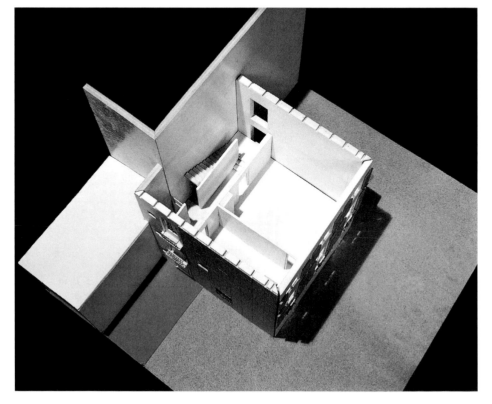

Hans Döllgast
1891–1974

The architect's house
Nederlingerstrasse, Munich
1953

Scale model 1 : 33 ¹/₃
Gerhard Breu

Döllgast's domicile is a narrow, three-storey end-of-terrace house, with a clear ground plan. A stair- and hallway, with a breadth of 2.75 m suitable as a living-area, runs the length of the house beside the dividing wall; on the east side is the entrance with a single-flight staircase, on the west are verandas overlooking the garden. On the first floor, a small hall-way with WC leads to the living-room and a combined kitchen and living-area; on the second floor, a vestibule with bathroom leads to two bedrooms. The rooms are also accessible from the hall-way.

On the ground floor, the passageway leads from the entrance down three steps to the studio with a large north window, to the garden and the boiler room, and on to the laundry-room, an extension with a lean-to roof.

This is a technically uncomplicated structure of single face-brick masonry from demolition sites. The concrete ceilings and lintels show on the exterior as grey strips. The stairs and landings are laid with Solnhofen slate, the rooms with grey linoleum. The walls and ceilings are of white plaster, except in the living-room, which has a white plywood coffered ceiling. The house was altered in 1989.

W. G.

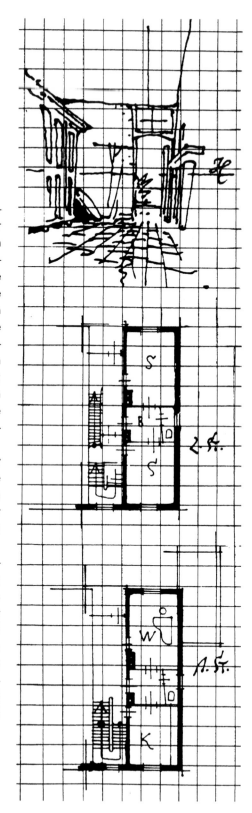

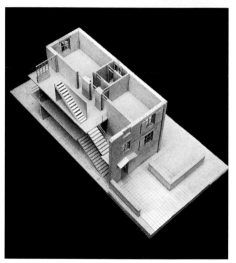

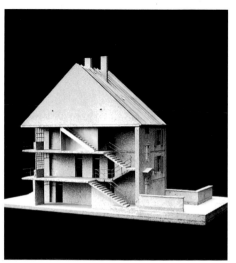

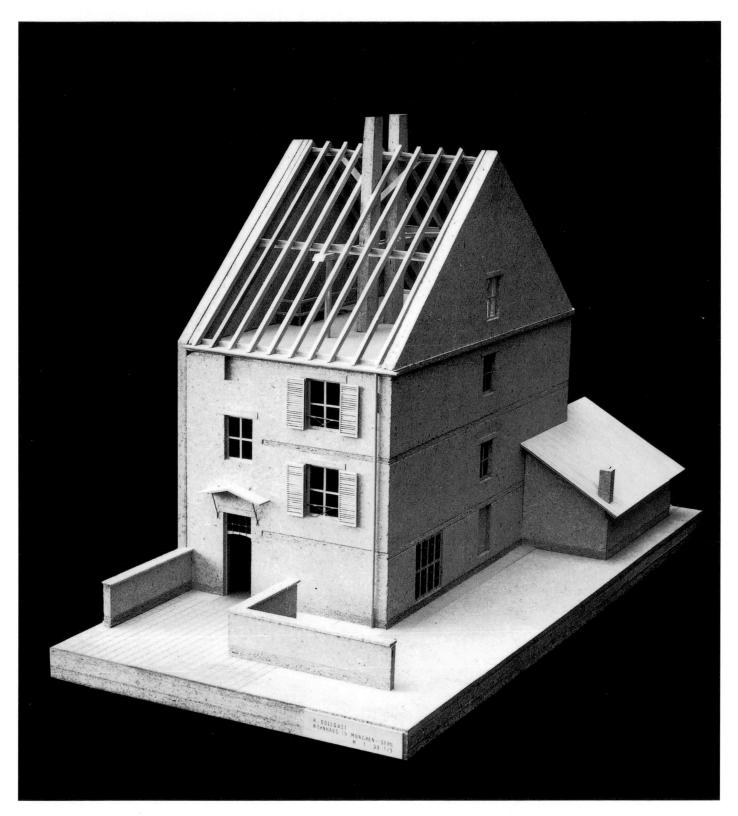

Hans Döllgast
1891–1974

Schloder house
Landshut
1957–59

Scale model 1 : 33 1/3
Ursula Müller
Doris Lackerbauer
Patrik Zeilhofer

"The site slopes south and is so narrow that one can only build upwards. The thing measures $8 \times 8 \times 8$ m, and has one large room on each floor. There was no intention of a rustic atmosphere; this appeared of its own accord. The whole style is as far from the precious as from the crude." (Hans Döllgast, Häuser zeichnen)

The house is situated on the steep southern slope of the Moniberg, near Landshut. From the road on the north side one can enter the middle level of the main three-storey section through a vestibule, or drive into the garage on the upper level of the extension. On the lower storey of the house is a studio, on the same level in the extension is the boiler room, and in the angle of the two structures is a veranda with a garden terrace. The bedrooms and bathroom are on the upper floor of the main house. Döllgast knew how to make the best of the sloping site. Elements of traditional Lower Bavarian architecture are apparent in the stark simplicity of the high-walled construction. Döllgast planned all the rooms down to the last detail and furnished them with his own designs. The Schloder house is still one of the best preserved houses by this architect.
F. P.

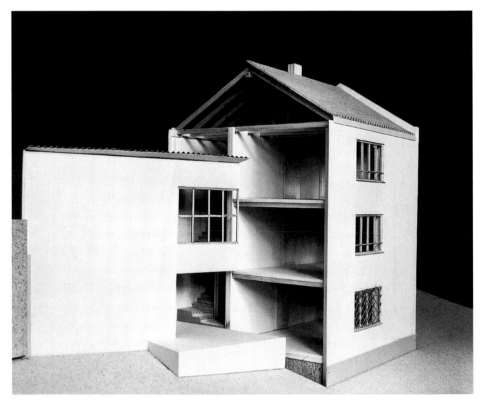

Theo van Doesburg
1883–1931

**Dance hall
Cabaret/ciné/bal "Aubette"
Strasbourg
1928**

Scale model 1 : 33 $^1/_3$
E. von Thermann

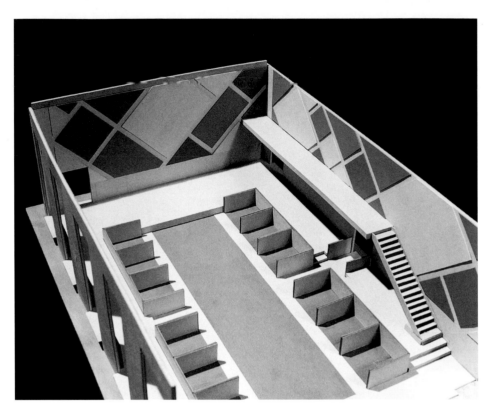

The scale model shows the large dance hall on the first floor of the Café de l'Aubette, a major restaurant and place of entertainment in Strasbourg, the décor of which represents one of the main De Stijl works.

"If anyone had asked me what I had in mind when I was designing this hall, I would have answered that I was trying to confront three-dimensional material space with diagonally coloured immaterial space." (Theo van Doesburg)

The dance hall is decorated with a modular colour composition. The spaces between the relievo coloured elements form a light-coloured linear network contrasting its obliquity with the static horizontal/vertical room. The idea is to "transcend" the walls and the one-sided cubic determining elements, such as the cinema screen and the side staircase and gallery. The floor, compartments and window side have straight horizontal or vertical coloured borders. Mirrors are mounted between the windows, and two parallel lighting strips provide artificial illumination. "The light and colour in this hall thus assumed also a functional significance, and since tables and chairs are only occasionally set up, the actual 'fixtures' consist only of colour and light." (Theo von Doesburg)
B. S.

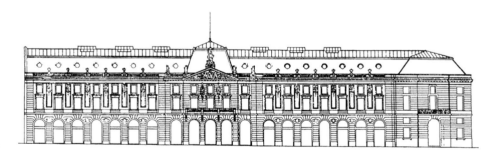

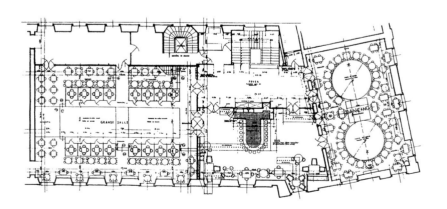

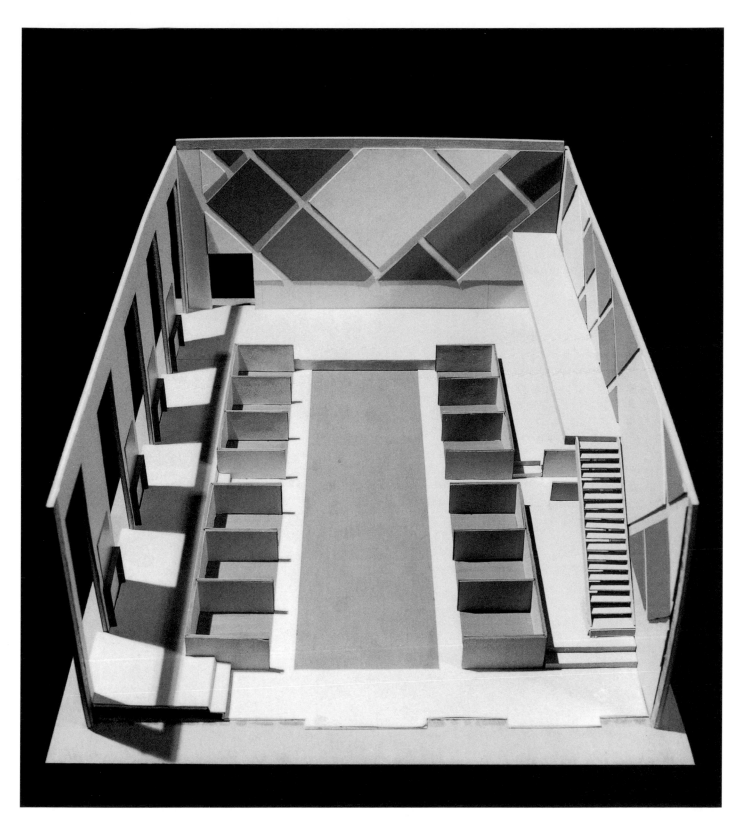

Theodor Fischer
1862–1938

Summerhouse
Schlederloh near Icking
1911

Scale model 1 : 33 ¹/₃
Hugo Daiber
Andreas Ulrich
Andreas Wahls

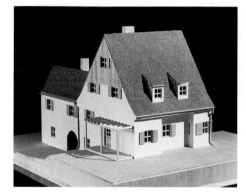

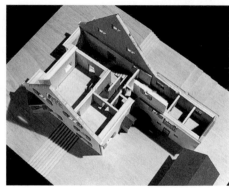

"Hardly anyone will realise that Theodor Fischer's house – a summerhouse he built for himself in a remote spot amongst trees high above the Isar in 1911 – was recently pulled down.

A reminder was given of its outstanding architectural significance two years ago, on the occasion of the comprehensive Theodor Fischer Exhibition in the Munich Municipal Museum. […] It was therefore hoped that, although the house had been officially passed for demolition, the owner (who had applied for a demolition order) would see reason. Then nothing more was heard. Now it is gone." (Letter from F. K. to the editor of the Süddeutsche Zeitung, 4 December 1990)

The modest house was cleverly adapted to the terrain. The living and utility areas joined to form a picturesque structure with a characteristic steep roof.

The house focused on the living-room with its tiled stove and corner oriel, reached through a spacious hallway. Five steps led to a slightly raised reading-room. The bedrooms were on the first floor.

F. K.

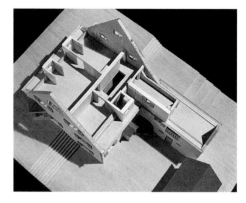

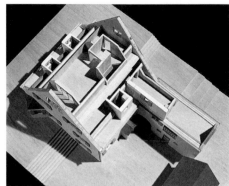

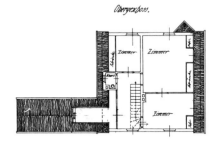

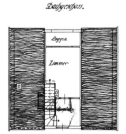

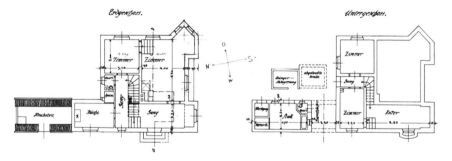

110

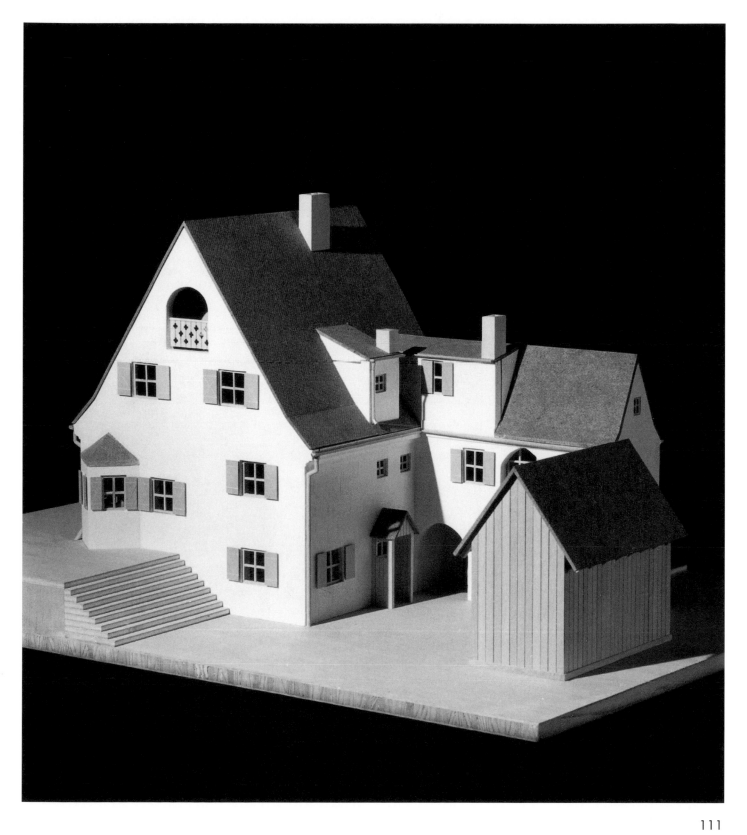

Josef Frank
1885–1967

House project
Salzburg
1924

Scale model 1 : 33 ¹/₃
Theo Schneider

This house is arranged round a square central courtyard on four successive levels rising from east to south. The concept of the house as comprising both place (immobility) and route (mobility) is exemplified here, inside and outside, by the linking of various levels and stairways. The "stasis of the centre" is abandoned in favour of a dynamic spatial arrangement. More than in many projects of dogmatic modernism, here the fourth dimension, time, has been successfully integrated. There evolves a new interpretation of the classical idea of the atrium house – permeated with great spatial and structural intensity.
M. J.

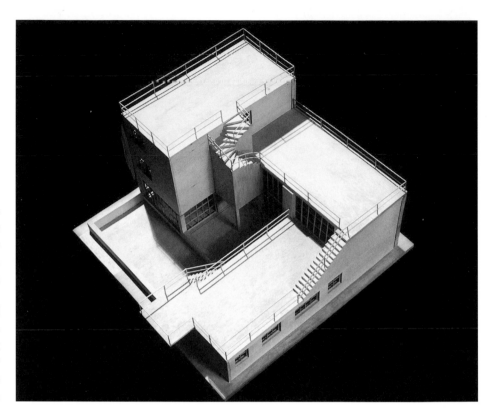

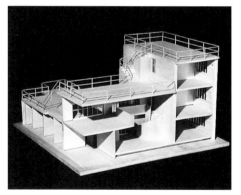

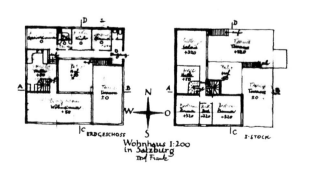

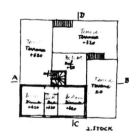

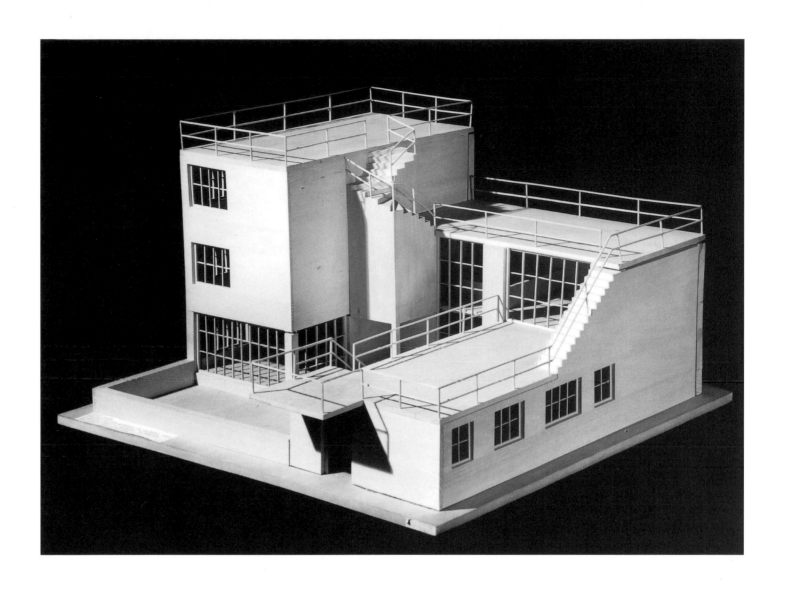

Josef Frank
1885–1967

Claëson house
Falsterbo, Sweden
1924–27

Scale model 1 : 33 ¹/₃
Wolfgang Zufall

In 1924, Josef Frank began planning the house for his sister-in-law Signhild Claëson in the southern Swedish town of Falsterbo, where he was to build five further houses by 1935.

The ground floor is divided into three lateral zones. Differentiated by projections and recesses, each division is given a characteristic form: the dining-area has a west-facing oriel with a veranda beside it, the living-room has a similar construction facing east, also with a large veranda leading on to the open terrace.

It is in the upper storey that the rectangular form (in the proportion 1 : 2) becomes clear; here again, terraces are added, and the three-part division is retained. Two bedrooms open on to the east terrace, and the interjacent bathroom is lit from the west.

In the centre of the house, the storeys are linked by a spiral staircase which leads up to a glazed wooden penthouse. Like the bridge of a ship, it is surrounded by a passageway which broadens into a terrace on the south side. Unlike the classically traditional Nordic houses designed by his contemporary Gunnar Asplund, this house stands at the beginning of the new era of functionalism in Sweden.

S. M.

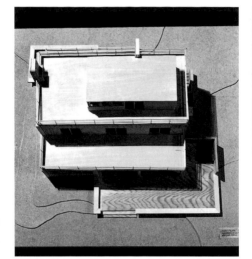

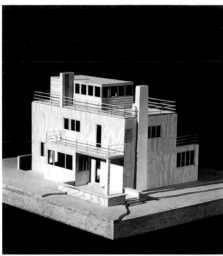

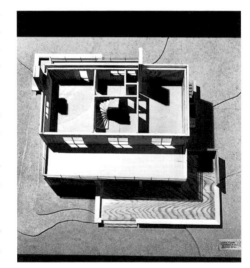

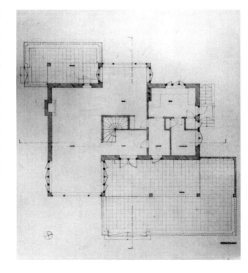

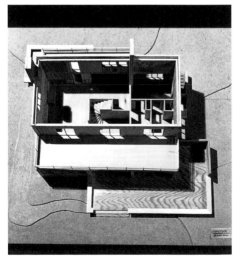

Josef Frank
1885–1967

House with a dance school for Mr. O., project Tel Aviv 1926

Scale model 1 : 33 ¹/₃
M. Agostini

Josef Frank's spatial idea of creating an organism determined by routes (mobility) and places (immobility) is also apparent in this project.

Terraced on three levels to the south, the structure follows the functions of the interior: behind the high two- and three-storey street façade are the apartment and the office, adjoining these the two-storey dance school giving on to the enclosed garden with pergola.

As one enters from the street, the route immediately begins to distinguish zones. Six steps lead up to the semi-private terrace, and a further step takes one on to the veranda. This gives access to the low duplex office-area; it also leads straight through a hall into the dance school and, at right angles, into the raised private quarters. Kitchen and dining-room on the ground floor and two bedrooms with bathroom on the upper storey enclose in an L-shape the office-area. Large roof terraces are accessible from both the dance school and the living quarters.

In the interior, the clear functional division of the three levels of the building has one structural link: from the mezzanine floor of the hall, a balcony projects into the dance hall, so that the apartment is linked only by visual contact, and remains self-contained.
S. M.

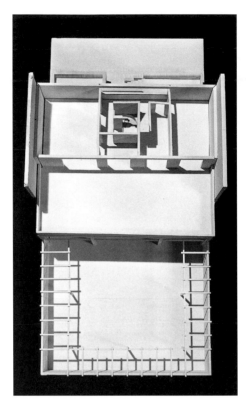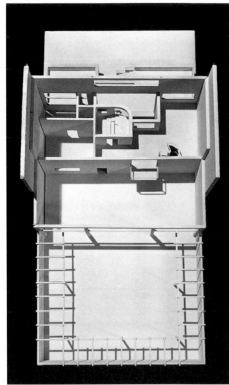

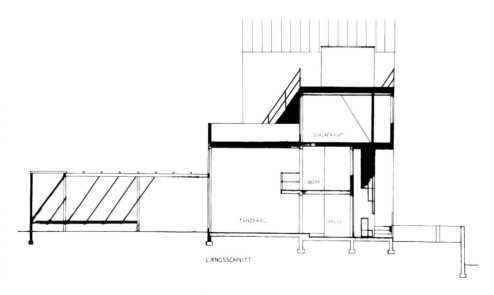

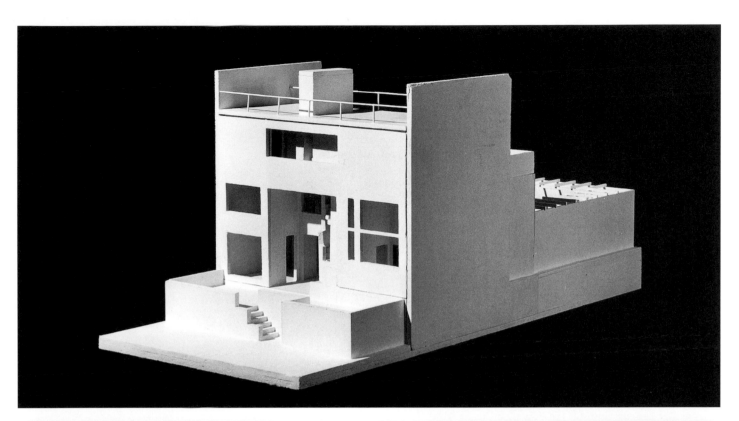

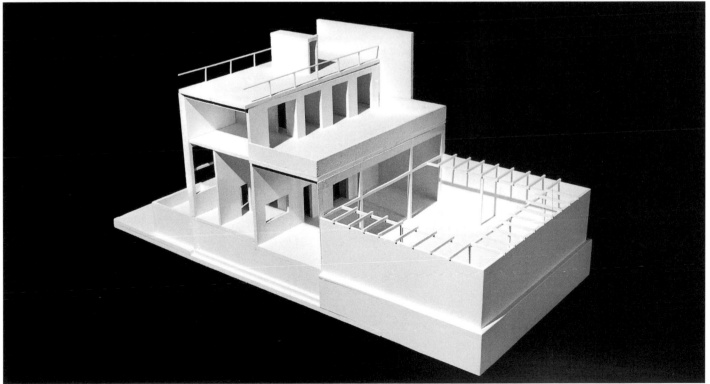

Josef Frank
1885–1967

**House project
Vienna XIII
1926**

*Scale model 1 : 33 $^1/_3$
Wolfgang Jandl*

In this project for a house in Vienna, Josef Frank designed a variation on the multi-storey atrium house. A two-tiered courtyard, roofed by the projecting upper storey, links the covered area on the entrance side of the ground floor and the roof terrace on the opposite side of the upper storey.

The three sides enclosing the courtyard contain on the ground floor the living-area arranged on different levels, and on the upper floor the bedrooms, on one level. The variety of relationships between enclosed and open spaces determines the free disposition of the interior and exterior routes and lighting that characterise the building. Josef Frank describes the relationship between transparency and a cosy home-like quality as follows: "I would certainly set store by having every room that is lived in equipped with windows in all directions, as far as possible, to mitigate the feeling of being shut in."
S. M.

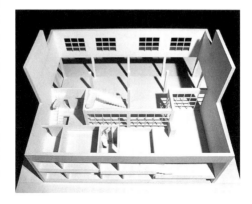

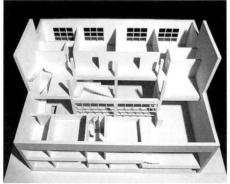

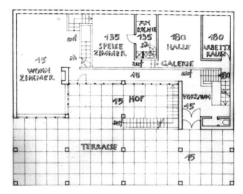

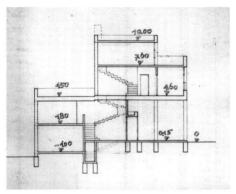

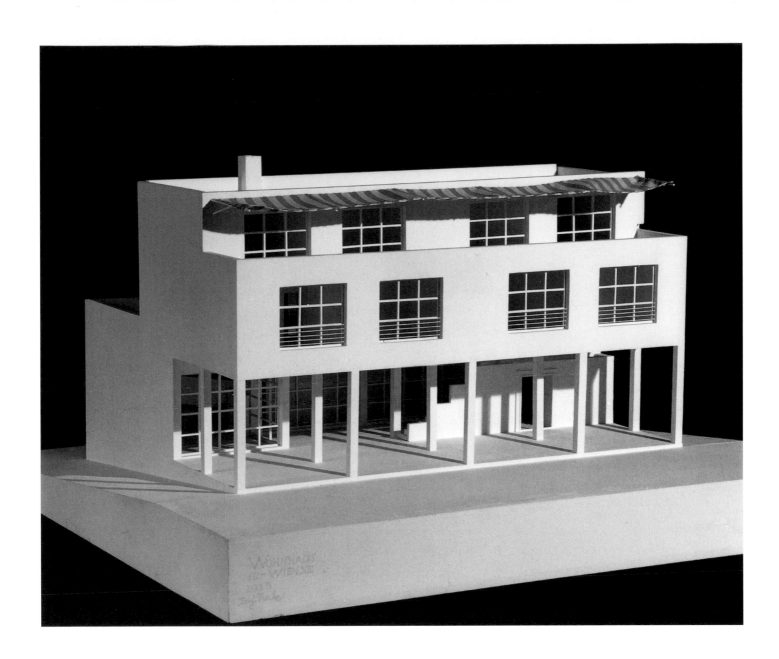

Josef Frank
1885–1967

Weissenhof housing estate, houses 26, 27, Stuttgart 1927

Scale model 1 : 33 ¹/₃
Moritz Haisch
Christian Kühnel

Josef Frank planned a pair of semi-detached houses for families with children and a maid. Two houses, mirroring each other, extend north-west to south-east. The light comes mainly from the south-west, the garden side. The entrance from the street is on the opposite side. Immediately behind the porch, a few steps lead from a small forecourt down to a large living-room with an adjoining sitting-area, kitchen, pantry and maid's room; a staircase gives access to the bathroom, two large bedrooms and one small one, with a balcony running the length of the house. Horizontal windows are for the architect the "natural" ones, "because we live in a horizontal world, and our eyes are placed side by side and not one above the other." The amount of light allowed to enter is designed more for orientation than for the even distribution of light. These cubic houses with flat roof and flush windows are of massive construction without wood: Feifel stones, plaster inside and out, Stephan ceilings, doors, metal frames and sliding windows. Experiments were carried with different energy concepts for the two houses: one with gas, one with electricity.
V. H.

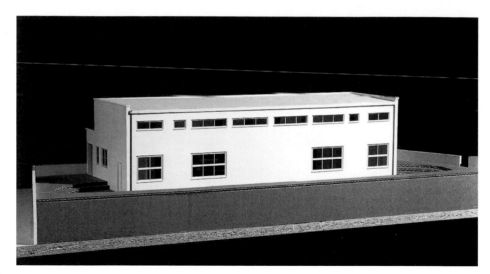

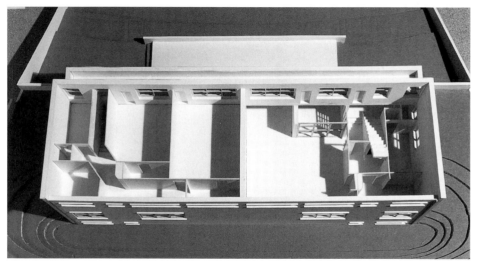

ERDGESCHOSS

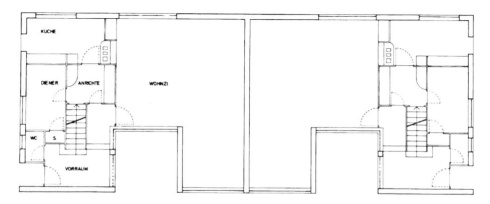

Josef Frank
1885–1967

Beer house
Wenzgasse 12, Vienna
1930

Scale model 1 : 33 ¹/₃
Martha Bilicka
Ellen Wild

Josef Frank realised this house in collaboration with Oskar Wlach in 1930.
In his programmatic article "Das Haus
als Weg und Platz" (1931), in which
he develops his idea of the house as
an organism determined by routes
(mobility) and places (immobility), Frank
wrote: "A well laid-out house is like
those fine old towns where even a
stranger immediately knows his way
around, and can find the town hall and
the market place without having to ask.
[...] The staircase forms the centre of
this house. [...] One enters the hall,
approaching the staircase which, since
it doubles back, offers its first steps to the
visitor. As he mounts them, he sees
through a large opening on the first
landing into the main room of the house,
the living-room. From this landing, the
staircase leads straight to the two more
secluded rooms connected to the living-
room: study and drawing-room. Here
the living-area ends. In order to emphasise this, the staircase now doubles back
once more, leading up to the next floor
with the bedrooms, and this makes for a
clear division of the house.
The route linking these [...] living-quarters
must be so varied that one is never
aware of its length." (Baumeister, vol 29,
1931, p 316ff)
S. M.

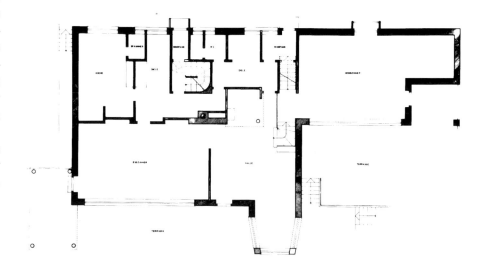

Josef Frank
1885–1967

Vienna Werkbund housing estate
Woinovichgasse 32
1932

Scale model 1 : 33 $\frac{1}{3}$
Herbert Hajek
Wolfgang Schebelle

Josef Frank, initiator and artistic director of the Vienna Werkbund housing estate, himself built a two-storey detached house with cellar, with a floor area of 100 m².

The entrance to this cubic structure with the upper storey set back, is up three steps on the west façade.

The ground floor is divided into three zones at right angles to the terracing: to the west, the entrance, kitchen and box-room, in the heart of the house the living-area, running the full length from north to south, and to the east the bedrooms, with the bathroom between them.

The open staircase on the one hand divides the centre of the house into the dining-area, connected to the kitchen and the cellar, and the living-area, leading out to the terrace and pergola; on the other hand, it links the north-south living-area on the ground floor with the studio at right angles in the upper storey, which is lit exclusively from the south and looks on to a terrace running the full width of the house.

S. M.

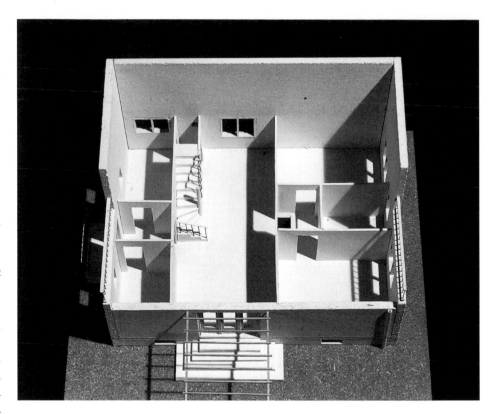

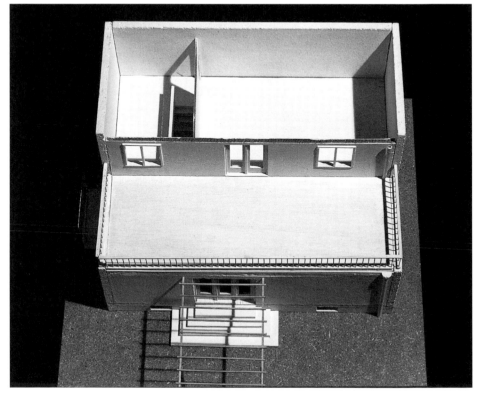

Josef Frank
1885–1967

Design for a house
1942/43

Scale model 1 : 33 ¹/₃
Detlef Schneider
Hans Uwe Schmidt

Josef Frank visited America in 1942/ 43, and this undated project shows clearly the influence of Frank Lloyd Wright, whom he greatly admired. It has striking similarities with the Ralph Jester house (1938), for which Wright constructed an ensemble of varied circles and cylinders on a level base.

Frank has three cylinders of different sizes emerging storey by storey, in descending order of height, from south to north, from a rectangular single-storey annexe containing a garage, a courtyard enclosed on three sides, servants' quarters and kitchen.

A circular terrace below the smallest cylinder leads into the hall, the intermediate area between the cylinders. The living-room – which, together with the dining-area three steps lower, occupies the largest cylinder – centres on the chimney-corner, which is lit from above by a circular lantern. The spiral staircase begins in the living-area, changes on the first floor to the glazed hall curving south and, enclosed in an added oval structure, leads to the second floor. In the smallest cylinder is a circular room with an adjoining circular bathroom, while the middle cylinder contains two levels, each divided centrally into two rooms with bathroom.
S. M.

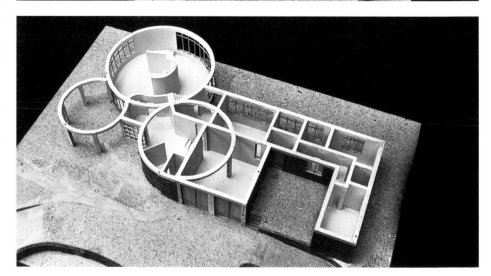

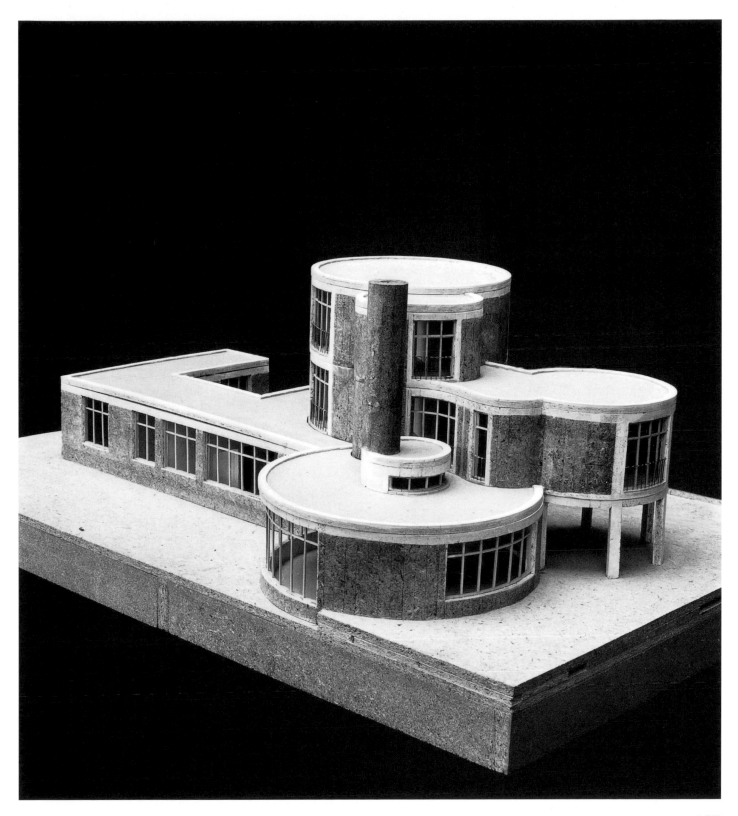

Josef Frank
1885–1967

**Thirteen imaginary designs for
Dagmar Grill
House no. 8
1947**

Scale model 1 : 33 ¹/₃
Eric Reumann

This house design belongs to the series of 13 imaginary designs for Dagmar Grill, Frank's partner during his last decade. These designs took shape in the course of correspondence between the two in 1947, and Frank continued work on them during the ensuing years. They range from free ground plan arrangements on rectangular bases, through "pagodas", to completely free ungeometric, apparently random forms.

House no. 8 is the most severe. The cubic structure is almost completely retained. Only two verandas, on the west and east sides, relieve the otherwise entirely filled construction grid. On the ground floor are the kitchen and the living-room, glazed to the south. A staircase leads to the first floor, where the rooms also face south. The large round window on the south side lights the bathroom, the one on the north side the hallway. On the second floor is the studio, glazed to the south and stepped back to form a west-facing terrace in the middle of which emerges the chimney rising from the ground floor, surmounted by a large "umbrella".

S. M.

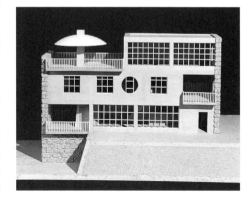

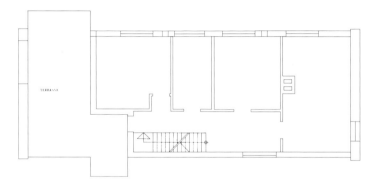

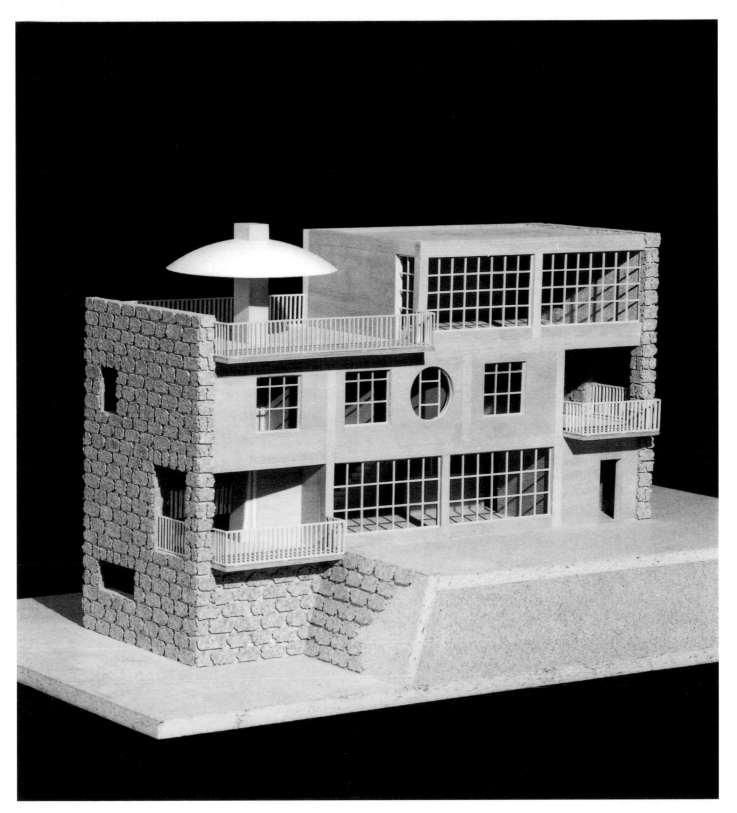

Josef Frank
1885–1967

Project "Double house" for Dagmar Grill
1953

Scale model 1 : 33 ¹/₃
Manfred Seif

This design also belongs to the series of 13. These are purely imaginary designs, and the numbering has nothing to do with their chronological sequence.

Taking into account the orientation, Josef Frank makes liberal use of his previously elaborated formal and spatial repertoire – for instance, the fireplace with a view in the Bunzl house in Ortmann, Lower Austria, and the alcove seat in the Wenzgasse house in Vienna. Particularly striking features are the colouring of the façades (sugar pink!), the shaping of the giraffe-like chimneys, the projecting staircases and the treatment of the garden façade, with two semicircular bays in the living-area. A west-east gradation in height completes the picture.

Here, as in the projects that followed, great store is set by the idea of "randomness", in accordance with his essay "Accidentism" (1958).

M. J.

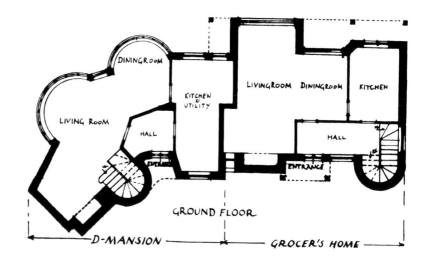

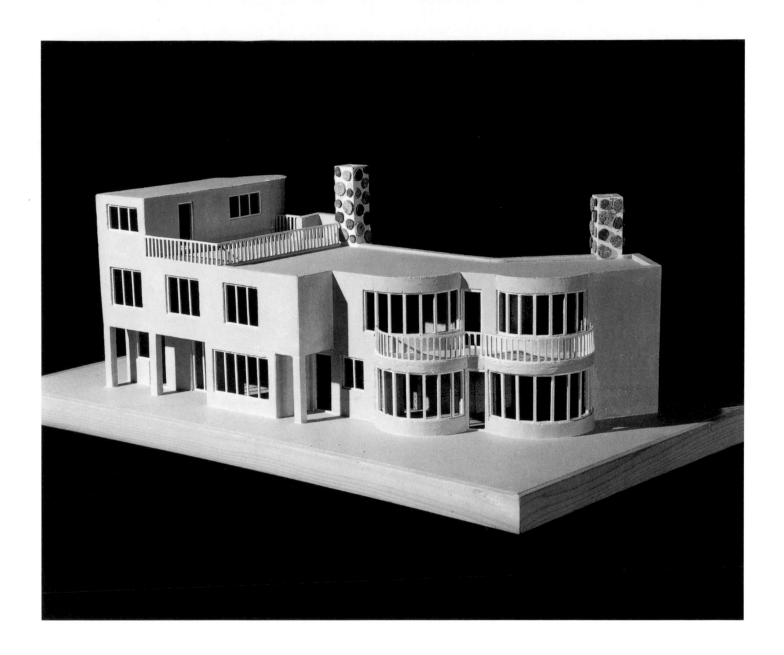

Bohuslav Fuchs
1895–1972

Fuchs house
Brno
1927/28

Scale model 1 : 33 ⅓
Gudrun Voerkelins
Rudi Meissner

This cubic four-storey building, conceived as one half of a double house, stands on a slope with a view over the city of Brno. It contains the architect's apartment and studio.

The living and studio-areas are separated by two sets of stairs. A straight stairway leads directly from the entrance up to the studio on the first floor.

The apartment rooms are on three floors (basement with garden terrace, entrance floor, second floor with a roof terrace on the third floor), and are connected by a spiral staircase adjoining the communal wall.

The house centres on the open, south-facing living-area with conservatory, with a gallery over the dining and sitting area bringing into relation the studio and living-area.

The conservatory and the entrance hall can be separated from the high room by sliding glass partitions. Large French windows lead on to the narrow balcony, above which the exterior openings are filled with glass bricks (with a window construction in the interior), affording the artist working in the studio gallery no direct view into the open.

B. S.

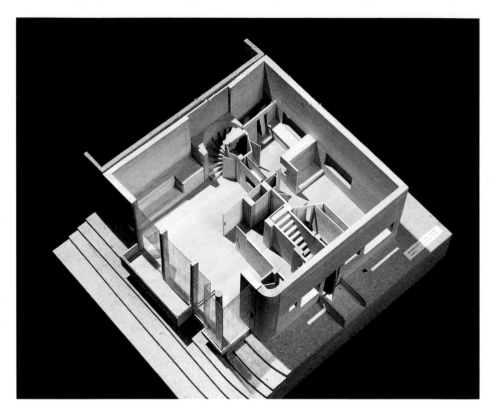

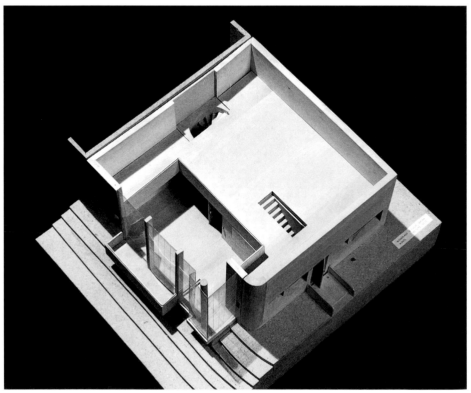

Architect unknown

Double house in Zlín
1933

Scale model 1 : 33 $^1/_3$
Jarmila Bernatek

Zlín, home town of the Moravian shoe-maker Thomáš Baťa, was carried along by the rise of his footwear company to become an incomparable example of urban development and architecture. In 1914, Baťa had commissioned Jan Kotera, the founder of modern Czech architecture, to build him a villa. After the First World War, Kotera's pupil F. L. Gahura worked out plans for regulating the future development of the workers' town, and these were carried out with unprecedented continuity until the 1950s. The most progressive powers in the country were architects. In 1935, Le Corbusier also elaborated an urbanistic design with blocks of flats in groups. This was, however, rejected by Baťa, who – in accordance with his motto "Work together, live separately" – preferred housing estates with detached houses. One of these designs is shown here as a scale model. It is a simple brick con-struction with wooden-beamed ceilings and a flat roof. The designers of these houses usually remained anonymous.

The factory, administration and com-munity buildings, on the other hand, were built as basic modules of 6.15 × 6.15 m, as ferroconcrete frames filled with brick. An impressive example is the 16-storey administration building built by Vladimir Karfik for the firm of Baťa in 1938.

F. K.

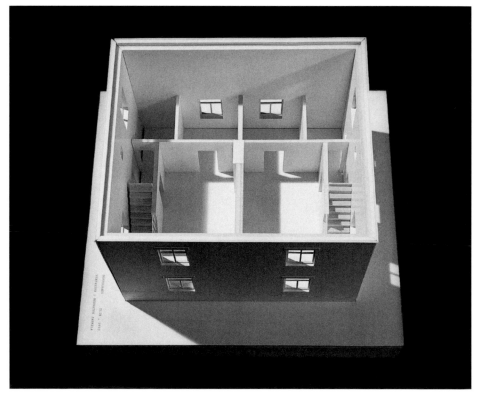

134

Johann Wolfgang von Goethe 1749–1832

Goethe house
Weimar, Frauenplan
1792 onwards

Scale model 1 : 33 $^{1}/_{3}$
Norbert Püls
Gerd Merkle

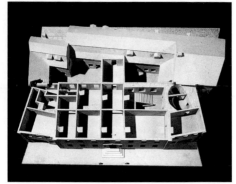

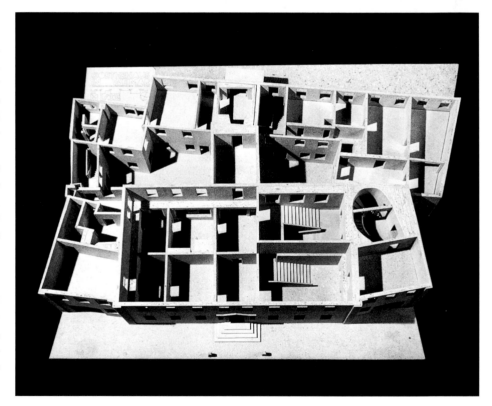

The garden house built by Goethe in Weimar influenced architects and architecture over the ensuing years. Goethe's house in the Frauenplan, on the other hand, although of eminent significance for literary historians, still awaits critical architectural examination. One might well call it an "early functionalist" house. After Goethe purchased the house, he altered it to suit his needs, linking the building that dominated the square with the raised garden wing. The size and character of the reception rooms at the front of the first floor distinguish them from the workrooms and servants' quarters.

The entrance, driveway, access and ascent by the main staircase (modelled on Italian impressions) contrast with the interior access to the private quarters by way of a spiral side staircase. Every structural alteration is based on a precise plan for living and working.

The differentiated colour schemes of the reception rooms are an important feature.

In contrast to the reception rooms is the splendid simplicity of the master's famous study, his library and small bedroom.

F. K.

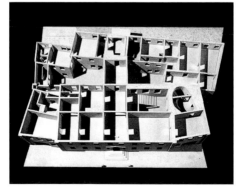
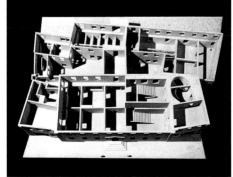

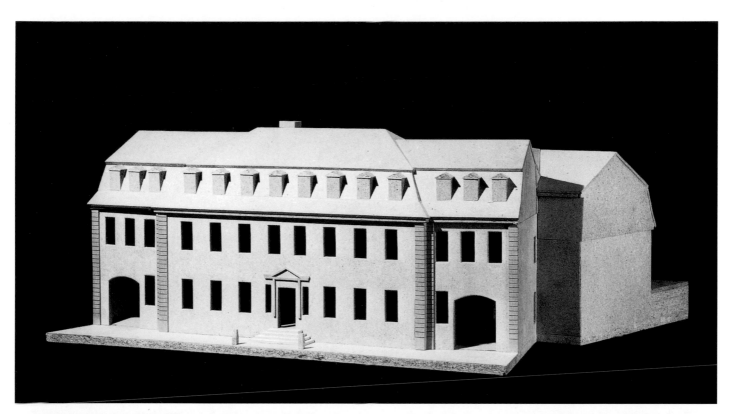

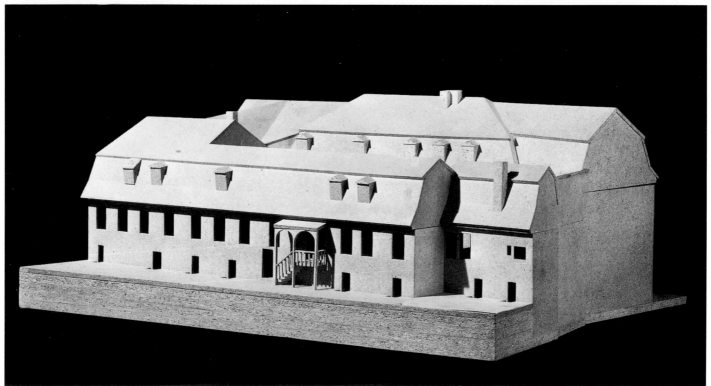

Eileen Gray
1878–1976

House E-1027
Cap-Martin, Roquebrune
1926–29

Scale model 1 : 33 ¹/₃
M. Bayat-Makou
B. Mund

Her first house, E-1027 – the name stands for the two designers, E. (Eileen), 10 (Jean), 2 (Badovici), 7 (Gray) – is on the French Riviera. Built parallel to the slope, it takes into account the topographical conditions. The slope falls away so that the living-area is supported on pillars, while the two-storey utility and bedroom-area is firmly planted in the ground. The entrance is on the north side. Going along the outside of the house, one reaches a covered forecourt. A curved wall leads the visitor into the house, while a separate entrance gives access to the tiny kitchen with a large covered outside cooking-area. Inside the house, one comes immediately to the living-room, the long side of which is glazed and can be opened on to terrace, sun and sea. Adjoining to the east is a study/bedroom with its own balcony. Bathroom and WC are between bedroom and kitchen. A spiral staircase, lit from above, leads from the roof down into the servants' quarters and a further bedroom with dressing-room, and on to the large terrace overlooking the sea. Ingenuity and flexibility in the fitting and furnishing complete the architecture.
S. M.

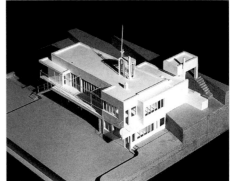

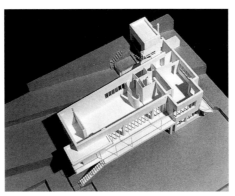

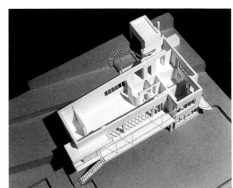

Hugo Häring
1882–1958

Vienna Werkbund housing estate Veitingergasse 71/73 1932

Scale model 1 : 33 ¹/₃
Dorothea Voitländer
Gesine Weinmüller

Hugo Häring arranges these semi-detached bungalow-type houses (76 m²/ 62 m² floor area) in three parallel rows. To the street side in the north he puts the utility rooms, including the kitchen, in a long, narrow row forming a backbone, while the living- and bedrooms face the garden in the south. This arrangement means that the north, west and east sides are almost completely closed, while the garden façade is glazed.

This allows a passive use of solar energy – an intention followed also by the pent roof opening towards the south, the effect of which is perceptible inside the house. Häring provides vents along the lintels; he maintains that architecturally, the three functions of a window – view, ventilation and light – could be more consistently carried out by separating them.

Glazed sliding walls between living- and bedroom enable extension of the living-area during the day.

A row of these houses was destroyed by a bomb in 1945.

S. M.

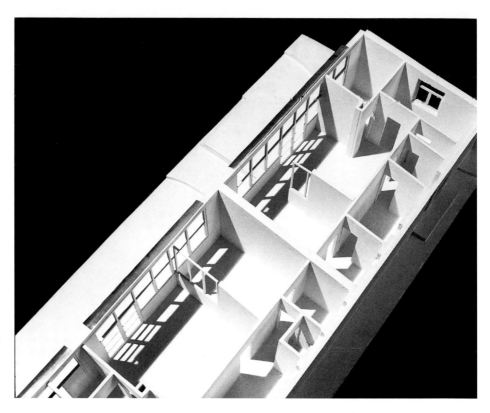

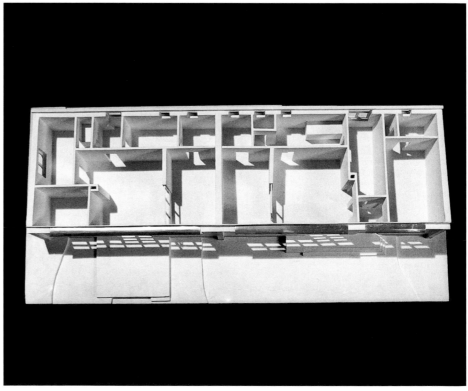

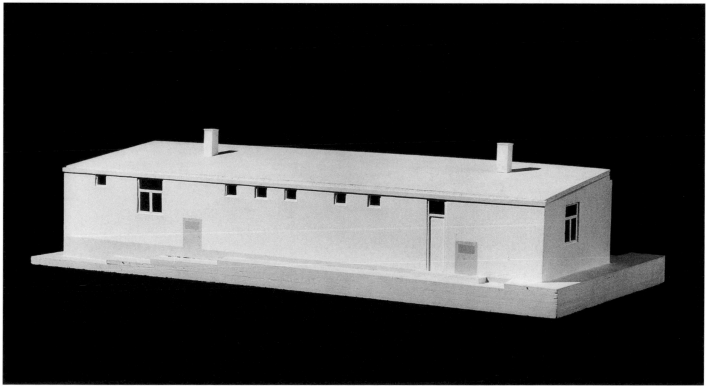

Josef Hoffmann
1870–1956

Vienna Werkbund housing estate
Veitingergasse 79/81/83/85
1932

Scale model 1 : 33 ⅓
Manfred Koronovsky
Christoph Grill

The four single-storey terrace houses designed by Josef Hoffmann, arranged to mirror each other, have a floor area of 57 m² and 71 m² respectively.

In accordance with his own elevated idea of living – namely, the noble villa – Hoffmann raises the ground floor eight steps above ground level, thus separating it clearly, like a "piano nobile", from the garden.

On the street side, the high glazed staircases lend rhythm to the otherwise uniformly flat façade.

The villa-type concept of this group is underlined on the garden side by the centrally situated open flight of steps and the slight recessing of the corner houses. The massive parapets shield the terraces from view and mark a clear threshold between living-area and nature.

The ground plans are similar to those of his flats, with the room functions often being interchangeable. The internal bathrooms of the two middle houses are lit through glazed openings in the roof terrace.

S. M.

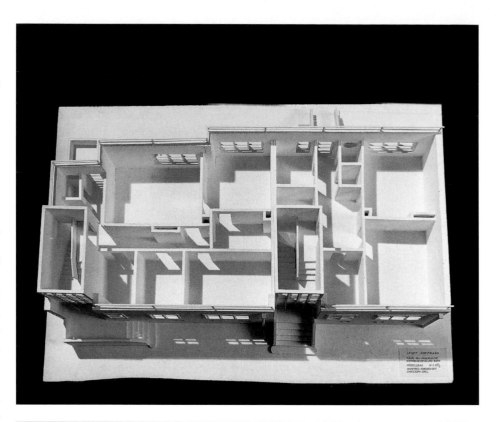

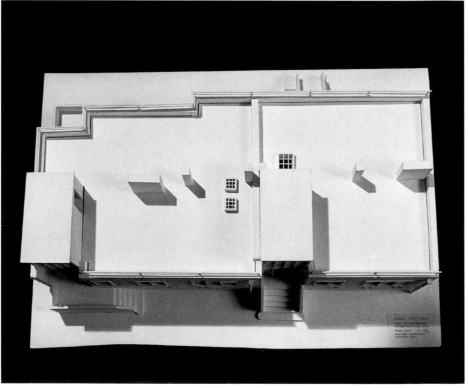

142

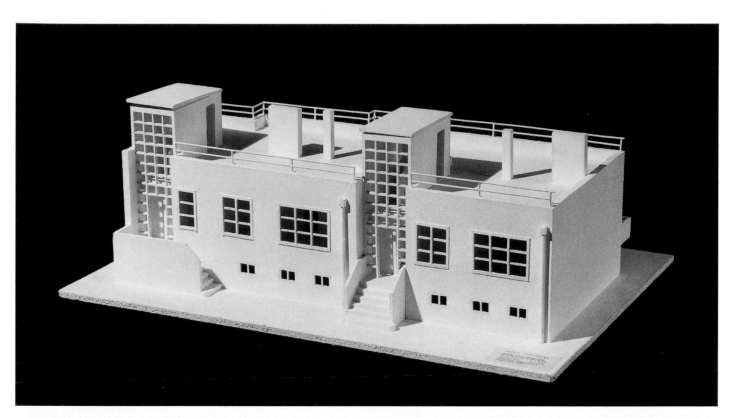

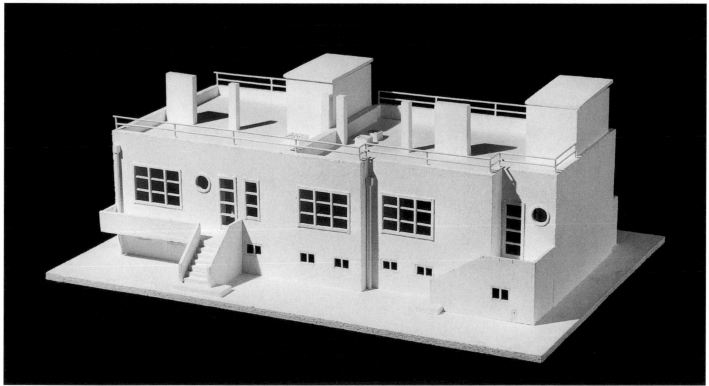

Clemens Holzmeister
1886–1982

House on the Hahnenkamm
1930

Scale model 1 : 33 ¹/₃
H. Rembeck
A. Schuster

Just a few paces uphill from the cable-car station on the Hahnenkamm stands the house on the rock. A stone base raises the frame structure, shingled in larch, above the winter snow.

In the entrance axis is the dining-area with the stove, forming the centre of the house. On the right is the kitchen. The children's room to the west and the living-room with adjoining veranda room to the east also form part of the latitudinal room when the sliding doors are open.

The economical distribution of space is functional and cosy, but not rustic. The sliding windows in the narrow veranda room give fresh air without causing draughts. The architect himself sat here making drawings and designs – for instance, the nearby mountain chapel on the Hahnenkamm (1964).

B. S.

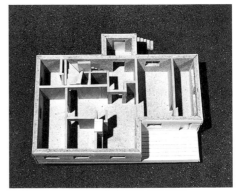

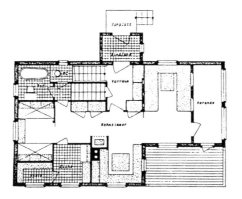

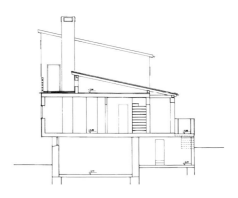

144

Louis I. Kahn
1901–1974

**Morris house project
Mount Kisco, New York
1957/58**

Scale model 1 : 33 ¹/₃
Ernst Ulrich Pfannschmidt

This project is based on a module of 1 : 4 inches. The 1-inch measure is applied to posts and slit openings, the 4-inch to wall elements and large openings. The front door is on the south side, which is closed in, with only a few slit windows; a vestibule leads into the two-storey entrance hall with stairway. On this level are the living-room and interior fireplace to the east, and the dining-area with anteroom, kitchen and laundry-room to the south. A separate adjoining cube contains the parents' bedroom with bathroom and study. These rooms are at different heights, the dining-area being highest, fireplace and bedrooms somewhat lower than the living-room. The four-flight staircase leads to a mezzanine cube with two bedrooms, bathroom and dressing-room, on to a bedroom with bathroom, and an open roof garden surrounded by protecting walls. The garage and the rooms with technical equipment are in the basement.

Vertical lamella-like protective elements to the east, slit windows in the south and large openings to the west give the rooms differentiated lighting, and thus a clear orientation.

V. H.

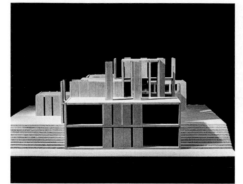
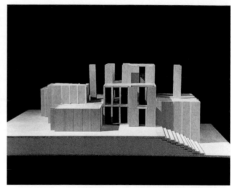
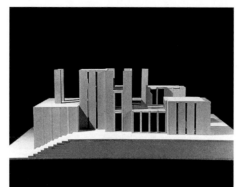
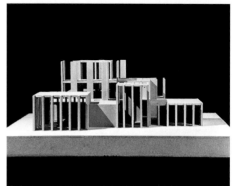

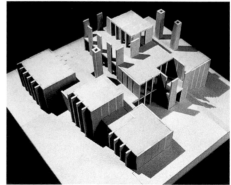
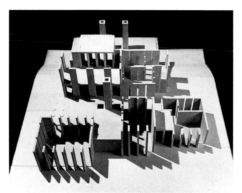
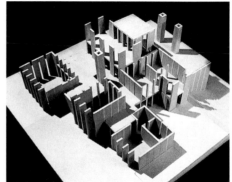

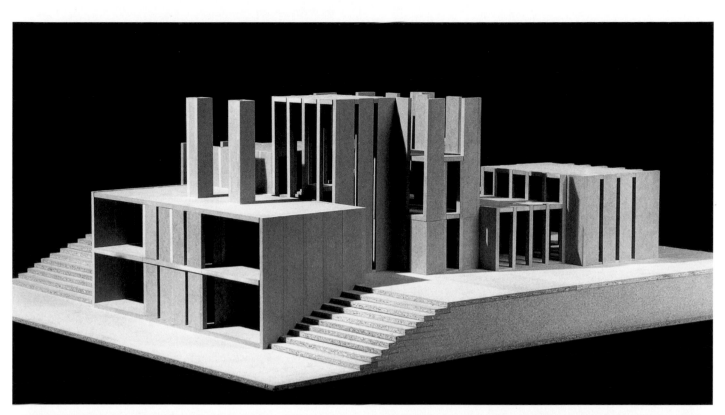

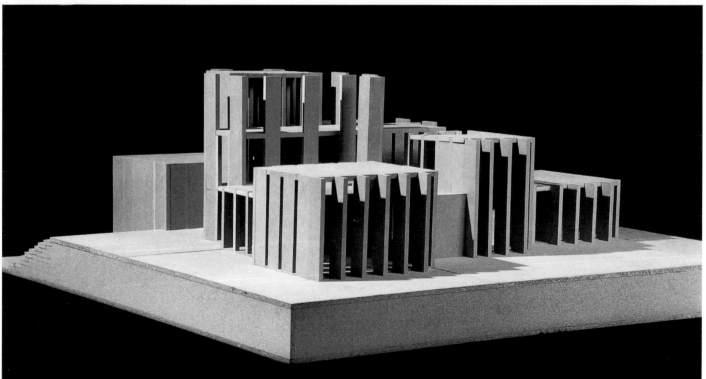

Louis I. Kahn
1901–1974

**Esherick house
Philadelphia, Pennsylvania
1965**

Scale model 1 : 33 ¹/₃

This building is a cuboid of simple proportions (44/32/18), with two free-standing chimneys. The interior is divided into two large and two small blocks (A-B-A-B). The two-storey living-room on the east side and the central staircase with gallery take up one half of the volume. On the west side, the large open cuboid contains the one-storey dining-room and above it the bedroom with a study which can be partitioned off; in the small closed cube are the utility rooms, such as kitchen, laundry-room and anteroom with WC on the ground floor, dressing-room, bathroom, lavatory and box-room on the upper floor. French windows, floors and stairs are of natural wooden elements, the walls have a dark plaster surface, and the pillar-like elements are made of bare concrete. The entire interior structure can be inferred from the south-eastern garden façade. Two closed cubes contain the utility rooms and staircase, two cubes open over both floors contain living-room, dining-room and bedroom. The large fixed flush window with small movable windows below and the recessed casements on either side with room-high shutters make for varied space-light relationships, as well as showing the diversity of the individual constructional elements and the overall ensemble.
V. H.

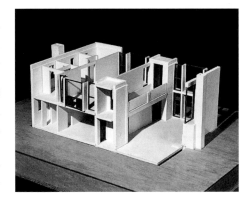

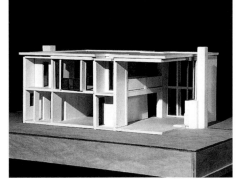

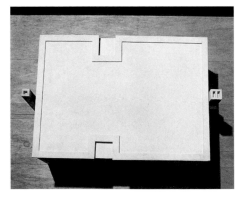

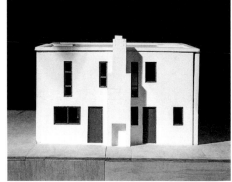

148

Adolf Loos
1870–1933

Michaeler house
Michaelerplatz 3, Vienna I
1909–11

Scale model 1 : 33 ⅓
Winfried Glasmann
Martin Hofmann
Johannes Iterman

The Michaeler house, six storeys high and combining business and living premises, stands in the centre of Vienna. When it was built, for the tailoring firm of Goldman and Salatsch, its plain exterior met with extreme disapproval because, given its prominent location opposite the imperial palace, it was felt to be provocative.

Today, this reaction is hard to imagine, since the lower part of the building is divided in classical proportions and costly materials were used. The top storey, with its steep mansard roof and cornice, can also be regarded as conforming with tradition. Disapproval can really only have been directed at the the upper, smoothly plastered section, with its clearly incised windows.

The inner courtyard, faced with white tiles and containing a free-standing lift shaft of steel and glass, is surprising for its modernity.

The model represents only the lower section with the business premises. This was designed in keeping with the overall plan, with a high hall and low adjoining rooms.

For decades, this part of the building was disfigured by alterations, and not until recently was it restored to its original form by Burkhard Rukschcio, for the Vienna Raiffeisen Bank.

F. K.

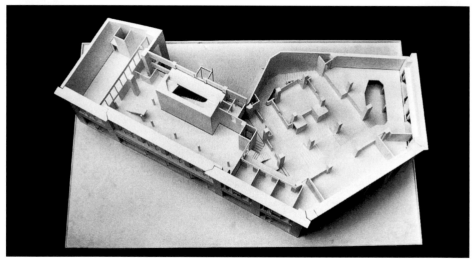

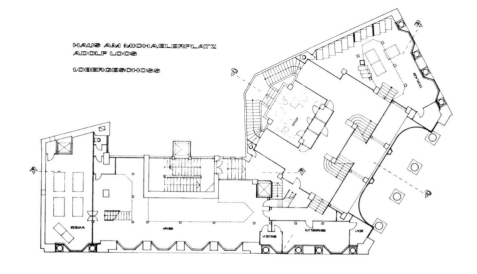

HAUS AM MICHAELERPLATZ
ADOLF LOOS

1.OBERGESCHOSS

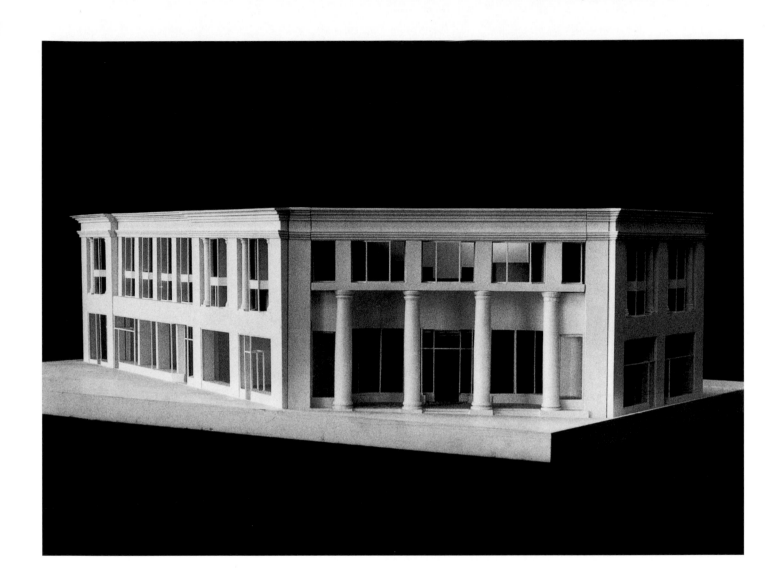

Adolf Loos
1870–1933

Steiner house
St. Veitgasse 10, Vienna XIII
1910

Scale model 1 : 33 ¹/₃
Anton Dollinger
Stefan Korinski

Apart from the Karma villa on Lake Geneva, extended 1903–06, this is the first dwelling-house built by Loos. It occupies a fixed place in 20th-century architectural history and established a precedent for modern architecture, due primarily to the blank cubic side facing the garden, with flat roof and clearly incised windows. (In 1913, Loos gave his famous lecture on "Ornament and Crime", first published in 1908.)

The street side had to conform to the prescribed storey limit, and Loos solved this problem by using a rounded metal roof.

In contrast to his later buildings, this house is still symmetrically organised as a classical form with lateral projections and a recessed garden terrace, the rooms being on one level. After the Second World War, it was disfigured by the addition of a gable roof, and not until the early 1990s was it restored to its original form by Burkhard Rukschcio. F. K.

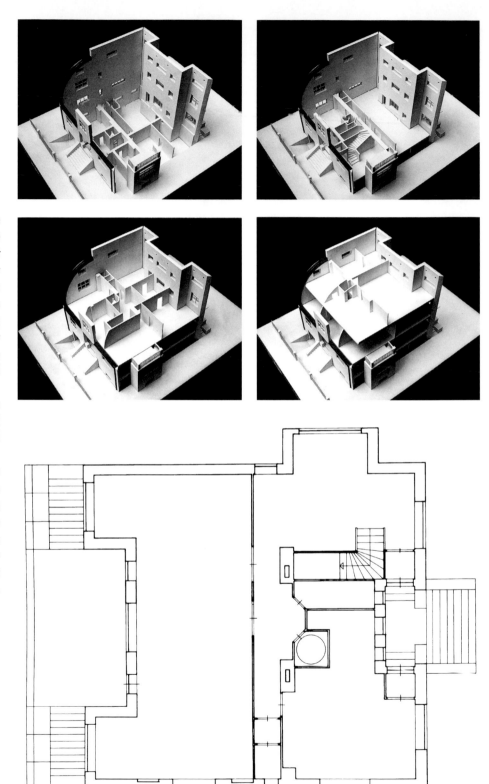

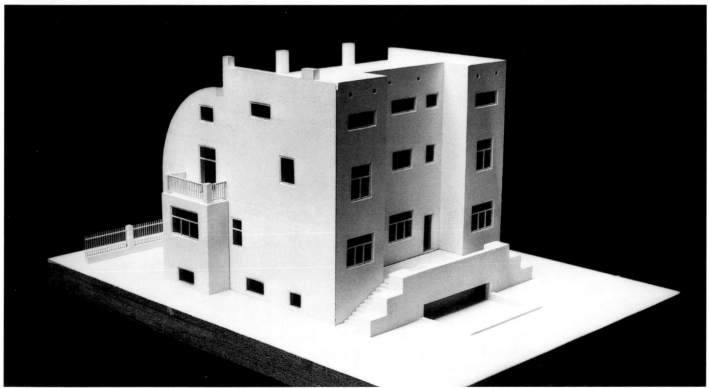

Adolf Loos
1870–1933

**Horner house
Nothartgasse 7, Vienna XIII
1912/13**

*Scale model 1 : 33 ¹/₃
Rudolf Eisenmann
Michael Müntzenberger*

Here the metal barrel roof makes both the top storeys seem like attics, so that the house appears to have one storey fewer because of the lowered gutter. Although the house is built on a slightly sloping garden plot, the rooms are on one level. The ground plan is almost square (10 × 11 m) and the construction, with load-bearing exterior walls and central pillar (which also serves as a chimney), but no load-bearing interior walls, anticipates that of the Rufer house, built ten years later.
F. K.

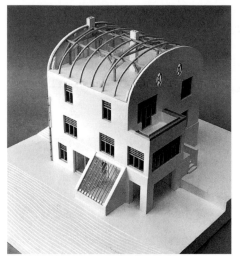

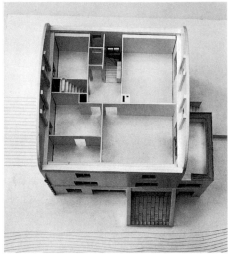

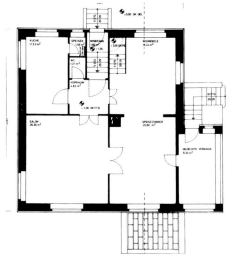

Adolf Loos
1870–1933

Scheu house
Larochegasse 3, Vienna XIII
1912/13

Scale model 1 : 33 ⅓
Franz Brenzinger
Dieter Schönberger

Loos's assistant Heinrich Kulka called this three-storey stepped cubic house "the first terraced house in Central Europe". The flat roof, made possible by the invention of the concrete-based fibreboard roof – which Loos called "the greatest invention in building for millennia" – allows the top storey of a house to be finished off with a horizontal surface.

The Scheu house has also been called a "growing house", because the stepped-back terraces offered the possibility of a partial superstructure.

The Scheu house is really a two-storey residence, since the third floor comprises a self-contained apartment accessible by a spiral staircase running from the base of the building.

The construction consists of load-bearing exterior walls and a central wall divided into pillars.

Here, too, the interior is determined by the uniform level of the rooms, although the built-in fireplace is set lower, as Loos had already demonstrated in his own apartment in the Bösendorferstrasse, in 1903 (today in the History Museum of the City of Vienna).

F. K.

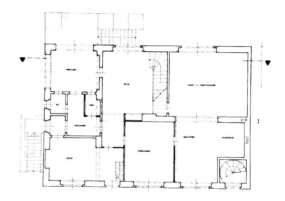

Adolf Loos
1870–1933

Mandl house
Blaasstrasse 8, Vienna XIX
1915/16

Scale model 1 : 33 ¹/₃
Karin Hesse
Bernhard Demmel
Sebastian Paul

Loos reconstructed an existing Viennese "cottage", adding a flat-topped annexe and a pavilion-roofed tower. The rooms, on individual levels, are arranged around a central duplex hall with a gallery. Loos varied the rebuilding of the existing staircase to make rooms accessible from intermediate landings.
F. K.

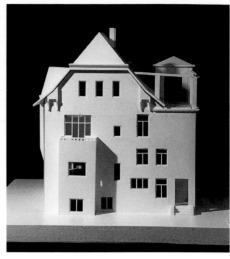

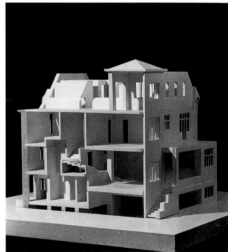
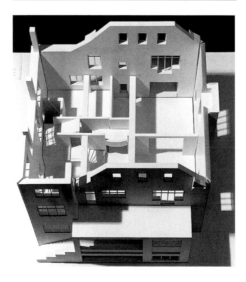

Adolf Loos
1870–1933

Strasser house
Kupelwiesergasse 28, Vienna XIII
1918/19

Scale model 1 : 33 $^1/_3$
Wolfgang Böll
Karin Grimme
Ulrike Pfaffelhuber

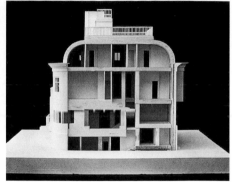
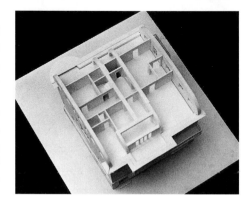

The reconstruction of this free-standing 3- to 4-storey cubic house as a villa already shows rooms on various levels, preparing the way for Loos's later *Raumplan* houses.

The top of the house is characterised by a terrace which, however, occupies only the centre part. The top storey spreads into view under a rounded metal roof similar to that of the Steiner and Horner houses.

Typologically, Dietrich Worbs describes it as a cubic house with varied-level rooms and numerous additional elements: oriels, balconies, loggias and a round tower.

F. K.

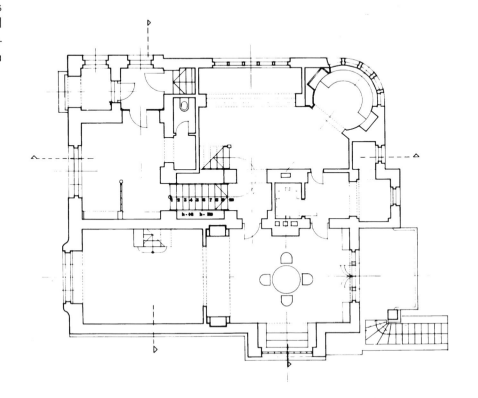

ADOLF LOOS - HAUS STRASSER
BÖLL GRIMME PFAFFELHUBER

Adolf Loos
1870–1933

**Heuberg housing estate
Röntgengasse 138,
Plachygasse 1–13, Vienna XVII
1921–24**

*Scale model 1 : 33 ¹/₃
Angelika Kern
Frank Schweser*

During this period, Loos was chief architect for the housing development authority in Vienna, and during the dawn of the First Austrian Republic, he identified with the aims of the Viennese movement for housing development.

His patented "house with one wall" provided the model for the Heuberg housing estate. His concept included wooden ceiling joists running from one dividing wall between the terraced houses to another, as well as façades made of self-supporting wooden framed walls.

The two-storey terrace of eight houses ends in classical style with corner extensions (the model shows only half the terrace). On the ground floor are kitchen/living-room, pantry, washroom, outside lavatory, hutch for small animals, and a hothouse connected with the kitchen garden. The bedrooms are on the first floor.

At this time, Loos advocated the "peat closet" and the theories of the Leipzig doctor Daniel Gottlob Schreber.

Today only remnants of the Heuberg housing estate are recognisable as the work of Loos.

F. K.

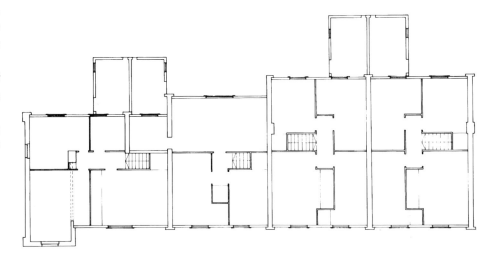

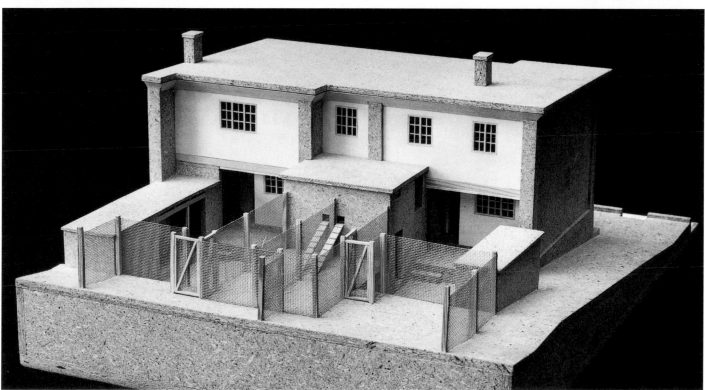

163

Adolf Loos
1870–1933

Housing development project (for London lecture) 1922

Scale model 1 : 33 ¹/₃
Richard Schewak
Maria Schiederer

At the time when the Heuberg housing estate was being built in Vienna, Loos gave a lecture on housing development in London, in March 1922, and designed for it this small terrace for an estate, with four adjoining houses. The ground floor includes porch, living-room, kitchen with boiler and bath, pantry, WC accessible from outside, hutches for small animals, and an open-air terrace. Both end houses have an additional study. On the upper floor are the bedrooms, with fitted cupboards and washbasins. A steep "Viennese stairway" with staggered steps leads to an additional attic room with a terrace.
F. K.

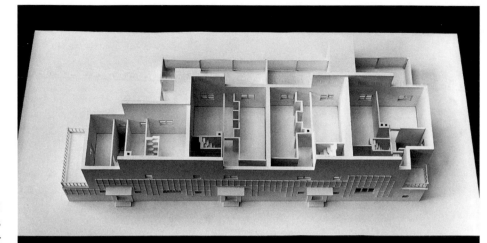

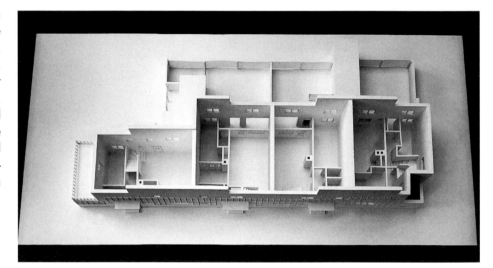

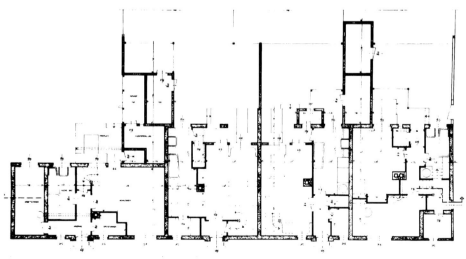

Adolf Loos
1870–1933

Housing development project (house types) 1921

Scale model 1 : 33 ¹/₃
Christoph Illig
Heidrun Naser
Franz Pillat
Clemens Reiter

For this project, Loos designed 5-metre types and 6-metre types, as well as 5.5-metre corner types, the uniform depth being 9.5 metres.

The staircase leading to the bedrooms on the upper floor always starts from the kitchen/living-room. Here Loos argued that, apart from the homeliness this afforded, it would make it impossible for the tenants to rent out rooms.

The constructional concept corresponds to the aforementioned principle of the "house with one wall".

F. K.

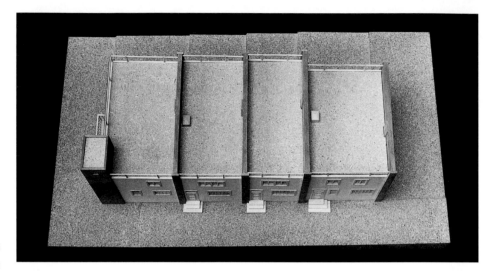

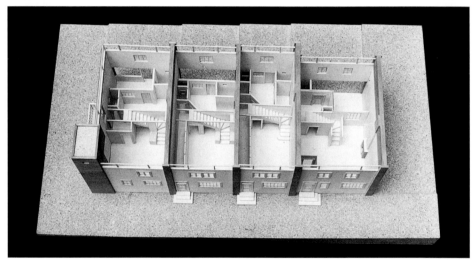

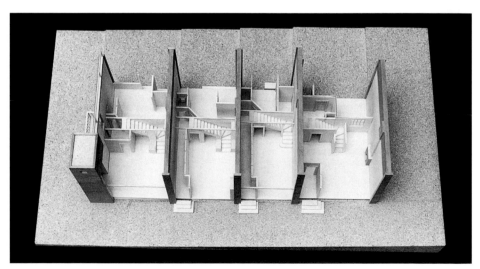

Adolf Loos
1870–1933

Haberfeld country house
Badgastein, Salzburg
1922

Scale model 1 : 33 ¹/₃
Peter Kupferschmidt

The stepped-back structure is classified along with the terraced houses, although the top storey has a gable roof. The lower brick walls support a wooden block construction with an Alpine roof, similar to that of the later Khuner country house in the Semmering region.

The central living-area affords access on the one side to Dr. Hugo Haberfeld's consulting-rooms, and on the other, up four steps to the raised music-area; beyond is the dining-room. Since the terrace above this is lower than the bedrooms it connects, the internal height of the dining-room is less than that of the living-area.

The design shows features of *Raumplan* (three-dimensional planning) and "partial symmetry" – concepts basic to the principles of Loos's work.

F. K.

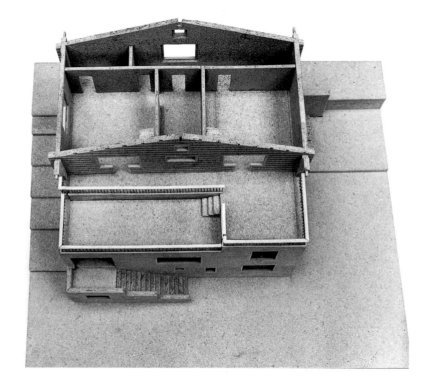

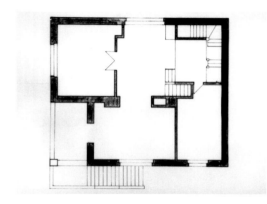

Adolf Loos
1870–1933

**Stross house project
Site unknown
1922**

Scale model 1 : 33 ⅓
Reinhard Bauer

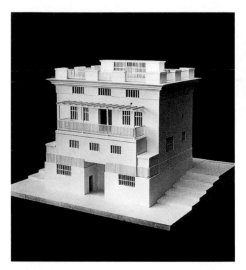
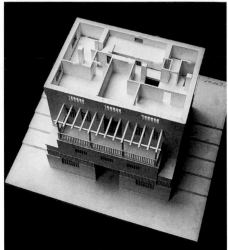

This well-proportioned cuboid town house, with a high, deeply recessed loggia, colossal inset columns and all the classical attributes, was designed concurrently with the blank cubic Rufer house. This might seem rather like "schizophrenia" on the part of the architect, but in fact Loos's entire work bears reference to classical antiquity and its repertoire of forms. Particularly when designing prestigious edifices, Loos took refuge in "enduring antiquity", but classicist examples are also to be found amongst his houses.

The exterior of the Stross house is characterised by strict symmetry and axiality. There is nothing strait-laced about the interior, however; here are the characteristic principles of *Raumplan*: different room heights on varying levels and precise calculation of movement involved. Hitherto, this design has been known only from the plan submitted; the three-dimensional model now brings us closer to the reality.

F. K.

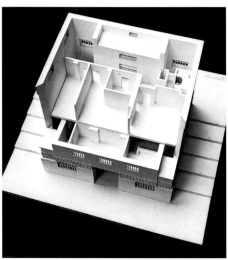
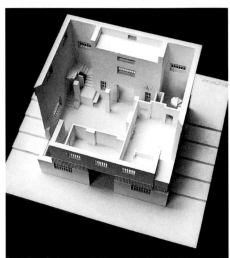

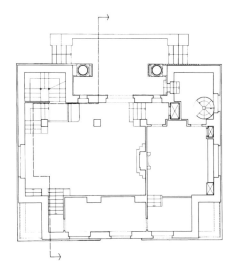

171

Adolf Loos
1870–1933

Steiner house
Chimanistrasse 26, Vienna XIX
c 1922

Scale model 1 : 33 ⅓
Heinrich Beck
Peter Lüdicke

The Steiner house is the reconstruction project for a house built on to the end of a villa-style suburban row. Loos gutted the house and built two projecting wings which are, however, reintegrated into the cubic form by a self-contained apartment on the top floor.
Characteristic of Loos's work are the classical cornice and the steps to different levels in the interior.
F. K.

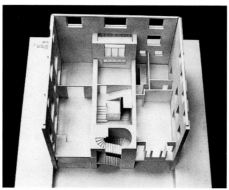
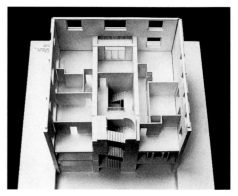

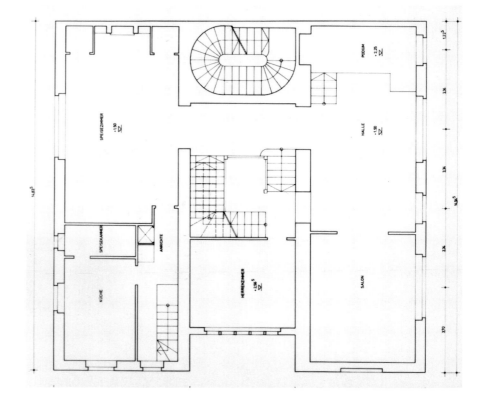

Adolf Loos
1870–1933

**Country house project
for Prince Leo Sapieha
Poland
1918**

Scale model 1 : 33 $^1/_3$
Ulrich Haas
Peter Schmid

The design for this two-storey country house with its steep, low-eaved thatched saddle roof shows lateral projections and a central living-area two storeys high. All the other rooms are placed in a U-form around this area, similarly to the Khuner country house. Below the surrounding gallery is the fireplace, in the centre axis; the staircase leading to the bedrooms on the upper floor starts in the living-area. The spatial concept is enhanced by further variations of level. F. K.

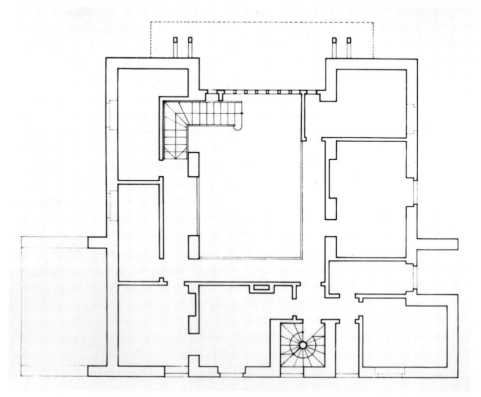

174

ADOLF LOOS LANDHAUS FÜR PRINZ SAPIEHA   M 1:33¹/₃   U.HAAS P.SCHMID

175

Adolf Loos
1870–1933

Terraced villa project
Site unknown
1918

Scale model 1 : 33 ¹/₃
Martin Münich

This flat cuboid building with inserted corner terraces on the upper storey stands on a site sloping down towards the garden.

The interior is generously proportioned. The central hall (11 × 14 m) derives its character from a large pool surrounded by steps and with a skylight above. A music room facing the garden extends along the back of the hall. The upper storey, accessible by a divided staircase as well as by a side, spiral staircase, is surrounded by a corridor.

The two main bedrooms and the bathroom and lavatory-area are fronted by roof terraces with pergolas.

F. K.

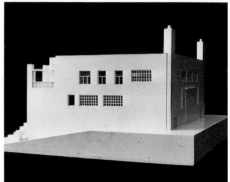
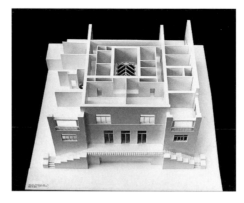
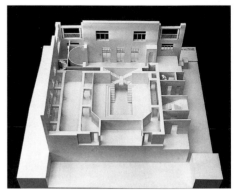
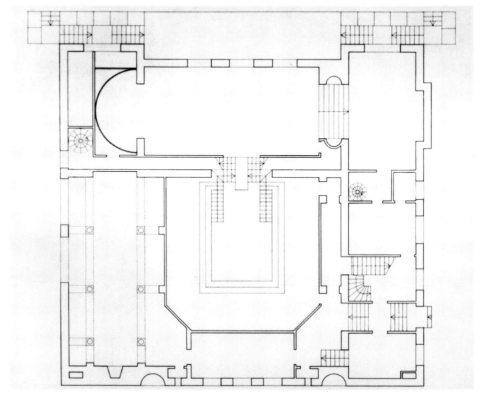

Adolf Loos
1870–1933
Assisted by Paul Engelmann
1891–1965

Konstandt house project
Johannesgasse, Olomouc
c 1919

Scale model 1 : 33 ¹/₃
Roland Klima
Josef Schuster

The classic villa-style architecture of this design for a house in Olomouc – native town of Paul Engelmann, who was a pupil of Loos and a friend of Wittgenstein – seems to set it apart from the rest of Loos's work during this period. The exterior shows all the classical attributes, such as lateral projections, oriels supported by caryatids, classical positioning of columns, portico, festooned attic, cornices and friezes. Appearances are deceptive, however, for the interior shows a variety still unusual for Loos's designs at this time.

The classical construction with its flat hipped roof conceals the interior progression and the sustained interest of the varying room levels.

Loos never really abandoned his classicism; in his later houses it is simply less evident.

F. K.

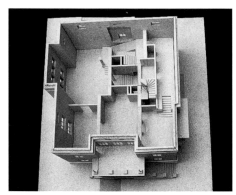

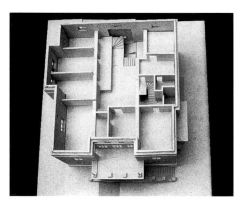
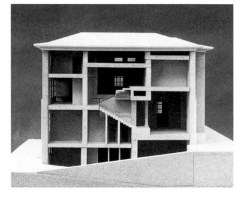
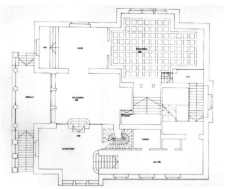
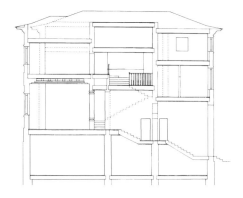

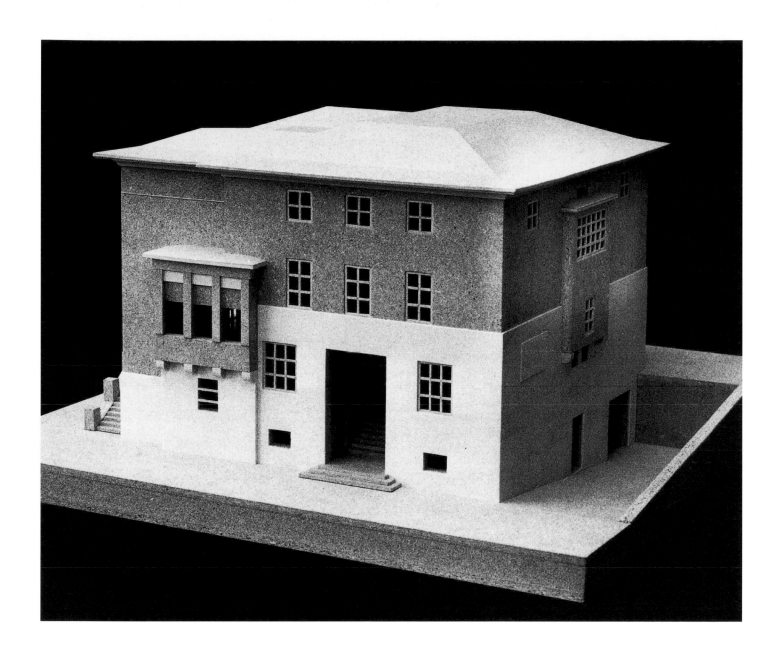

Adolf Loos
1870–1933

**Bronner palace project
Block in Grimmelshausengasse,
Bayerngasse, Kellergasse,
Vienna III
1921**

*Scale model 1 : 33 ¹/₃
Reinhard Bäumler
Thomas Mücklich*

Loos's entire planning concept is contained in this classical construction in the style of a baroque garden villa. Lateral projections, cornices, pillared façade, open layout of staircases, driveway, and the raised attic on the central section combine to lend an impression of grandeur.

It is in the interior layout that Loos's concept shows to effect – in the central hall with its raised platform, in the complex system of individual stairways and the various levels of the rooms comprised in the different functional areas.

F. K.

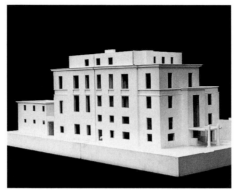

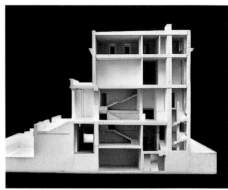

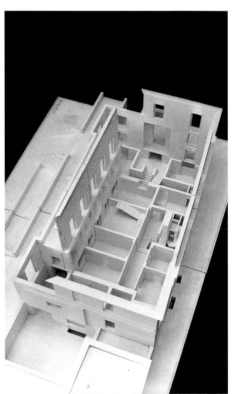

Adolf Loos
1870–1933

Palace project
Address unknown, Vienna
1921

Scale model 1 : 33 $^1/_3$
Reinhard Bäumler
Thomas Mücklich

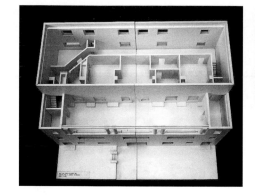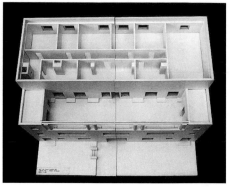

This building, designed in the same year as the Bronner palace, dispenses with all classical details and demonstrates a smooth, block-like, stepped form. The difference between them is, however, less than one might think, since the interior development and progression of the rooms, with inset columns, is just as grand in effect. A lateral entrance hall takes one into the main hall and on into the dining-room; on the left of the main hall, steps lead up to the salon, which has a smoking-room to the left and a living-room with a fireplace to the right. The hall links the various levels, and stairs lead from it up to the sleeping-quarters, which are fronted by a terrace with pergola between two corner projections. A further storey for servants and utility rooms tops the garden façade with an unbroken horizontal border, since the windows face the street.
F. K.

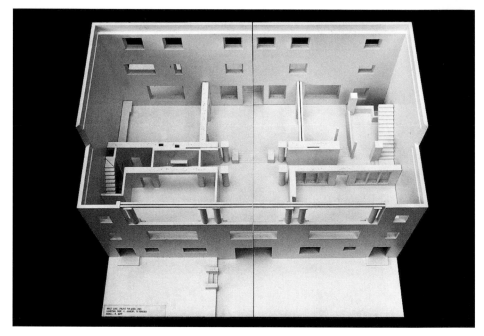

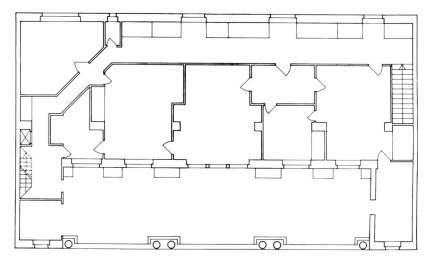

Adolf Loos
1870–1933

Rufer house
Schliessmanngasse, Vienna XIII
1922

Scale model 1 : 33 ¹/₃
Anton Putzhammer

The cubic structure of this house (11 × 11 × 12 m) with its recessed roof terrace provides perhaps the clearest demonstration of Adolf Loos's radicality.

Though from outside the house looks small, its internal capacity is surprisingly large. The interior of the cube reveals a wide variety of room heights and levels grouped around a central load-bearing chimney. Music-room, library, bathroom, bedrooms, children's rooms and utility rooms are all individual units, but otherwise the entire house is a single air-space. Everything is cleverly dovetailed; according to function and significance, each compartment is allotted not only a specific area but also a specific height. The conception of the house is entirely in keeping with what Heinrich Kulka called *Raumplan*.

The Rufer house probably best fulfils Loos's principle that a house should be designed from the inside outwards. The exterior cube appears to have quite arbitrary openings and windows in no particular order, but they are placed optimally for the interior distribution of rooms.

F. K.

2. OBERGESCHOSS

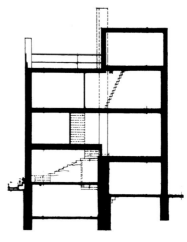
SCHNITT

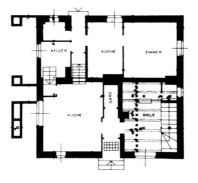
ERDGESCHOSS

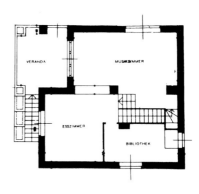
1. OBERGESCHOSS

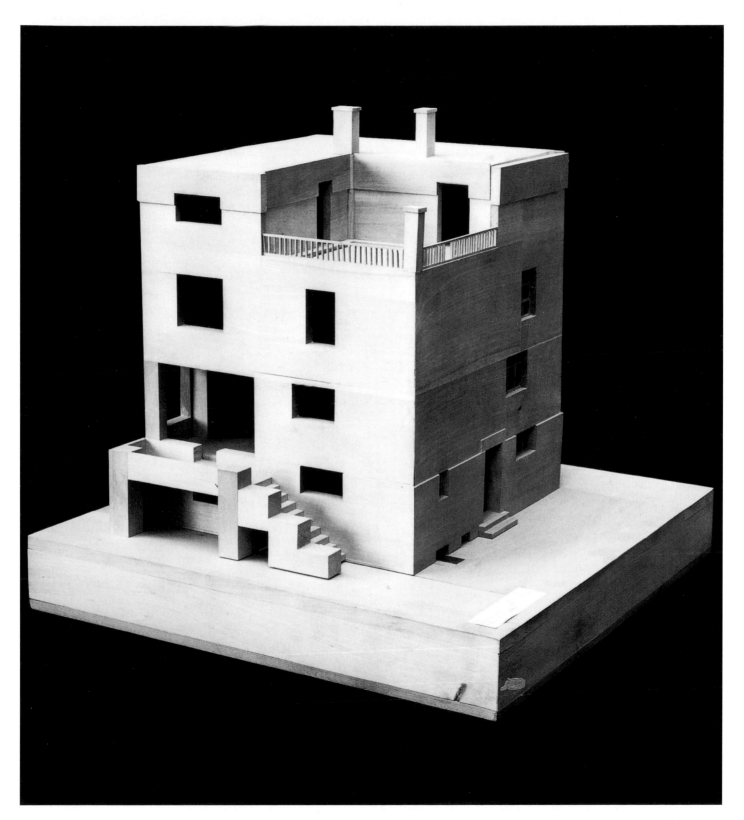

Adolf Loos
1870–1933

**Moissi villa project
Venice Lido, Italy
1923**

*Scale model 1 : 33 ¹/₃
Axel Moser*

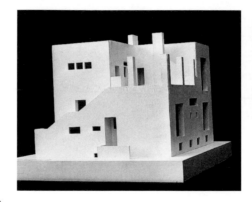
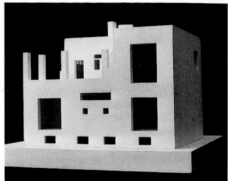

This villa, designed for the actor Alexander Moissi, is cubic in structure, with a recessed terrace bordered by a pergola. Here the living-quarters are in the upper storey, probably to give a better view, and the bedrooms are on the floor below. A special feature is the integrated outside stairway branching off from the entrance, replacing the usual side stairway. A spiral staircase leads to the living-quarters, arranged in an L-shape around the terrace and including a dining-area with a dumb-waiter, a music-area and a sitting-area with an open fireplace recessed under a staircase leading from the terrace to the roof. Once again, worthy of note are the staggered levels and the ventilation of the internal bathroom above low dressing-rooms adjoining the bedrooms. This house confirms the theory of Loos's Mediterranean inspiration for his house design.
F. K.

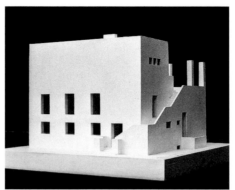
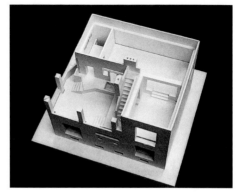

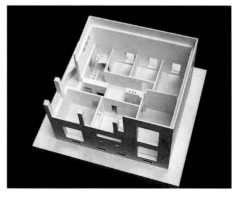
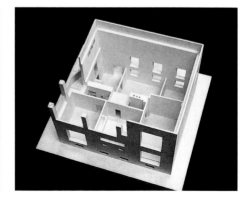

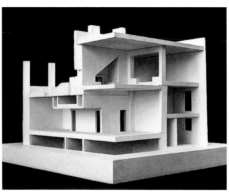
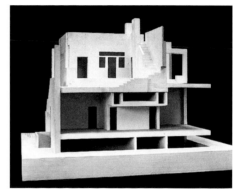

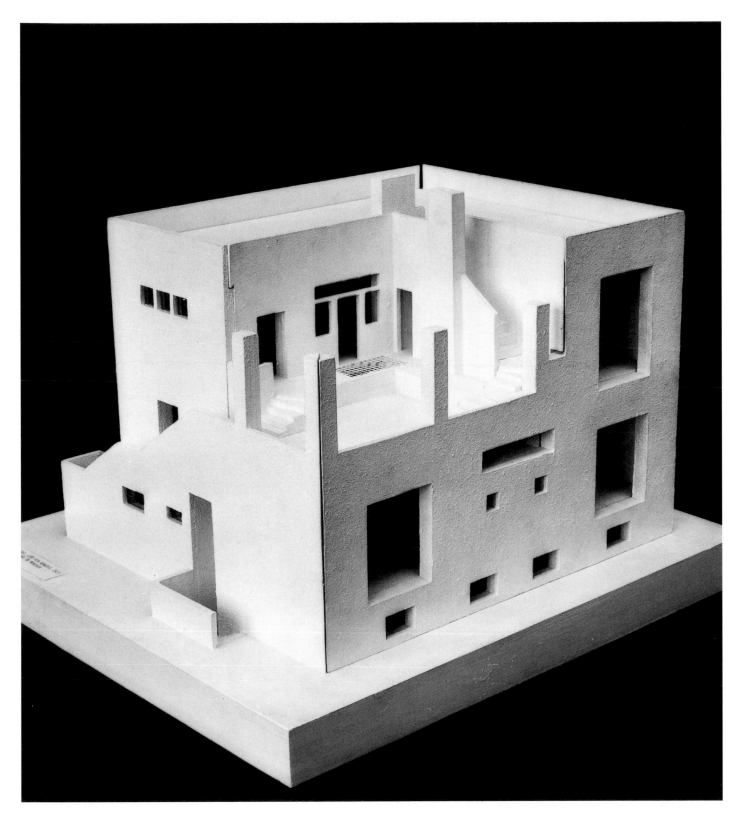

Adolf Loos
1870–1933

**Spanner country house
Rotes Mäurl 270,
Gumpoldskirchen, Lower Austria
1924**

Scale model 1 : 33 ¹/₃
Ulrike Lambrecht
Martina Reininger

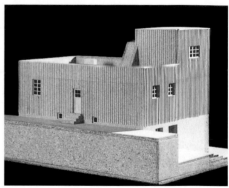

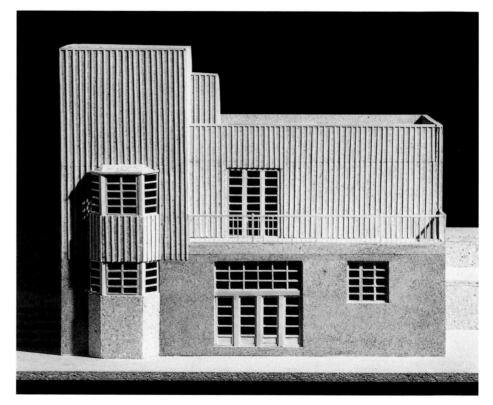

Situated in the vineyards of the southern Vienna Woods, this stepped terraced house with its square tower is simple in construction. "A cheap wooden house painted green and white", was Heinrich Kulka's terse description in his book on Loos (1931).

Hall, living-room and dining-area adjoin the terrace on the lower level. The hall lies four steps below the rest of the ground floor, and is open towards the raised dining-area. The three bedrooms on the next floor are accessible by a corridor from a staircase parallel to it. The upper part of the tower contains a further room and the water-tank. The vertical dimension of the tower is emphasised by bow windows. In 1938, pitched roofs were superimposed upon the original flat roofs.

F. K.

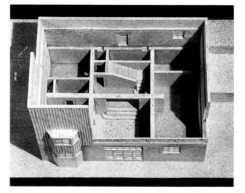
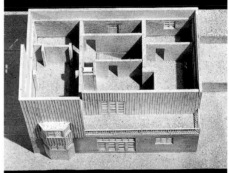

Adolf Loos
1870–1933

**Simon villa project
Vienna XIX
c 1924**

*Scale model 1 : 33 ¹/₃
B. Natterer
P. Schröpf*

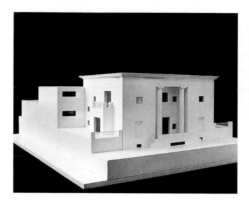
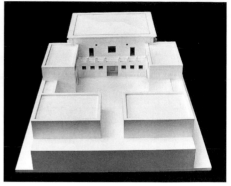
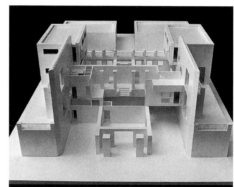
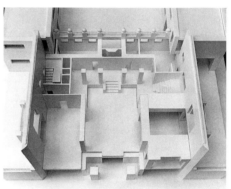

This classical building complex is approached via a *cour d'honneur*, the wings of which have been omitted in this model. The villa itself is thus a long way from the street. In other villa projects by Loos, the utility and servants' quarters are situated in the basement or the attic storey; here they are in separate low buildings. The entrance to the house is through a porch in the centre axis, from which steps lead down to the smoking-room, the library and the living-area.

At the head of the stairs in the hall is a row of columns. On the garden side, the centre axis is marked by a deeply recessed loggia two storeys high, with colossal inset columns.

F. K.

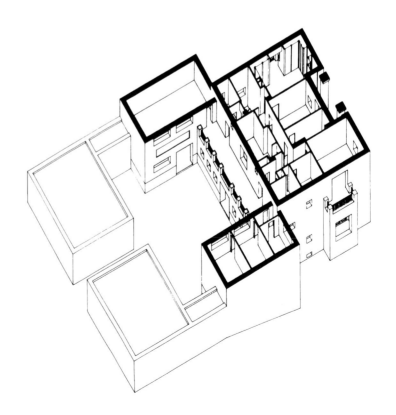

Adolf Loos
1870–1933

**Residential complex project
Inzersdorferstrasse
(now Kennergasse, Bürgergasse,
Staudigelgasse, Favoritenstrasse),
Vienna X
1923**

Scale model 1 : 33 ¹/₃
Barbara Eberhardt
Gerald Olgemöller
Monika Rehmus

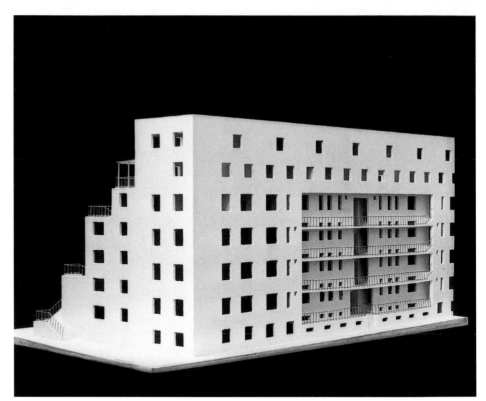

It remains a great sin of omission that this urban residential complex was never realised. With this building, Loos offered an alternative to the concept of the Viennese "superblock":

"In this project I have apartments that occupy two floors. This is not an invention of mine. [...] It is very important for people not to have their living-quarters next to their sleeping-quarters [...]. They then imagine they have a house of their own. This increases people's self-esteem. The two terraced houses, one behind the other, have raised walkways accessible by an outside staircase. Each apartment has its own entrance from the walkway, and its own pergola for sitting outside in the evening. The children can play safely on the terrace [...]."

"I have always longed to build a terraced house like this for workers' flats. I find the fate of proletarian children from their first year until they go to school particularly hard. The prison of the child locked in at home by its parents should be opened up by the common terrace, which enables neighbours to keep a lookout." (Adolf Loos)
F. K.

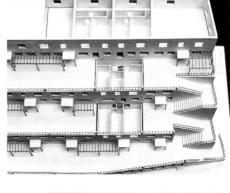

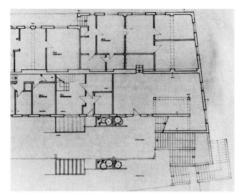

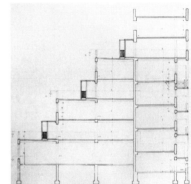

192

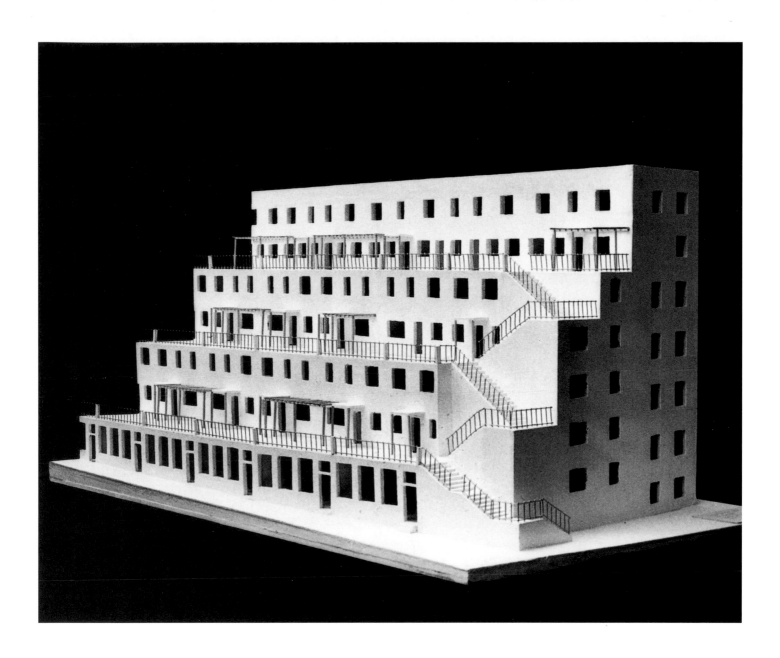

Adolf Loos
1870–1933

**Villa Verdier project
Le Lavandou, near Toulon,
France
1923**

*Scale model 1 : 33 ¹/₃
Monika Lassak-Georgii
Franz Tadaeus Lassak*

This villa project is classified amongst the terraced houses. Two semicircular oriels divide the garden façade of the long rectangular building. The house centres on a duplex living-room with a U-shaped gallery round it. Sliding doors give access to a terrace between the oriels, with steps down to the garden. Under the gallery, along the centre axis, the living-area has a chimney-corner. There is a roof terrace in front of the upper storey.
F. K.

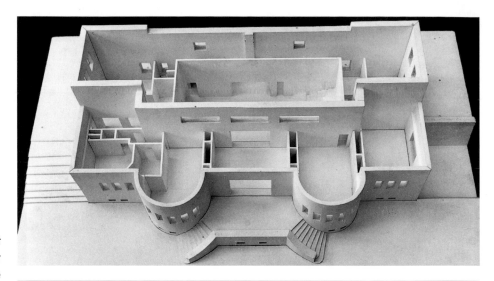

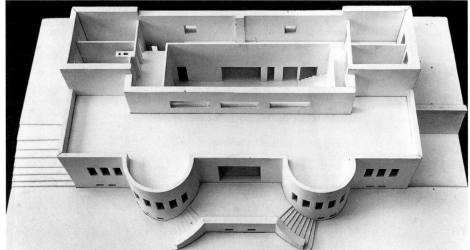

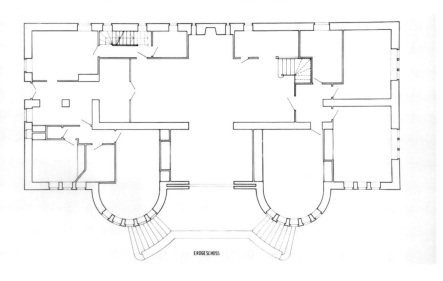

194

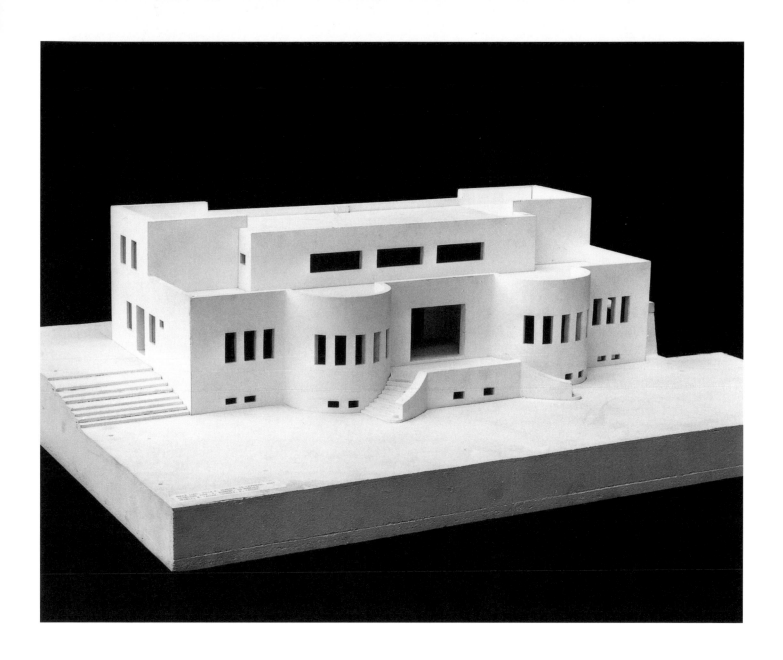

Adolf Loos
1870–1933

**Project: group of 20 houses
Promenade des Anglais, Nice,
France
1923**

*Scale model 1 : 33 ⅓
Stefan Hennemann
Helmut Kipf*

This project is reminiscent of the terraced houses project for the municipality of Vienna. The stepped formation in two, three and four storeys of the differently-sized units avoids the problem of unused space that arises in municipal blocks. Each apartment has its own terrace. The model shows only one "branch" of the design; several such "branches" were planned, "growing out" of a five-storey "backbone" (north wing).

A wide variety of living-quarters has been evolved here; nevertheless, during the construction of the model several unresolved cavities were formed, probably due to lack of detail in the preliminary design phase.

F. K.

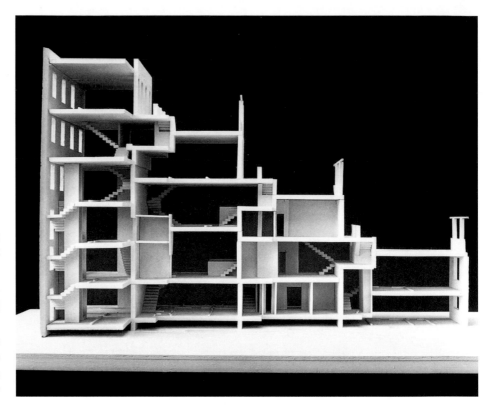

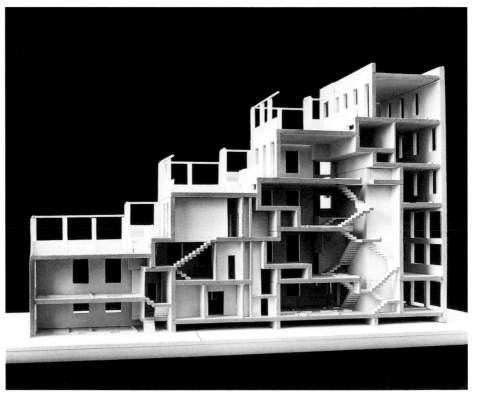

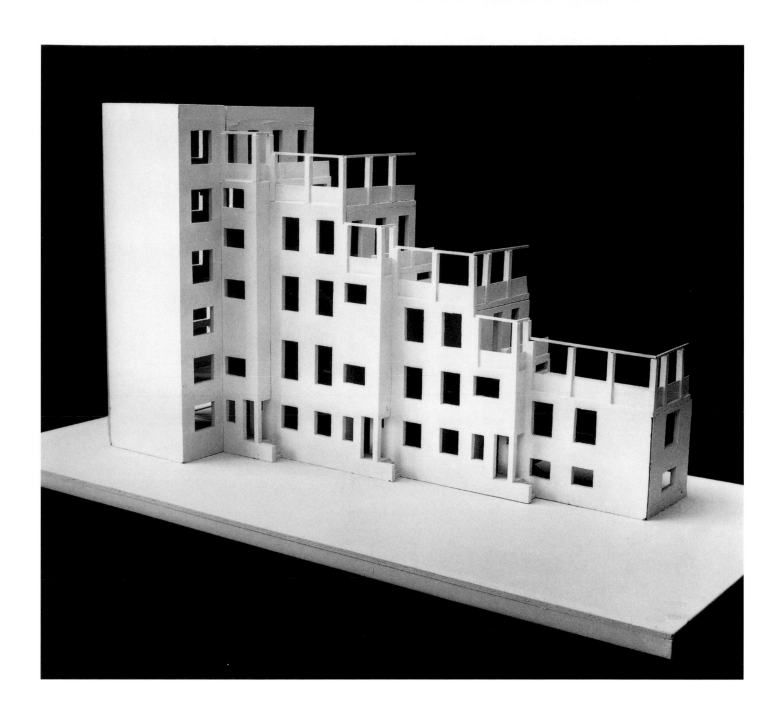

Adolf Loos
1870–1933

**Villa Plesch project
12, Berges de la Prairie,
Croissy-sur-Seine, France
1924**

*Scale model 1 : 33 ¹/₃
Karl Reinhard
Falk von Tettenborn*

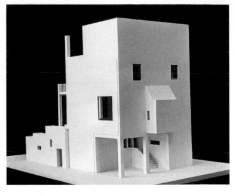

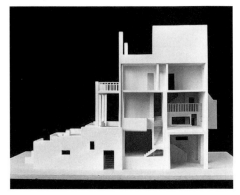

The high, square-based main structure
with roof terrace descends in a series of
levels continuing through the garden in
front, emphasising the character of the
terraced villa. The concept of staggered
levels is continued in the interior of the
house, using the 2 : 3-storey device often
found in Loos's later work. The chimney-
corner projects squarely in the middle of
the entrance façade.
In the lower living-area, the load-bearing
interior walls are divided into pillars.
The elevation of the building on ground
supports is unique amongst Loos's house
designs.
F. K.

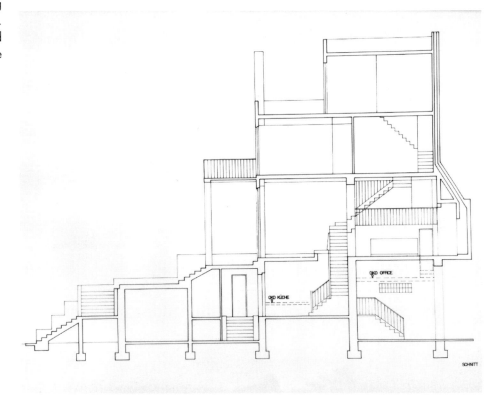

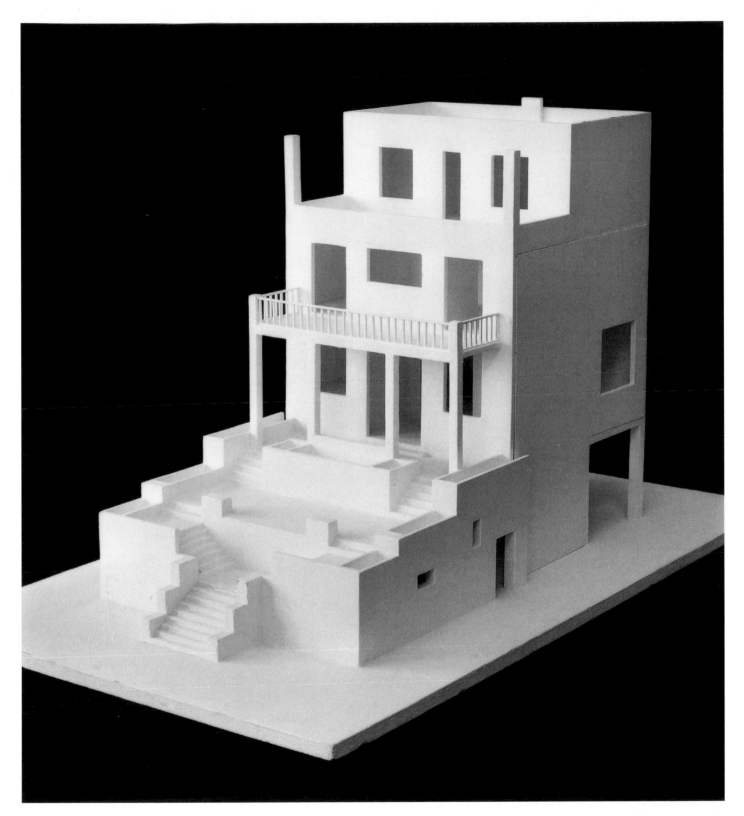

Adolf Loos
1870–1933

Tristan Tzara house
15, Avenue Junot, Paris XVIII
1925/26

Scale model 1 : 33 ¹/₃
Hans-Peter Hebensberger
Sibylle Hüther

This Paris house, built for the Romanian writer and Dadaist Tristan Tzara, combining living-quarters, studio and a rented flat on the first floor, is situated on a street sloping up to Montmartre, and takes advantage of the difference in height between street level and garden. Seen from the street, the plinth is two storeys high, built of natural stone like the adjoining supporting walls of the grounds. The slightly concave street façade is symmetrical in construction, with a recessed entrance; the upper section of the house, blank and cubic, is accentuated by a loggia. As seen from the street, this house has altogether an extremely distinctive appearance. The rear side descends in terraces to the garden. The interior shows the mastery of Loos's late work (Moller house, Vienna, 1927/28; Müller house, Prague, 1929/30) in accordance with the *Raumplan* concept and with regard to spatial differentiation.
F. K.

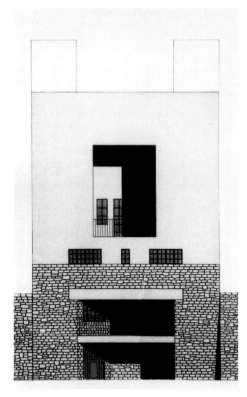

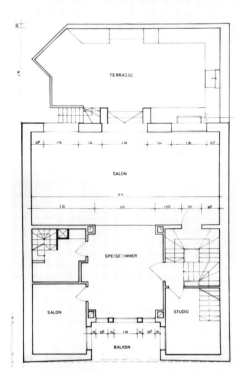

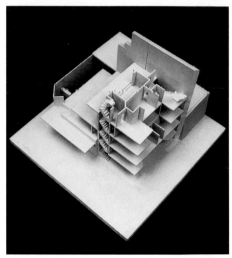

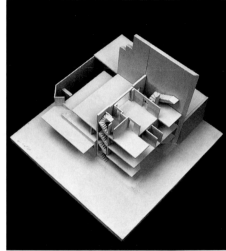

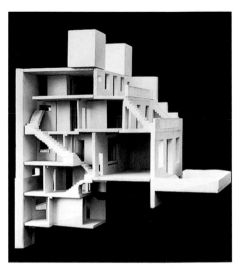

Adolf Loos
1870–1933

Rosenberg house project
Avenue Junot,
Rue Simon Dereure, Paris XVIII
1925

Scale model 1 : 33 ¹/₃
Joachim Peithner
Peter Krogoll

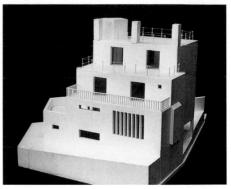

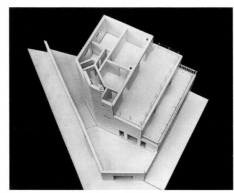
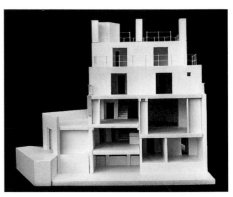

This house was planned for a triangular site near the Tzara house on Montmartre. Since, unlike the Tzara house, it was to be detached, the ground-plan is developed in all directions.

Three stepped-back terraces and a roof terrace give a cubic impression. The various room levels and heights are linked by several flights of stairs. The first floor comprises the spacious living-room with added recessed fireplace, and the dining-room with floor level 1.1 m higher but the same ceiling level.

A spiral staircase runs the whole height of the house, giving access to a self-contained flat on the top floor and continuing to the roof terrace.

During the construction of the model, inconsistencies appeared, such as too little headroom in passageways. Those mistakes would have had to be eliminated during the building of the house.

F. K.

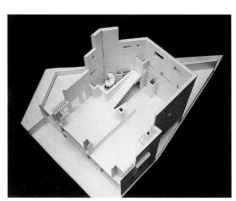
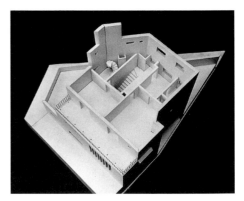

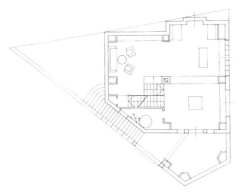

202

Adolf Loos
1870–1933
Assisted by Jacques Groag

**Moller house
Starkfriedgasse 19,
Vienna XVIII
1927/28**

*Scale model 1 : 33 $^1/_3$
Reinhold Brunninger*

The Moller house is one of Loos's late residential buildings in Vienna, and also one of his most mature works.

Seen from the street, the free-standing four-storey construction is block-like; the garden side is cubic, with stepped-back terraces. The central oriel and the symmetrically placed openings un-mistakably characterise the street façade. In this house, Loos makes masterly use of progression and partial symmetry combined with *Raumplan* staggered heights and levels.

The music room and the higher-level dining-room are linked by a sliding door and extensible steps. The bedrooms, on the upper floors, have built-in wall units, and balconies or terraces in front.

The Moller house has for some years now been the residence of the Israeli ambassador.

F. K.

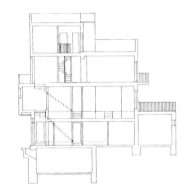

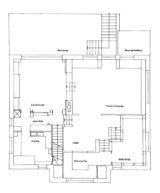

Adolf Loos
1870–1933

**Josephine Baker house project
Paris
1927**

Scale model 1 : 33 ¹/₃
G. Bittorf
M. Burer

This house – unfortunately never realised – for the dancer Josephine Baker was to have been created by reconstructing and combining two existing houses. Josephine Baker intended to have a small club attached to her living-quarters, and the distribution of the rooms is consistent with this division. The private rooms were to be on the second floor, taking up only a small part of the premises. All the rest, with salon, dining-room and café, were to be used by the guests. From the entrance at the base of a round tower, one would have walked up a grand staircase to the reception rooms on the first floor. The centrepiece was to be an indoor swimming-pool lit from above, with a surrounding gallery from which the bathers could be watched through glass walls.

The cubic upper part of the house and the round tower were to have been executed in black and white marble stripes.

F. K.

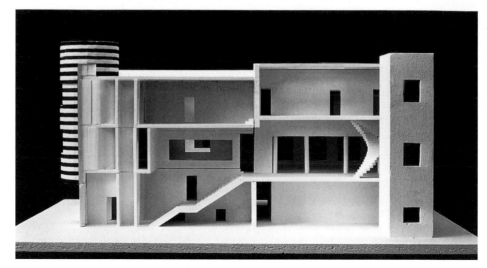

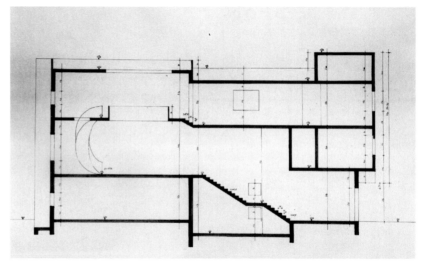

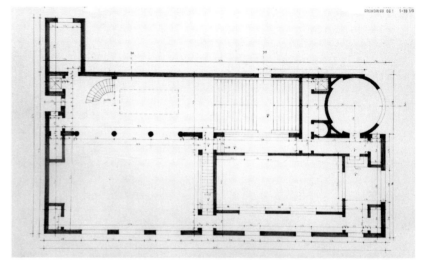

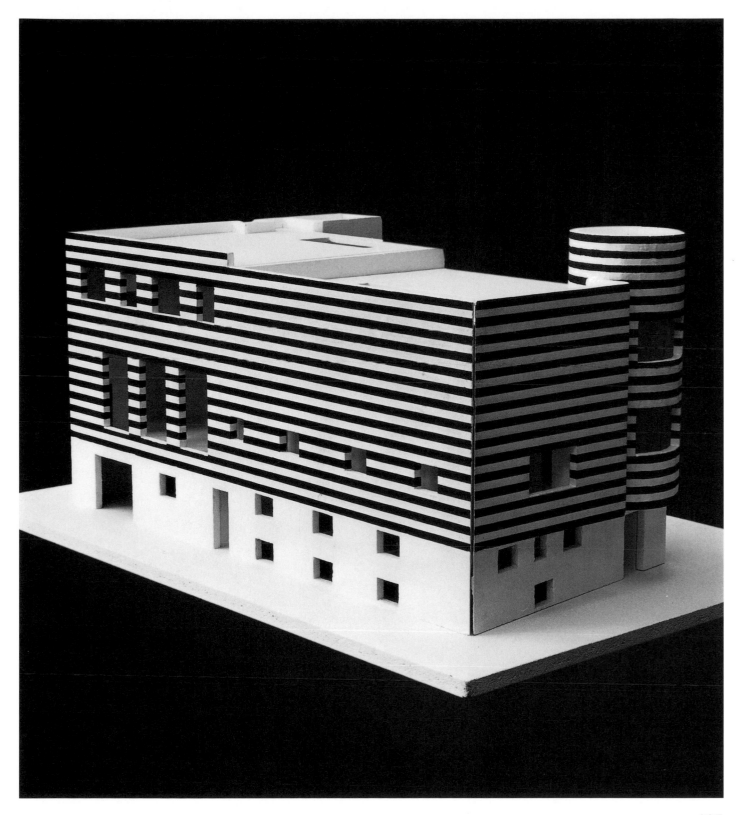

Adolf Loos
1870–1933
Assisted by Karel Lhota

**Müller house
Stresovicka 842 (now 820),
Prague XVIII
1928–30**

Scale model 1 : 33 ¹/₃
S. Habermann
B. Peters
Andrea Düchting
Martin Junk

The Müller house in Prague is the ideal-typical realisation of Loos's terraced villa with the *Raumplan* concept developed to the full. Again, the garden façade has a distinctive character.

The house is built on a steep slope, the differences in height being compensated for by terraces. The entrance is on the bottom floor. The route through the house holds many surprises, and can be regarded, in a higher sense, as functional. The high living-area, running the entire width of the house, forms the centre, leading on one side to the raised dining-room and on the other to the raised drawing-room and the library. A further double side staircase affords access to every part of the house, and is linked in the living-area with the other stairways; the well has a skylight. From the wide roof terrace, a "window" opening looks on to the Hradčany.

Here Loos has achieved perfect accord between exterior form and complex interior planning.

F. K.

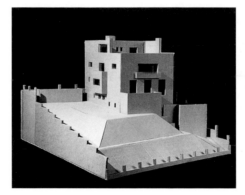
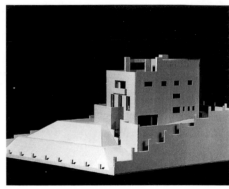

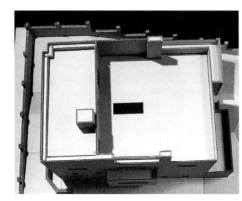

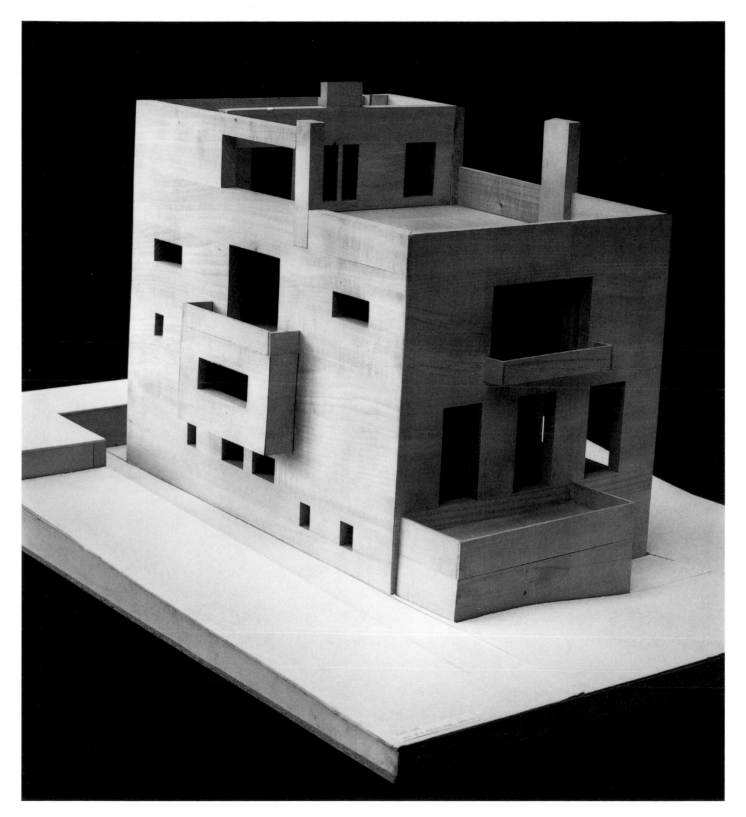

Adolf Loos
1870–1933
Assisted by Heinrich Kulka

Double house for the Werkbund housing estate Woinovichgasse 13/15/17/19, Vienna XIII 1929/30

Scale model 1 : 33 ¹/₃
Lutz Becherer
Andreas Kampik

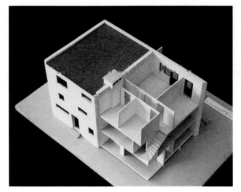

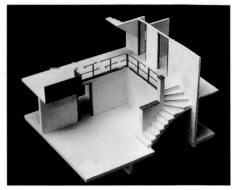

The Vienna Werkbund housing estate was originally planned for construction on a different site. The estate, and with it Loos's double house, was completed in 1932. Although these houses are small (6 × 8 m), he has nevertheless succeeded in creating a duplex living-room as the centre of the house, with side-rooms angled round it.

The houses are entered through a very low porch under a gallery. The staircase leading to the first floor starts in the living-room and continues in a different place to the sleeping-quarters on the top floor, with balcony.

Seen from outside, the high living-room and the gallery become apparent by an L-shaped window, which is mirrored in the adjoining house – as indeed is the entire construction.

F. K.

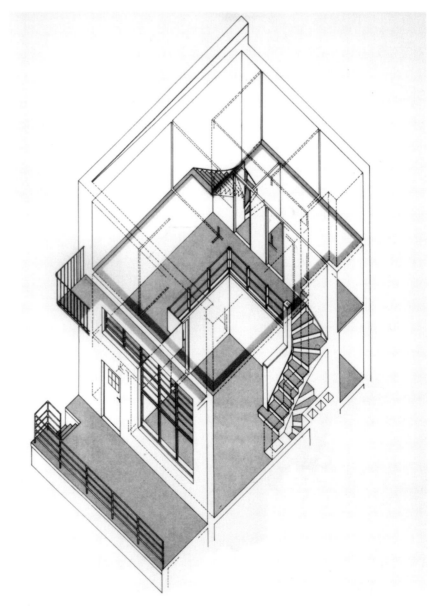

Adolf Loos
1870–1933

Project for a double house for the Werkbund housing estate Woinovichgasse 13/15/17/19, Vienna XIII
1931

Scale model 1 : 33 ¹/₃
Peter Buchberger
Hans Pichlmeier

During the building of the Vienna Werkbund housing estate, Loos was in the south of France. Heinrich Kulka therefore directed the planning and construction of the semi-detached houses; with the help of Kurt Unger, Loos tried to prescribe this new design for the execution, but it arrived too late, the houses being already under construction.

This design offers an equally economical concept for symmetrically constructed semi-detached houses, using a clear 2 : 3-storey device. The high living-room corresponds to two normal low-ceilinged stories, with the sleeping-quarters above.
F. K.

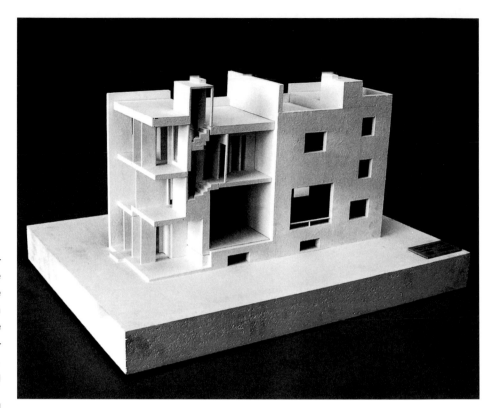

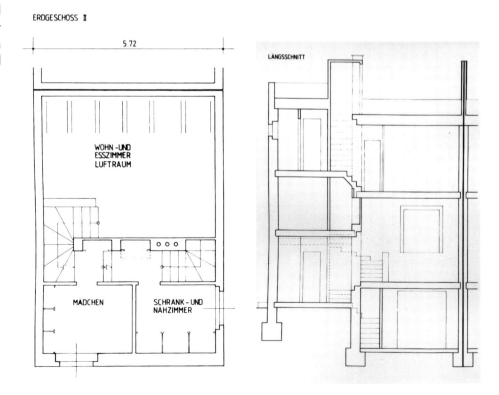

ERDGESCHOSS II

5.72

WOHN-UND ESSZIMMER LUFTRAUM

MÄDCHEN

SCHRANK-UND NÄHZIMMER

LANGSSCHNITT

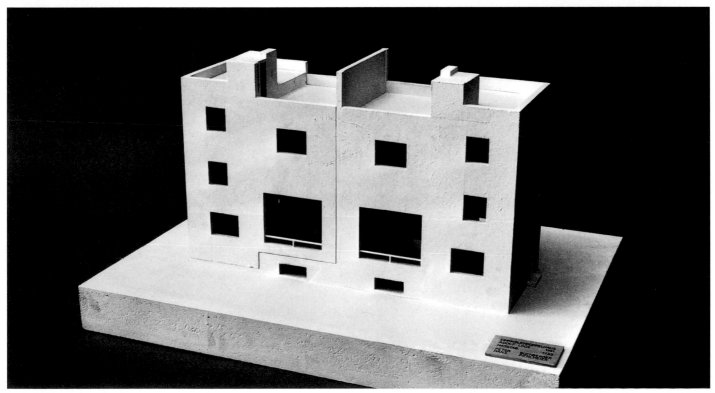

213

Adolf Loos
1870–1933

Detached house project
Site unknown (Paris?)
1930

Scale model 1 : 33 $^1/_3$
Sabine Fuderer
Christine Huber

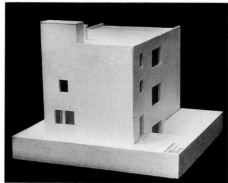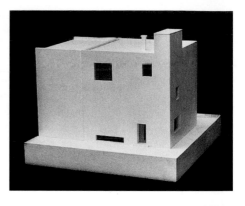

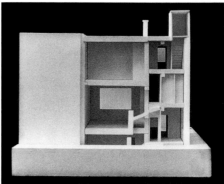

The cubic construction (9 × 9 × 9 m) could serve either as one of a semi-detached pair or as the end of a terrace. The openings in the street façade indicate a 2 : 3-storey interior distribution, but the large living-room, running the full width, is different in height from the vestibule, in order to allow room for the garage below.

An open-newel staircase leads to a mezzanine floor with servant's and guest rooms. The staircase continues via an intermediate landing to the sleeping-quarters, with further steps down to the guest room and bathroom. Attic stairs lead up to the roof terrace. The house has neither balconies nor terraces.

F. K.

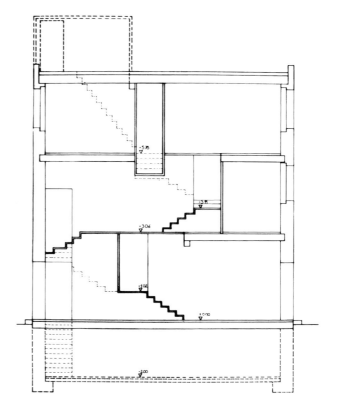

215

**Adolf Loos
1870–1933
Assisted by Heinrich Kulka**

**Khuner country house
Kreuzberg, near Payerbach,
Lower Austria
1929/30**

*Scale model 1 : 33 ¹/₃
Anton Hohenadl
Franz Rauch*

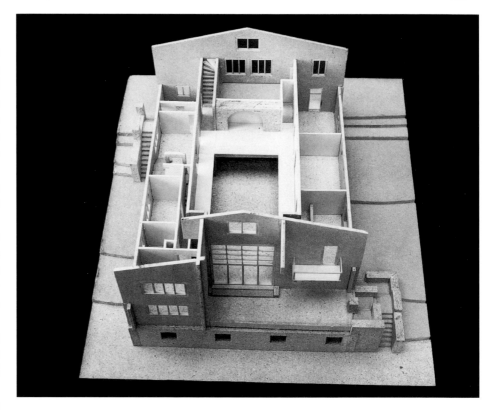

Here, in one of his last buildings, Loos shows masterly use of the idea of the duplex living-room with U-shaped surround. Since this country house is situated in the mountains of the Semmering region, it is built of wooden blocks on a stone base, and has an Alpine-style saddle roof with a shallow slope.

The living-room is surrounded on three sides by a gallery which gives access to the bedrooms.

Below this, on the central axis of the room and the house, is the fireplace, to one side of which opens the dining-area with kitchen. The attic contains further rooms, and affords access to a sunterrace raised over the roof-ridge.

The rooms, each decorated in a different colour (red, blue, yellow), have fitted cupboards and wooden-beamed ceilings.

Built as a country house for a large family, it now makes an ideal guesthouse, the "Pension Alpenhof" run by the Wurdack/Steiner family.

The two-storey house built down at the road for a gardener is also built of wooden blocks, but with a pent roof, and serves to round off the small ensemble.
F. K.

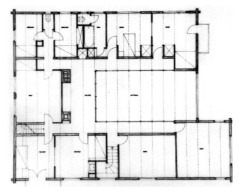
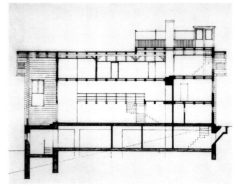

217

Adolf Loos
1870–1933

Cubic house project
Site unknown
c 1929

Scale model 1 : 33 ¹/₃
Martin Ehrmann
Stephan Jacoby

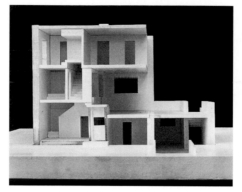
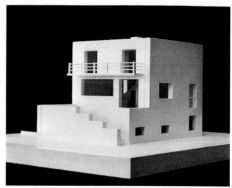

Built on to the garden side of the three-storey cubic construction (8 × 8 × 8 m) is a garage which also serves as a terrace for the raised living-area. The balcony of the upper storey with sleeping-quarters runs the full width of the house.

The distribution of windows, as seen from outside, indicates a variety of levels in the interior.

The open-plan living-room, with a raised dining-area, the study (accessible from a landing) and the open stairway leading to the bedrooms are all planned with great economy of space. For the major Adolf Loos Exhibition in 1989/90, the house was reconstructed full-size in the inner courtyard of the Albertina Museum in Vienna, by Hans Puchhammer (of the Technical University, Vienna), in order to demonstrate the fundamental precision of the work involved. The cubic house is also an example of optimum utilisation of the cube.

F. K.

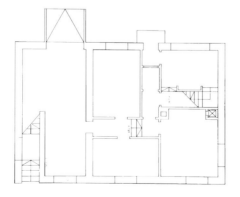
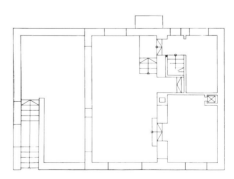

219

Adolf Loos
1870–1933

**Bojko house project
Neblingergasse 8, extension of
Hummelgasse, Vienna XIII
1929/30**

Scale model 1 : 33 ¹/₃
Helmut Rosskopf
Andreas Streibl

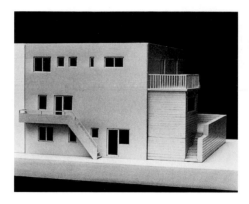

Projecting on one side of this three-storey cuboid terraced villa is a glazed veranda below a balcony running the full width of the house.

The house is planned to be built on to the side of an existing building, the entrance being on the narrow side. The living-room combines with the 90 cm higher dining-room to form a communal area taking up the entire length of the house. From here a stairway leads via an intermediate landing to the smoking-room, and on to the first floor with four bedrooms.

F. K.

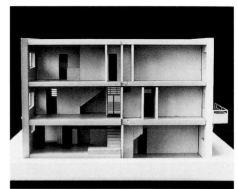

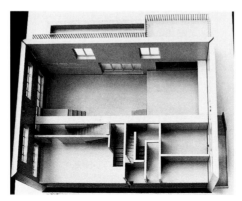
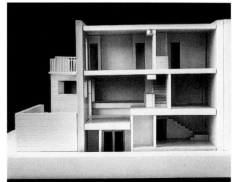

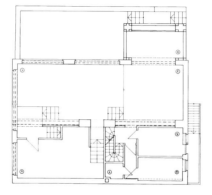
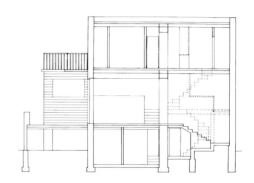

Adolf Loos
1870–1933

**Fleischner villa project
Plot no. 323, West Carmel by
Haifa, Israel
1931**

*Scale model 1 : 33 ¹/₃
Siegfried Englhardt
Ludwig Wappner*

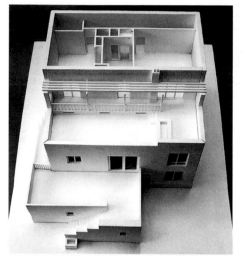

The cubic terraced villa, planned to
stand alone on a north-facing slope, has
in front a raised garden terrace with its
own steps.

This design for Fleischner, a doctor,
bears similarities to the doctor's house in
Badgastein, designed ten years previously.

One side of the house is taken up by the
surgery and waiting-room, while the
living-area with a raised platform
dominates the centre. The bedrooms
above afford access to a terrace running
the entire width of the house.

This design, too, shows a cleverly devised
system of staggered and reduced storey-
heights.

F. K.

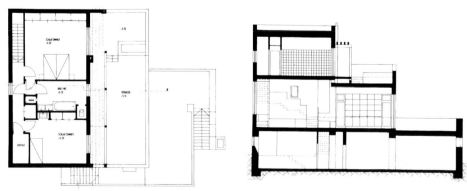

Adolf Loos
1870–1933

"The last house" project
Site unknown (Prague?)
1933

Scale model 1 : 33 ⅓
Roland Dobras

"Loos always wanted to build an American-style wooden house. He claimed that wood, which has today been replaced by other building materials, will in future be the material most in use for family houses – and not only in the country, but also in town."

Here František Müller, a Prague building contractor for whose family Loos had some years previously built the Müller villa and for whose daughter this wooden house was designed, refers to a legacy which Loos did not live to see realised.

The wooden house with shed roof was to be constructed on a brick base. The horizontal overlap wooden cladding was to be painted with green oil-based paint, the window-frames white.

Even this wooden house with its small ground area (70 m²) shows all the attributes of *Raumplan*.

F. K.

Adolf Loos
1870–1933

**"The last house" project,
(variant)
Site unknown (Prague?)
1933**

*Scale model 1 : 33 ¹/₃
Ulrike Fischbacher*

The almost cubic, free-standing construction is arranged in 2 : 3 storeys – a
variant of the wooden house with shed
roof planned for the daughter of František and Milada Müller.

This design, too, is for a wooden house
with framed walls clad on both sides,
and wooden-beamed ceilings.

On the garden side is a flat terrace, and
a balcony stretches in front of two of the
upper-storey bedrooms. The flat roof is
accessible via a small superstructure.

The high living-room with raised dining-
area takes up the full width of the house.
The staircase leads via an intermediate
landing to the sleeping-quarters and
raised bathroom.

Probably neither of these "last house"
designs was ever carried out.

F. K.

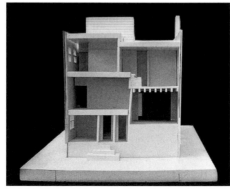

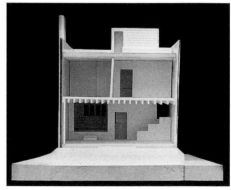

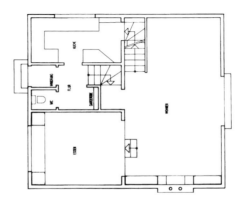

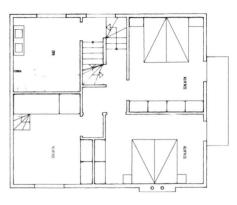

Hans Luckhardt
1890–1954
Wassili Luckhardt
1889–1972

**Am Rupenhorn Colony,
house no. 1
Berlin
1928**

*Scale model 1 : 33 ¹/₃
Hans Peter Grad
Andreas Houzer*

This house stands along with two others on the site at Heerstrasse 55, on the Am Rupenhorn corner, close to the Havel lakes. The simple cubic form of the structure is extended upwards, so that the high roof garden offers a wide view over Spandau and the Brandenburg woods.

The steel skeleton construction allows a variable arrangement of the dividing walls to form a large living-room or several smaller rooms. The utility rooms occupy the entire basement, and a wide terrace sweeps out over the garage. On the ground floor, the large living-room is completely glazed to the south. On the upper floor are the bathroom, WC and bedrooms. The roof is designed as a terrace with pergola.

A prefabricated steel skeleton frame is filled with slabs of pumice – a new construction material at the time. There is no interior separation of utility and living-rooms, which increases the living-area considerably. Particular importance is given to the effect of the colour and material of the exterior, which was protected against weathering.
V. H.

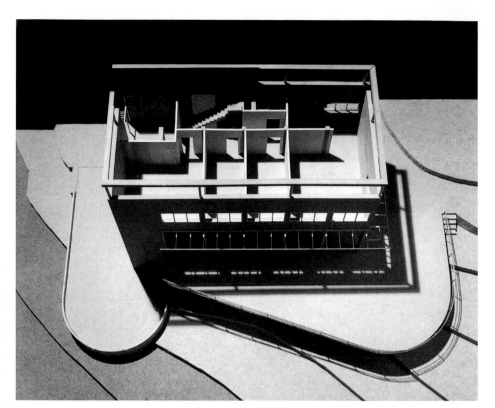

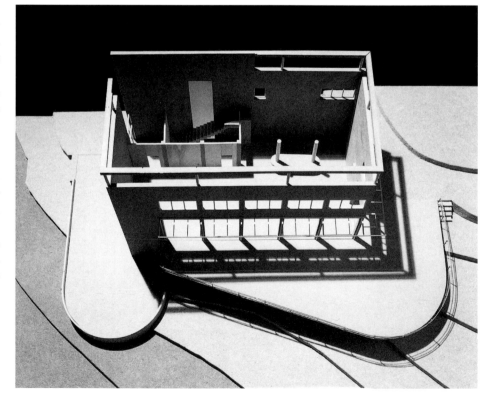

André Lurçat
1894–1970

Vienna Werkbund housing estate
Veitingergasse 87/89/91/93
1932

Scale model 1 : 33 ¹/₃
Thomas Seibert von Mengersen
Christian Solbrig

It was André Lurçat, not Le Corbusier, that Josef Frank invited to represent France in the Vienna Werkbund housing estate. He built four three-storey terrace houses, each with a floor area of 68 m² on a base of only 38 m². The almost windowless north façade towards the street derives rhythm from the semi-cylindrical projecting spiral staircases; the south façade, facing the garden, has strip windows along the whole width.

The ground floor contains the offices in the east section, the west part being occupied by a covered outside area – which, ten years later, had been walled in by almost all the residents.

The living area begins on the first floor, with living-room, kitchen and pantry; above these, on the second floor, are the two bedrooms with interjacent bathroom. Passages are kept to a minimum by exterior placing of the staircases. For the furnishings, Lurçat planned fitted cupboards and fold-out beds, but these were never installed.

S. M.

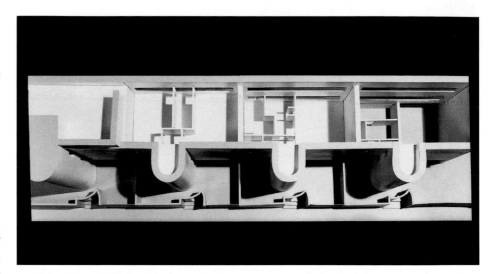

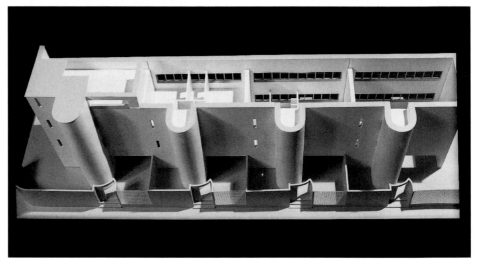

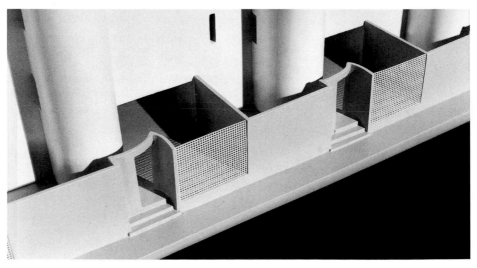

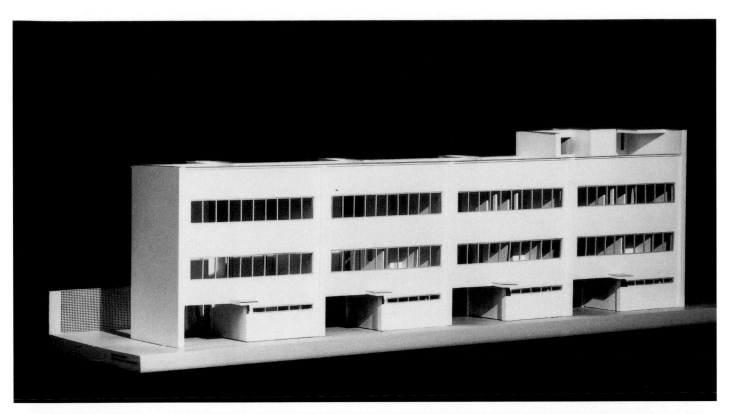

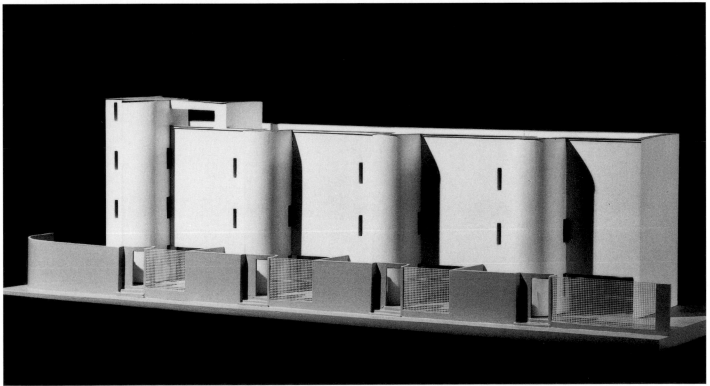

Ernst May
1886–1970

May house
Frankfurt am Main
1925

Scale model 1 : 33 ¹/₃
Clemens Lenz
Gerhard Knapp

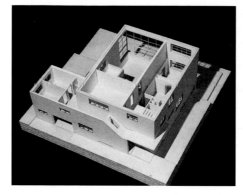
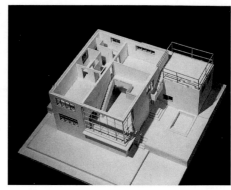

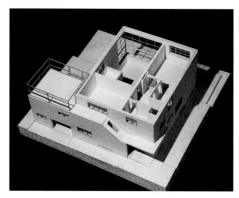
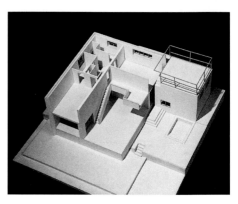

Ernst May was town councillor responsible for building and construction in Frankfurt am Main from 1925 until 1930. In residential building, his main concern was the distinction between the functions "living and eating" and "sleeping and hygiene". During his term of office, Grete Schütte-Lihotzky developed the so-called "Frankfurt kitchen". In 1925, he built a house for himself near the centre of the old town (the "Römer" area). It consists of a simple two-storey cube and a low two-storey annexe set a few steps down, with a maid's room on the upper floor and garage and library on the lower. In the sheltered corner between the main building and the garage is the swimming-pool. Immediately behind the main entrance at the north-east corner, the hallway and staircase separate the two functional groups. The hallway leads in the ground floor to the "living and eating" area and the partly two-storey living-room with staircase and gallery. A spacious three-flight staircase leads to the bathroom and bedrooms on the upper floor. From the living-room gallery, an outside staircase leads up to the roof terrace; curtained off, this can also be used as an open-air sleeping-area.
V. H.

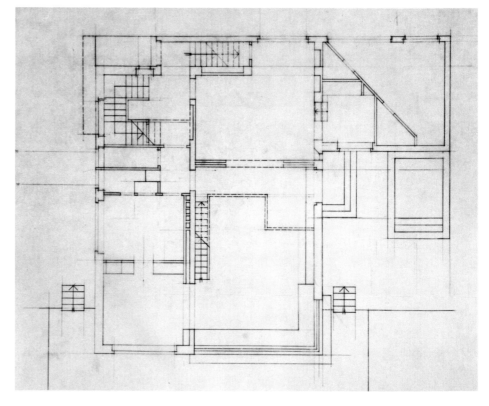

233

Richard Meier
1934

**Douglas house
Lake Michigan
1971–73**

Scale model 1 : 33 ¹/₃
Mathis Künstner
Peter Franz
Florian Plank

The Douglas house stands in the shelter of a dense conifer forest on a steep and remote site on Lake Michigan. The dramatic dialogue between the whiteness of the house and the blue-green hues of water, trees and sky not only gives the building a powerful presence but also, through the stark contrast, enhances the beauty of the landscape.

From the road, only the roof and the top storey are visible. The upper bridge leads into the entrance hall, which looks down to the lower living and eating-areas and out to the large terrace, which – along with other elements of the house – makes visual allusion to a ship. The sleeping-area faces the slope, and is linked by a gallery to the rest of the interior. A second, lower bridge ensures circulation from the living-level back to the ground, then leading by way of a staircase and a ladder to the beach below.

T. B.

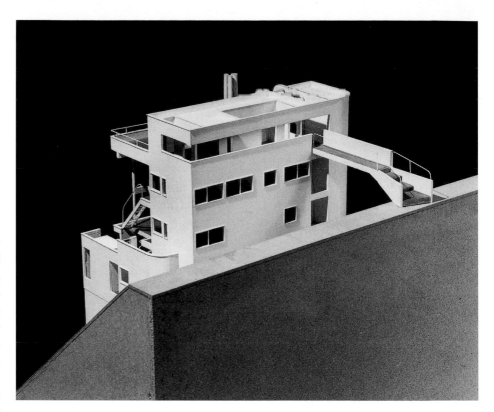

Konstantin Melnikov
1890–1974

**Exhibition pavilion
Paris
1925**

*Scale model 1 : 33 ¹/₃
Marion Becher*

Melnikov made his international debut with the Soviet pavilion at the 1925 Paris Arts and Crafts Exhibition, where Le Corbusier, for example, made a name for himself with the "Esprit Nouveau" pavilion. In this context, Melnikov's work appears completely independent. The building is designed within an elongated rectangle, and the effect of diagonally arranged ascending and descending staircases, together with the symmetrically adjoining exhibition rooms, is one of impressive dynamism. Thus he fulfils the motto: "Build movement" – a revolutionary demand at the time.

The open thoroughfare derives rhythm from the wing-like roofing, the inset tower accentuating the vertical dimension. The laws of perspective governing visual perception are taken into account. It is surprising that the pavilion was erected without complicated details, as a wooden frame construction with diagonal struts. The symbolism of the building is evident in inscriptions, in the "hammer and sickle" and in the colour scheme, a vivid red and blue.

F. K.

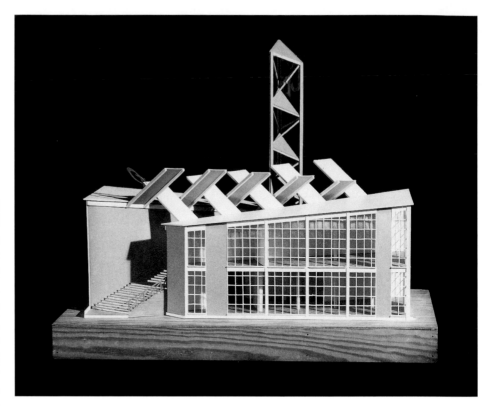

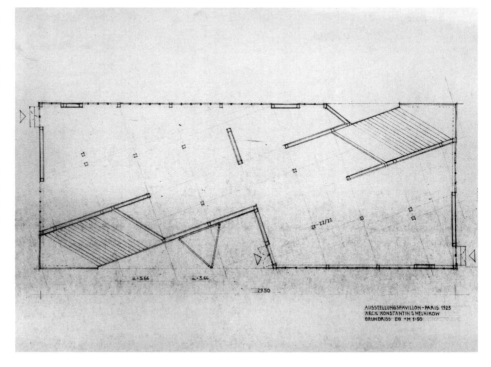

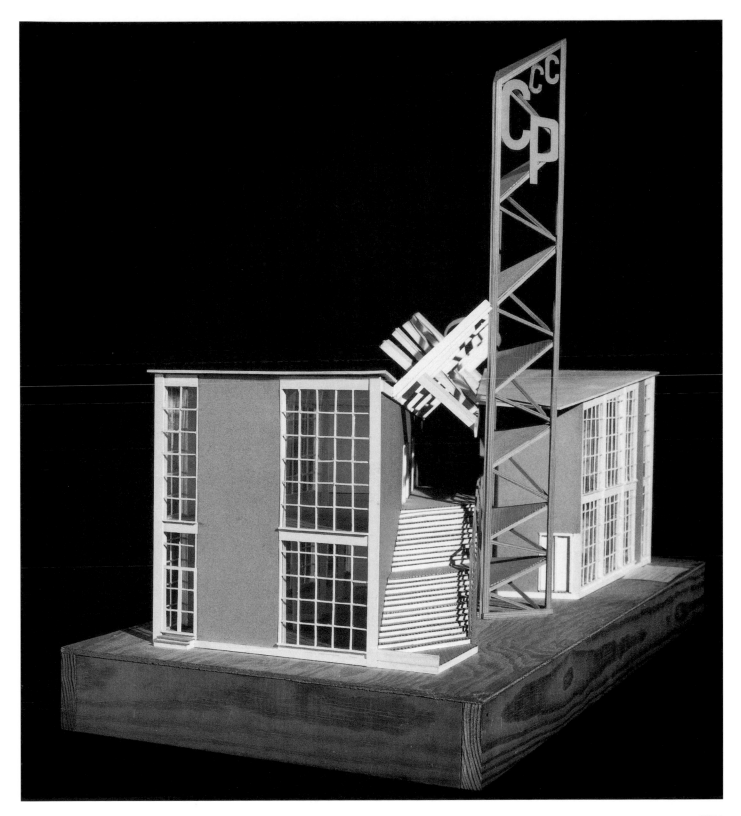

Konstantin Melnikov
1890–1974

**The architect's house
Moscow
1927**

Scale model 1 : 33 ¹/₃
Joachim Ganzert
Axel Lehmann

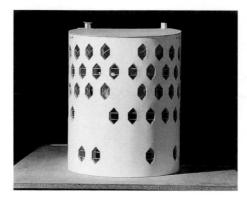

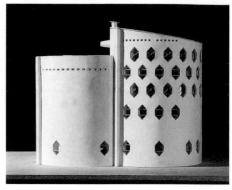

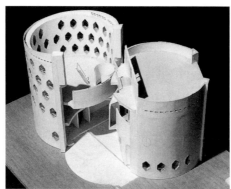

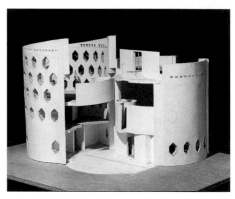

Two interpenetrating cylinders form the basic concept. In the spatial construction, the overlapping section is annexed on the one hand to the living-room, lit by one large window, and on the other to the studio, lit by individual rhomboid windows. Under the title "The Architecture of my Life", Melnikov wrote in 1966: "It was neither to reproach nor to flatter the order which has created a common, uniform life for all of us, that in 1927 I built for myself in the centre of Moscow a house with the inscription
KONSTANTIN MELJNIKOV
ARCHITECT,
which lays emphasis on the particular significance of each single one of us. Our house, an individual statement of a personality, stands proudly amidst the breakers of the huge unharmonious buildings of the capital, and throbs with the pulse of today, as though it were a sovereign unity. I am alone, but not lonely; secluded from the noise of millions of human voices, the inner worlds of mankind open up. I am now 76 years old, and I am in my own residence. The silence it commands preserves for me the view right into the farthest distances of the past."
F. K.

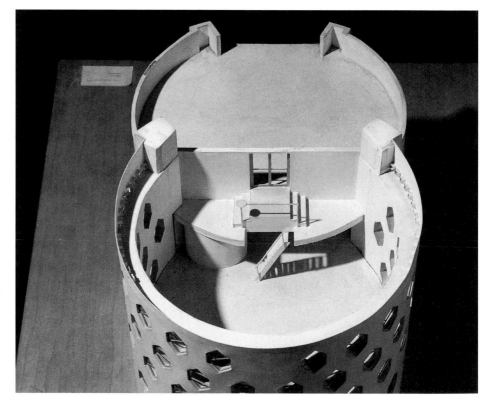

239

Konstantin Melnikov
1890–1974

**Residential units in a hotel for 100 guests
1929**

Scale model 1 : 33 ¹/₃
Rudolf Henseli

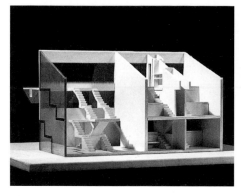
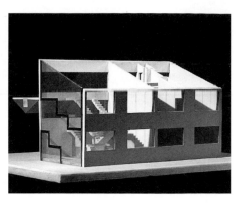
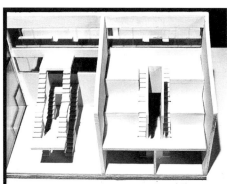
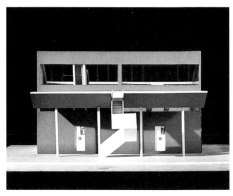

The hotel project is a part of an ideal plan designed by Melnikov for "the green city", including a transport network and facilities for "collective recreation" and sport.

The scale model represents an excerpt from the "Hotel for 100 guests", showing a dynamic two-section ground plan with a central rhomboid hotel foyer. In cross-section, the spatial and lighting arrangement and the use of oblique surfaces in the two-storey part containing the rooms – arranged alternately along each corridor – bears Melnikov's radical architectural signature.
F. K.

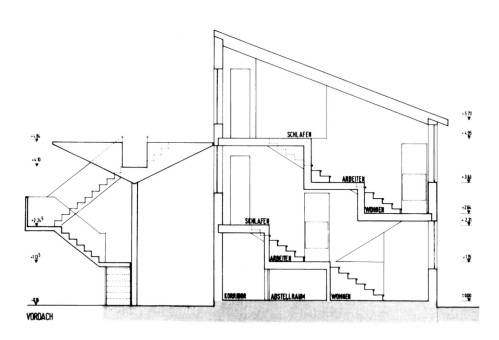

240

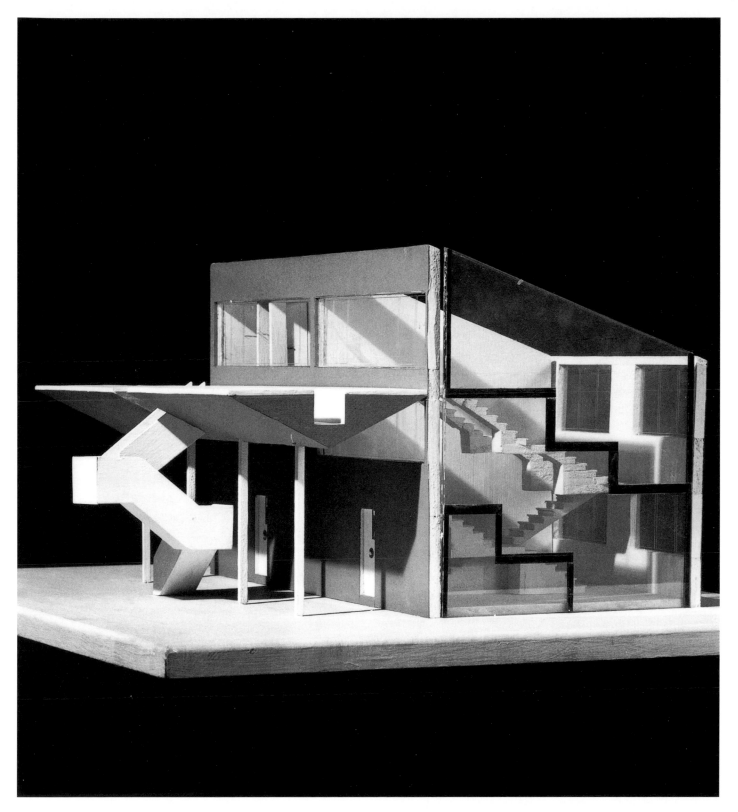

Ludwig Mies van der Rohe
1886–1969

**Lange house
Krcfcld
1928**

Scale model 1 : 33 ¹/₃
M. Mayer
B. Zankhuizen

The Lange house lies parallel to the street, on which the entrance is marked by a projecting canopy. On this side, regardless of the strict correspondence between ground plan and façade, the upper storey is broken by strip windows lighting a long corridor. On the garden side, the supporting brick wall of the terrace forms the boundary of the platform upon which the house is raised – a device frequently employed by Mies. The façade is broken by the generously proportioned rectangular window openings that link interior and exterior space. The almost conventional character of the house suggests a compromise with the building contractor, since Mies does not achieve here the consistency of his earlier brick buildings. His experience as a bricklayer is evident; for all doorways and window openings and for all interior and exterior measurements he uses a principle based on the measurements of the individual brick and bond.
T. B.

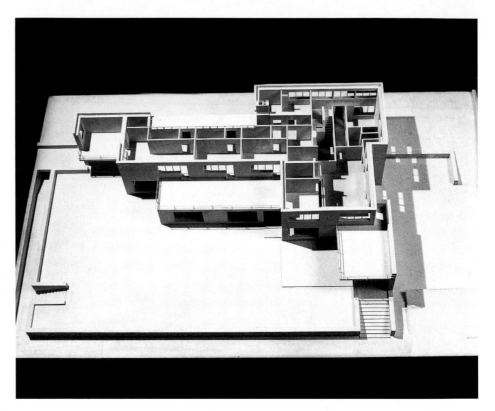

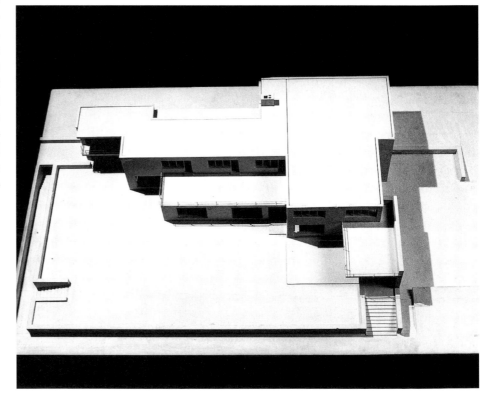

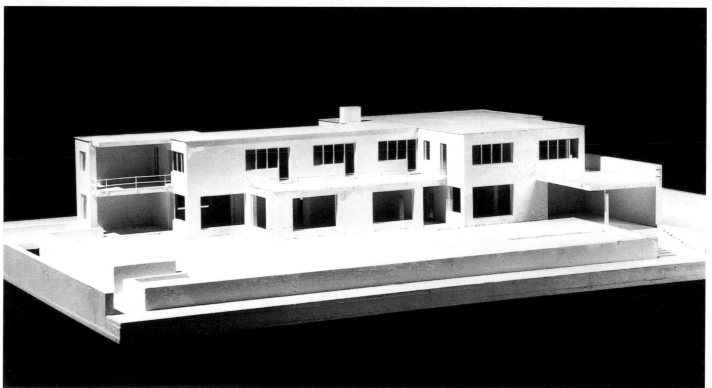

Ludwig Mies van der Rohe
1886–1969

Tugendhat house
Brno
1928–30

Scale model 1 : 33 ¹/₃
Rolf Krebs
Joachim Renner

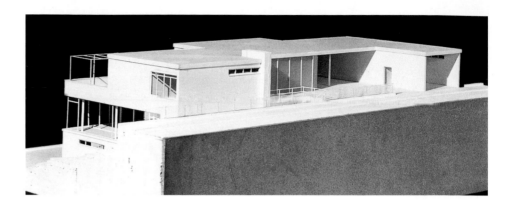

Mies designed the Tugendhat house con-currently with the Barcelona pavilion. The parallels between the two designs are particularly significant in the inter-action of the dividing walls and façades with the vertical cross-ribbed supports.

Since the house is built on a slope, only the top storey of the three can be seen into from street level, so access to the house is from here. Between the garage and the bedroom wings, the building opens out to give a panoramic view over the town.

In front of the bedrooms is a terrace with pergola and patio. From the entrance hall in the top storey, a spiral staircase enclosed by a milk-glass wall leads to the living-area, starting with the music room, and in the diagonal, the view over the town is framed by a cylinder panelled in markassa wood and a white-and-gold onyx screen.

The complexity of this large room becomes apparent only gradually. Intimacy and seclusion increase from the downhill-facing glass wall to the more closed-in library fronting the slope.
T. B.

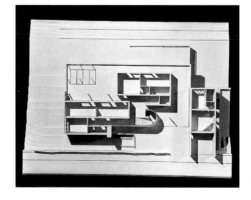

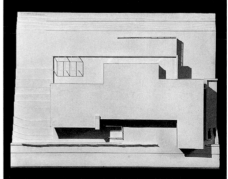

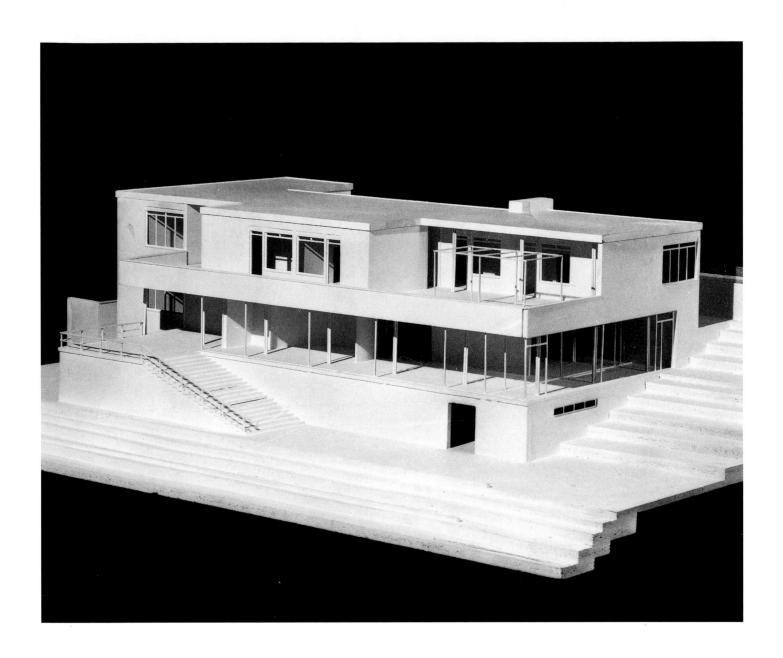

Ludwig Mies van der Rohe
1886–1969

**Project for a house with three courtyards
1934**

Scale model 1 : 33 ¹/₃
Christian Schnurrer

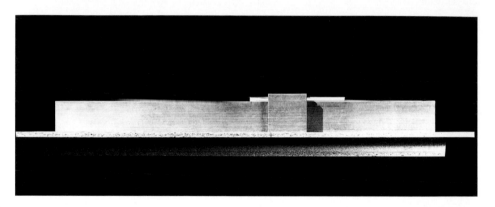

In the courtyard house project, a brick wall encompasses a rectangular site, forming self-contained living-quarters, one section of which is covered by a flat roof supported by the wall and by slim pillars. The system of supports in the interior allows optional room division. The arrangement of the various living-areas is based on the principle of inter-connecting interior glass partitions and exterior open areas within a fixed boundary. One courtyard is designed as an entrance-area and large garden, while the two others are more like atria. All the walls are set on module lines, the basic unit being the brick. The exterior appearance is completely determined by a windowless brick wall; only the chimney and the roof sections relieve the cubic form.
T. B.

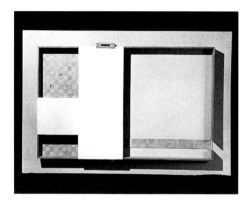

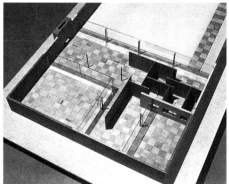

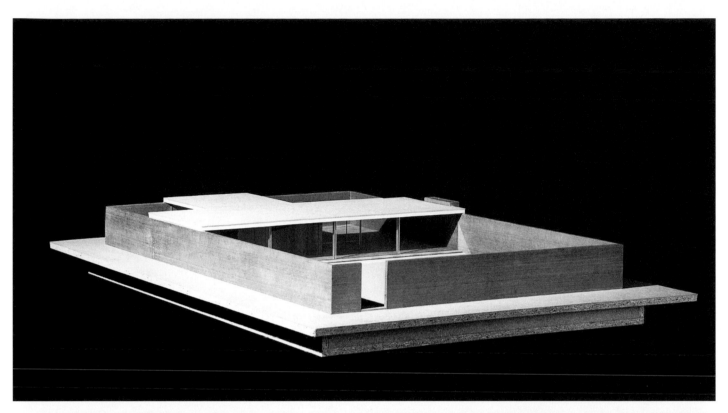

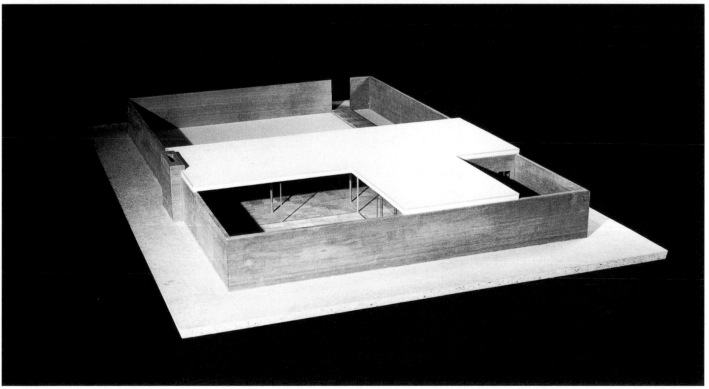

Richard Neutra
1892–1970

Vienna Werkbund housing estate
Woinovichgasse 9
1932

Scale model 1 : 33 ¹/₃
Christian Einhellig

Richard Neutra designed this detached single-storey house with a floor area of 61 m² in 1930, during his "guest performance" at the Bauhaus in Dessau.

In keeping with Neutra's partiality to industrial building processes, this was planned as a steel frame construction with wallboard interior and shotcrete exterior (cf Neutra's Lovell Health House, Los Angeles, 1927–29). It was in fact built with the plastered hollow-block walls prescribed for the entire housing estate.

The ground plan is characterised by the sequence of three functional areas: first the utility area, with entrance, kitchen and cellar stairs; then the living-area, fronted by a terrace; and adjoining this the sleeping area, with bathroom, box-room and bedroom with its own entrance.

The roof terrace is accessible from the terrace by way of an outside staircase, and the high pergola frame on the northwest side lends the house character.
S. M.

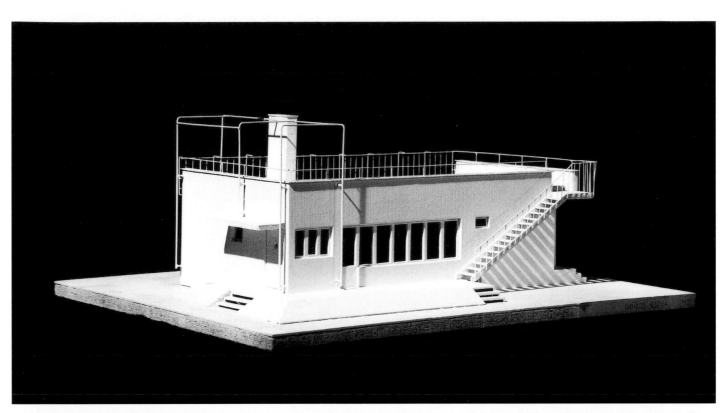

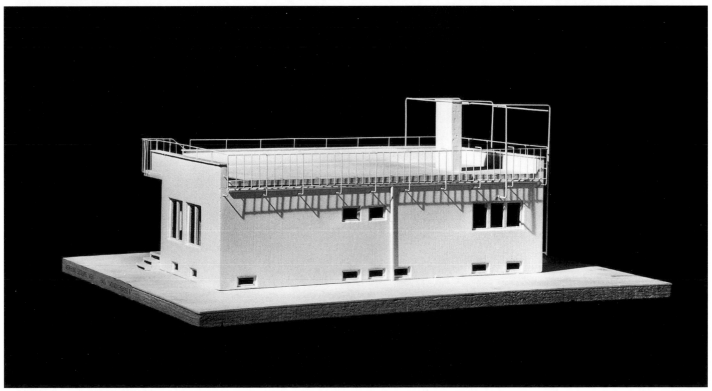

Robert Örley
1876–1945

**Detached house
Lannerstrasse 14, Vienna XIX
1904/05**

*Scale model 1 : 33 ¹/₃
Robert Kammergruber
Nikolaus Meissler
Andreas Sternecker*

This small but imposing house asserts itself amongst the villas of the 19th district. Permeated with a powerful geometry, its symmetry is harmonious in ground plan, elevation and structure. Behind the dignified, self-assured exterior lies a high degree of interior intimacy. The central two-storey hall is lit by a lantern with a base of finely-barred coloured glass. The independent craftsmanship of Robert Örley's work is apparent in details such as the garden veranda or the invisible surrounding ventilation ducts for the underground exterior walls of the basement. This building expresses a style of architecture which requires no questioning because it has already said all there is to say.
R. K./A. S.

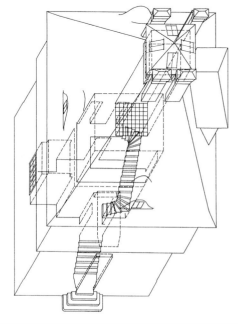

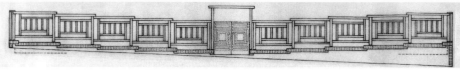

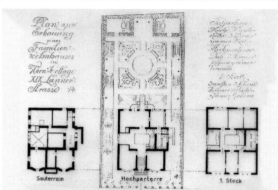

250

Jacobus Johannes Pieter Oud
1890–1963

**Weissenhof housing estate,
houses 5, 6, 7, 8, 9
Stuttgart
1927**

*Scale model 1 : 33 ¹/₃
Wolfgang Kahle*

Mies van der Rohe commissioned the
Dutch architect to build a group of five
terrace houses. Oud designed economical structures (approx. 5 m wide),
their layout strongly influenced by the
requirements of urban development. The
apartment borders on two narrow
streets: to the north with access to the
utility-rooms for services and deliveries;
to the south, garden, porch and living-
quarters. Courtyards (3 × 3 m) provide a
semi-communal area, with bicycle shed
and laundry room with drying-room
above, lending rhythm to the terrace.
The functional design of the interior
bears an individual stamp: the arrangement of fitted and walk-in cupboards, the
kitchen with dining-area, independent
access to all bedrooms, some also
leading directly to the bathroom, etc.
Oud describes this detailed planning in
the Werkbund publication "Bau und
Wohnung" (1927).
B. S.

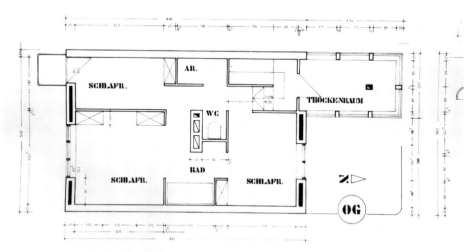

REIHENHÄUSER · WEISSENHOFSIEDLUNG · STUTTGART

Jože Plečnik
1872–1957

Project for a house near Belgrade
1936

Scale model 1 : 33 ¹/₃
Wolfgang Albert

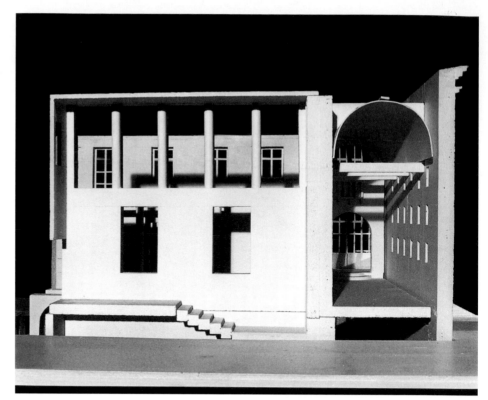

The street façade of the Villa Dimnik on the Nova Ulica has an open two-storey portico with a rectangular fluted pillar supporting the centre front, two lateral projections and at the rear a further recessed wall with four symmetrically spaced columns. A massive cornice, behind which a pent roof slopes down to the garden side, tops the house on three sides. The various rooms have windows of different sizes.

The house is entered from one end of the portico, up the balustraded staircase parallel to the façade, and into a hallway. To the left, steps give access to a flight of stairs leading to a spacious landing and on, over four wide steps, to the rooms in the upper storey. To the right, a vestibule leads to rooms on a slightly higher level and to the long, barrel-vaulted main room, which has a veranda in front and an interior balcony accessible from the upper floor. This two-storey room is lit by a large east window and 18 small windows regularly spaced in the south wall.

V. H.

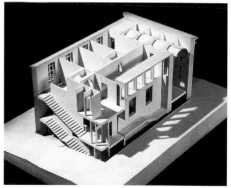

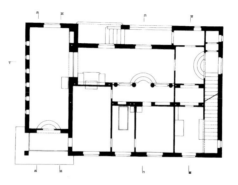

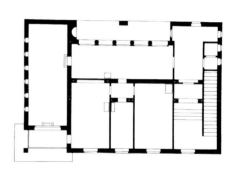

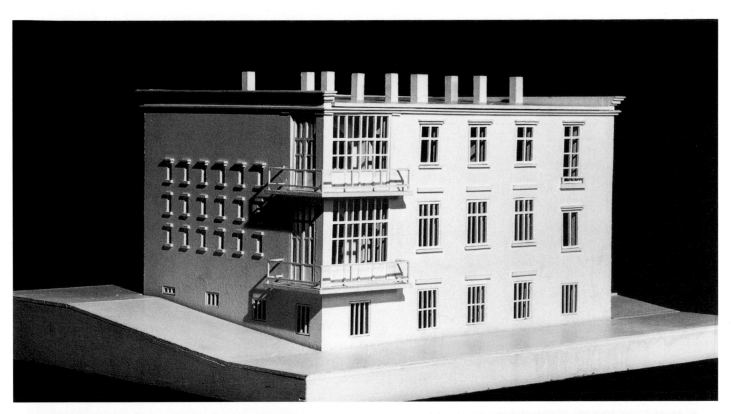

Jože Plečnik
1872–1957

Project for a house
Ljubljana
1940

Scale model 1 : 33 ¹/₃
Hans Dotter
Ernst Schneider

This elongated structure (5 × 16.5 m) is situated on a long, narrow site (approx. 15 × 75 m). Its pent roof slopes lengthwise from the two-storey side with the entrance porch, to the three-storey garden façade.

On the ground floor, the axis from the entrance leads through a long corridor, past the single-flight staircase, kitchen and bathroom, to the large main room, which has one window in each of the three outside walls and a fireplace in the centre of the rear wall. Parallel to the corridor, lit by a small window below and a large one above, a staircase with intermediate landing leads to the upper floor with two rooms, the main one of which is lit from the garden side by a single large studio-veranda window.

The design of the façades is developed from the interior. Since the windows are placed in relation to the interior axis, one lateral façade has five sections (six pilasters), the other six sections (seven pilasters), with windows of varying sizes between – but of course, two opposite façades cannot be seen simultaneously.
V. H.

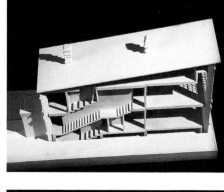

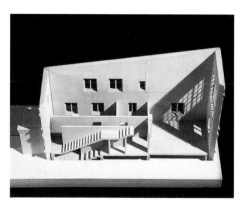

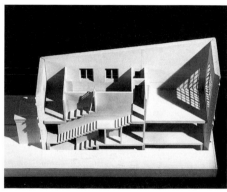

256

257

Ernst Anton Plischke
1903–1992

Vienna Werkbund housing estate
Veitingergasse 107/109
1932

Scale model 1 : 33 ¹/₃
Arnd Westphal
Urs Friedrich

Plischke designed these two-storey terrace houses with 57 m² floor space for the Werkbund housing estate in Vienna in 1932.

In comparison with most of the other houses on the estate, these show clearly Plischke's endeavour not to see the façade – according to the "Zeitgeist" – as a surface, but to break up the strict cubic form by giving it sculptural detail. This conception of architecture is fulfilled both by the cuboid projections for porch and staircase on the street side (extending the floor space of this tiny house) and by the recess for balcony and terrace on the garden side (offering increased privacy). The ground floor contains kitchen, pantry and – one step lower – full-length living-room; on the upper floor are a box-room and full-length bedroom, with bathroom and WC in the entresol.
S. M.

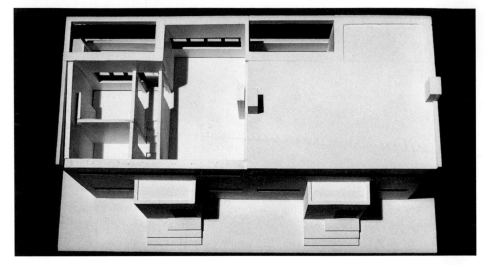

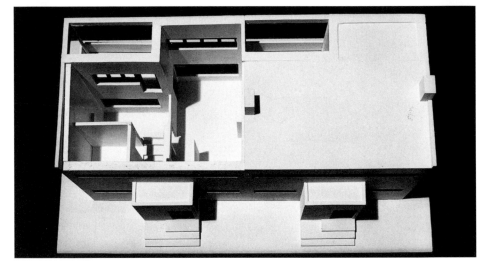

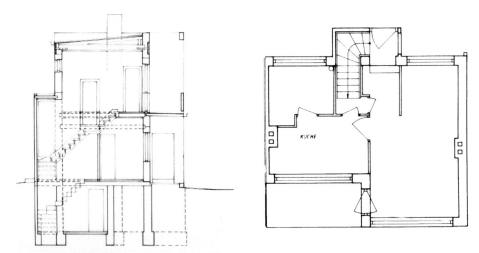

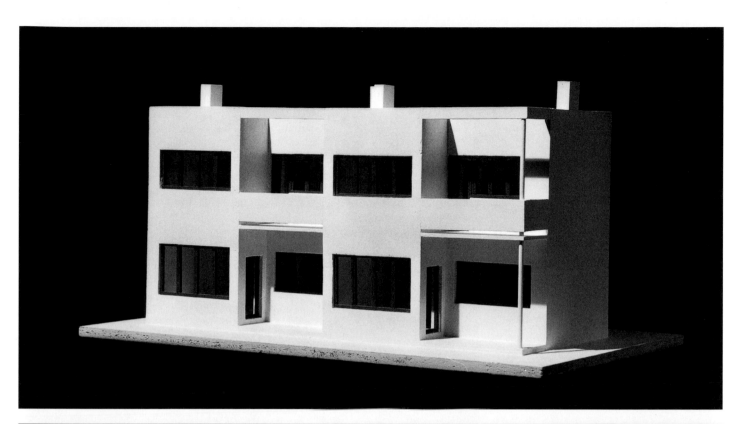

Ernst Anton Plischke
1903–1992

Peter house project
Hietzing
1936

Scale model 1 : 33 $\frac{1}{3}$
Elisabeth Szablinski

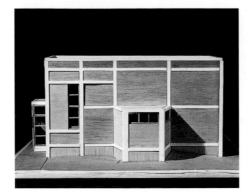

The plot intended for the Peter house project was completely flat, so that a spatial concept independent of external conditions was required.

The interior structure of this small house is determined by four open levels. One enters the house on the lowest level, through a porch with a coat-rack, into the hall, which leads to the kitchen with adjoining maid's room, and on to the living- and dining-area with fitted bench. From here, steps lead up to the raised living-room and on through an entresol with study, to the upper floor with interlinking sleeping compartment and bathroom.

The prefabricated concrete frame construction lends variety to the façades, showing how the design was developed from interior to exterior. Despite the asymmetry in the garden façade, a balance is achieved with wall surfaces, window openings and movable grilles.

In this project, Plischke makes clear the relationship between the four poles of architecture: volumetry – spatial concept – functional planning – construction.
V. H.

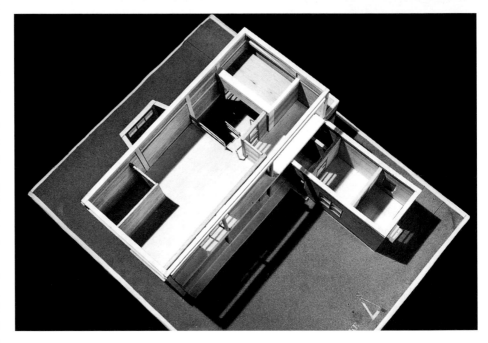

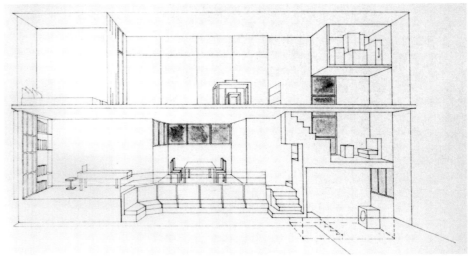

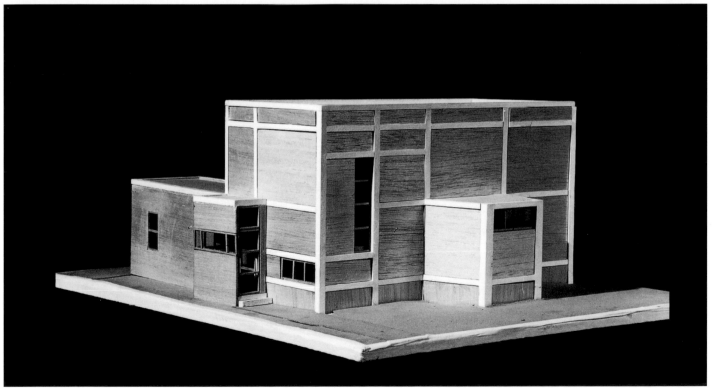

Ernst Anton Plischke
1903–1992

Gamerith house on the Attersee
Upper Austria
1933/34

Scale model 1 : 33 ¹/₃
Christoph Kreutzer

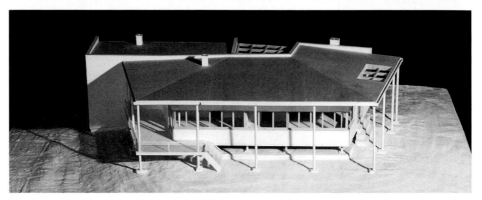

This house, with studio and house-keeper's flat, stands at the top of a hill. To the north, behind the house, is wood-land; the south looks over meadows to the lake. The building evolves from the landscape. The outline of the house was first marked out with a wooden frame-work, which was also used to determine the angles of the outlook recess, to give a view consisting of $^1/_3$ sky, $^1/_3$ land, $^1/_3$ lake.

The ground plan follows the contours of the slope. To the south are the living-room with terrace, bedroom, studio with east exit; to the north, bathroom and housekeeper's flat (bedroom, kitchen/living-room, separate entrance and WC), with hall and kitchen in between.

Under the housekeeper's bedroom is a small cellar accessible from outside.

The roof has a wide overhang, pro-tecting the strip windows on the south side from the summer sun.

The house is a light wooden con-struction, reminiscent of the Japanese tradition. The solid wood floor is raised above ground level, over concrete foundations. Other features are free-standing supports, wooden walls and a flat metal roof raised above the ceiling and resting on slim supports.

W. G.

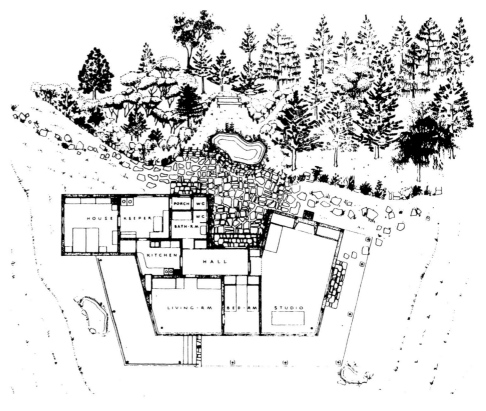

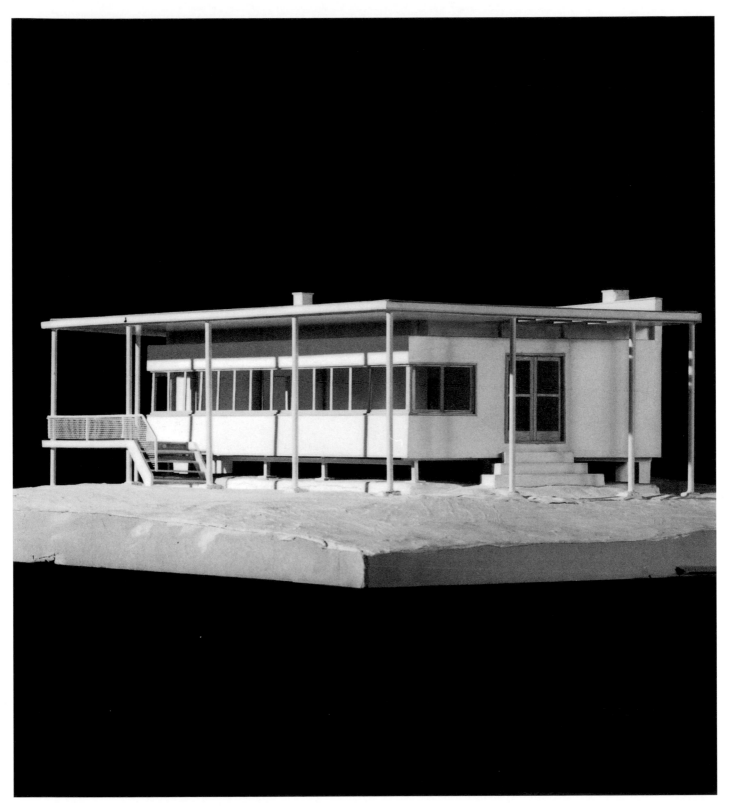

Gerrit Rietveld
1888–1964

**Schröder house
Utrecht
1924**

*Scale model 1 : 50
Hans Stark*

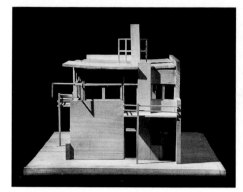

In 1924 Gerrit Rietveld, who joined the De Stijl group in 1919, developed this corner house of a traditional 19th-century terrace, in close collaboration with Truus Schröder-Schräder, who had commissioned it.

The basic cuboid form is resolved into vertical wall and railing elements, supports and projecting horizontal slabs. For all linear elements, Rietveld chose red, blue, yellow and black; for all plane surfaces, white or grey.

In the conception of the ground plan, there is a deliberate contrast between the ground floor, divided by solid walls into functional areas for eating, studying and working, and the upper floor, the living-area.

As in the traditional Japanese house, this upper storey can be used as one single room, or be divided by sliding and folding screens into several functional areas (living-room, hall, three bedrooms). The staircase, bathroom and WC are the only fixed elements.

Julius Posener wrote: "Colour and form are elements of composition in which the solid elements are devalued, while a precisely balanced system of planes and lines becomes centrally important."
S. M.

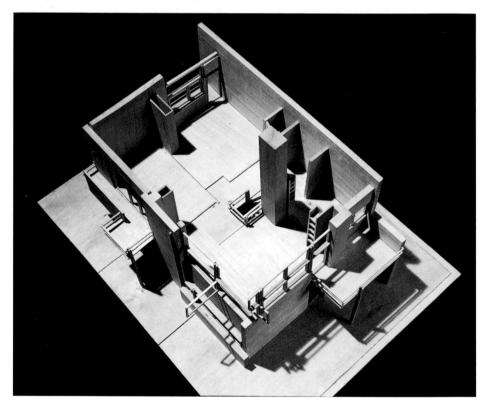

Gerrit Rietveld
1888–1964

Vienna Werkbund housing estate Woinovichgasse 14/16/18/20 1932

Scale model 1 : 33 ¹/₃
Kilian Keller
Luitpold Weishar

Representing Dutch architects, Gerrit Rietveld built a terrace of four houses facing north-south, with three storeys and cellar, each with 101 m² floor space on 46 m² ground area. Unlike André Lurçat, Rietveld tried to divide this type of house not strictly into floors, but with interlinking spaces. Rooms of various shapes, sizes and heights, as well as stepped-back balconies and the projecting entrances combine to form a spatial organism.

The north-facing half, with two low storeys (kitchen and hall on the ground floor, bedroom and bathroom on the first floor), is topped by a high, stepped-back room in the attic fronted by a balcony.

The south half, facing the garden, is characterised by a high, well-lit living-room with a terrace on a lower level, and bedrooms in the two upper storeys. The attic storey also has a stepped-back balcony overlooking the garden.

The connecting element is the square, two-flight newelled staircase, with eleven steps in the north half and four extra steps for the height difference in the south half.

S. M.

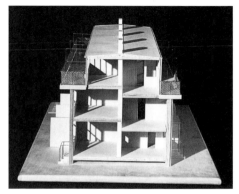

Hans Scharoun
1893–1972

Weissenhof housing estate, house 33, Stuttgart
1927

Scale model 1 : 33 ⅓
Ulrich Hoffmann

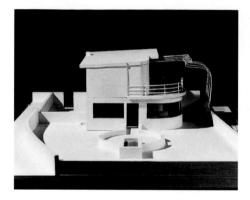
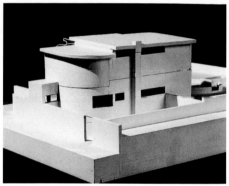

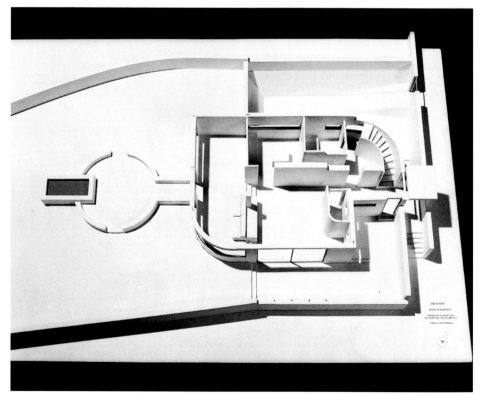

"The two-storey house belongs to the group of the smallest detached houses on the estate. Its arrangement must be clear; its absolute and relative scale should give the effect of spaciousness, leaving a definite impression on visitors, who should not remember simply a 'tour of rooms'.

This is what I have attempted to achieve: through a clear separation of living, sleeping and utility quarters; through marked differences in the measurements of the living-room and bedrooms; through the combination of various functions in one room; through the inter-action of the axis running the length of the house, as a line in contrast to spatial extension (the end of this axis in the garden was intended to be an oblong pool, which for reasons of economy was not executed); through the shape of the living-room, designed to give a feeling of space beyond the boundaries of the walls; through taking account of this particularly beautiful landscape.

Similar trains of thought – besides questions of utilisation – lie behind the design of the utility section. Here, too, I tried to retain the overall impression of this section. Thus the maid's cubicle is placed as a small compartment in the larger room. The actual kitchen, too, is designed just as much on considerations of scale as on those of purpose."
(Hans Scharoun, Die Form, 1927)
B. S.

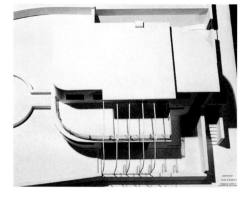
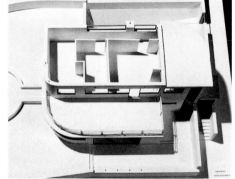

Hans Scharoun
1893–1972

**Schmincke house
Löbau, Saxony
1933**

Scale model 1 : 33 ¹/₃
Sebastian Kruppa
Robert Nickel
Erhardt Lindemann

The elongated east-west design of the house evolved naturally from the lie of the land. On the south side are the road and the factory buildings of the industrialist Fritz Schmincke; on the north side, the house opens on to an old English-style garden.

The utility wing (with maid's room, kitchen and pantry) and the staircase in the two-storey hall are angled at 30° from the axis, to the south-west; similarly the dining-area in the open living-area, to the north-east.

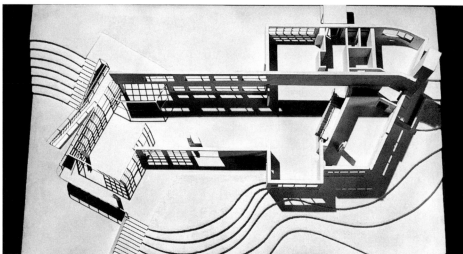

The floor with the living-quarters and the floor with the sleeping-quarters both end in a balcony with a particularly fine view over the garden – the idea behind the angle chosen for this wing.

The lower living level is reserved for the reception rooms.

The hall contains not only the open dining-area, but also the children's play-area opposite, which can be partitioned off.

At the north-east corner, the metal skeleton construction has stairs rather like accommodation ladders, leading from the garden to the terrace decks. Circular recesses in the ceilings of these contain coloured lights, which at night mirror the north-east tip of the house in the garden pond, like the bow of a ship.

B. S.

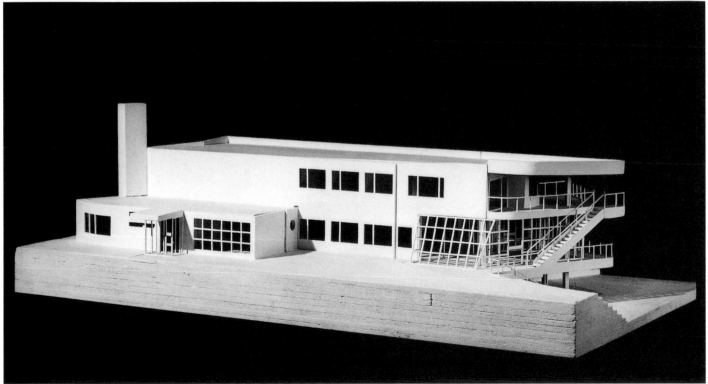

271

Hans Scharoun
1893–1972

**Baensch house
Berlin Spandau
1935**

Scale model 1 : 33 1/3
Karl Käufl
Elfriede Müller
Birgit Sorge

This site, on the Weinmeister Heights west of the River Havel, slopes down steeply south-eastwards from the road and offers an excellent view.

In the three-section fan-shaped ground plan, the axis of the house is at an ideal angle from the line of the road, and the ground plan segments follow the natural lie of the land. The entrance is in the north-west of the house, with the utility section to the left. The diagonally extending hallway is bordered on one side by the oval dining-room (with a circular vaulted ceiling), and on the other by the study, which has a separate entrance, and forms part of the hall when the sliding glass partition is open. An open staircase leads up to the sleeping quarters. The actual living-room is three steps down, its convex glass wall opening on to the landscape.

Under the increasingly restrictive practice of the planning departments in the Third Reich, a sloping roof was compulsory. Here the apparently conventional gable roof, as seen from the street, develops a freely sweeping silhouette towards the garden. The gable edge is given a bright red facing; sliding wooden shutters on rails are operated by winders from the interior, thus counting as a piece of "technical equipment".
B. S.

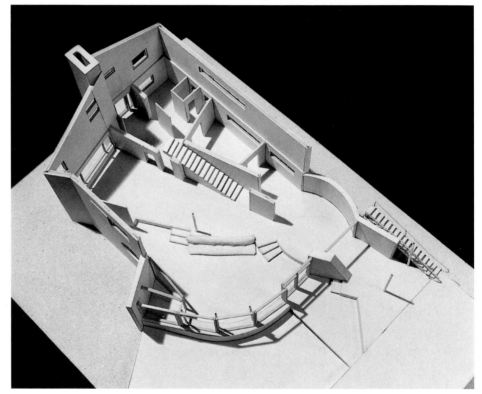

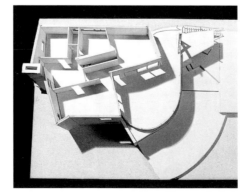

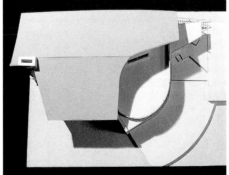

Rudolph M. Schindler
1887–1953

Log cabin project
1916/17

Scale model 1 : 33 ¹/₃
Franz Madl

Schindler designed this little holiday summerhouse before he entered Frank Lloyd Wright's office.

In its axial conception, it follows the pattern of the pavilion containing smaller units. The projecting building rests on three recessed pillars of natural stone, so that it seems to hover above the ground. The block construction is clearly brought out by the long overlaps at the corners, as well as by the visible roof and floor timbers. The narrow horizontal windows are formed by omitting a few rows of timbers. The whole conception of this house is based on a module of four feet in both the vertical and the horizontal, an idea used by Schindler in a more refined form in his subsequent buildings.

T. B.

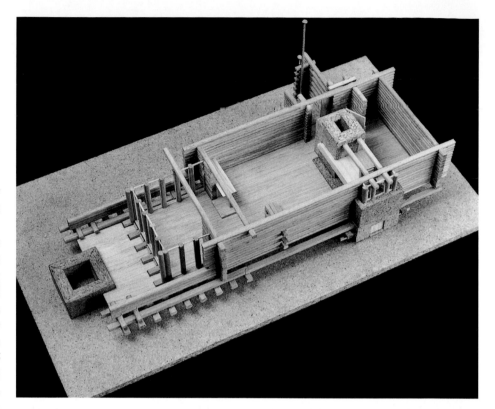

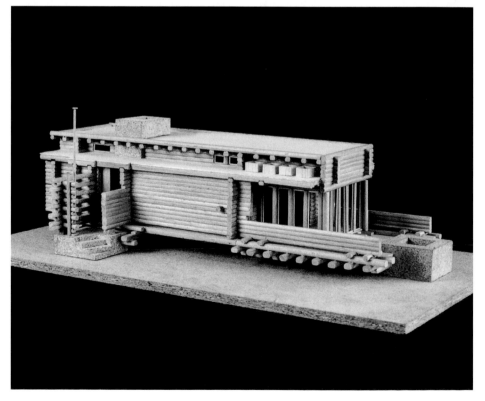

Rudolph M. Schindler
1887–1953

Schindler house
Los Angeles
1921/22

Scale model 1 : 33 ¹/₃
Rudolf Brandes
Pia Schlaghaufer

The Schindler house was conceived as a co-operative double house for the Chase and Schindler couples.

The open plan is divided into two L-shaped types, each with two private withdrawing areas and an enclosed courtyard with its own fireplace. During the summer months, this is used as the living-room, when the outer walls are opened by means of sliding doors. Above the entrance, there are open verandas for sleeping. At the junction of the two L-shapes, the planning includes a communal kitchen, the couples sharing responsibility for meals in alternate weeks.

The simple construction of the house is determined by the use of concrete floors and walls. The redwood ceilings have wooden supports on the side facing the courtyard. Throughout the courtyard sides of the house, fanlights are inserted between the two ceiling levels, giving a cool stream of air under the roof.
T. B.

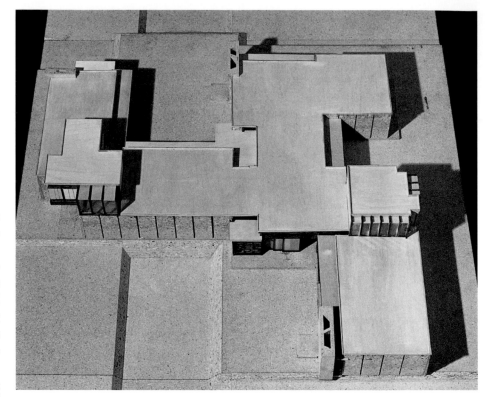

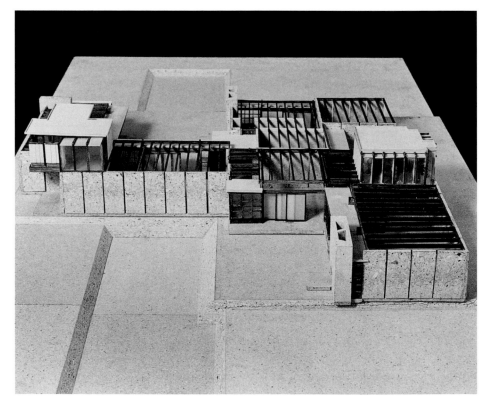

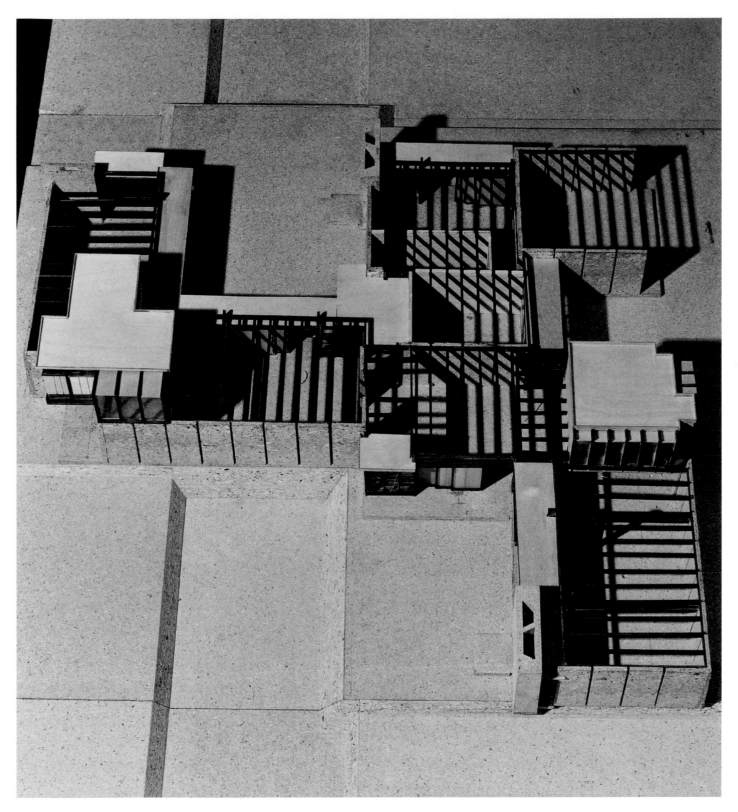

Rudolph M. Schindler
1887–1953

**Pueblo Ribera house
La Jolla
1923–25**

*Scale model 1 : 33 ¹/₃
Klaus Gürtner
Christian Hartmann
Angela Rissler*

The whole complex is formed by twelve U-shaped Californian-style houses, grouped so that each house has a small courtyard with garden. A service road runs through the centre of the site, providing access to the garages.

The ground-floor rooms open on to the garden. Grouped around the central living-room are entrance, kitchen and small dining-area, bedroom and bathroom. An outside staircase leads from the courtyard to the open attic storey, which is designed as a veranda for living and sleeping.

Here, too, Schindler experimented with concrete walls, made by the so-called "slab-cast" process, in which horizontal shuttering lined with roofing-paper and fixed with triangular battens is moved up vertical wooden columns. This gives the finished wall the characteristic horizontal grooves between the cast layers.
T. B.

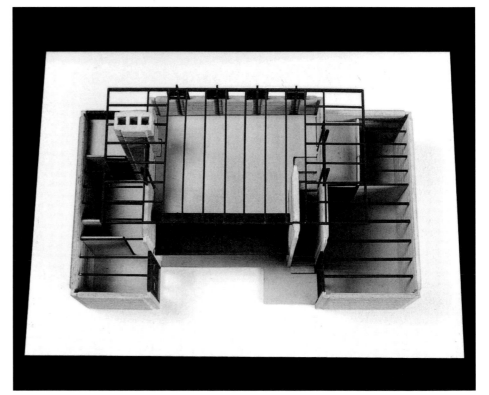

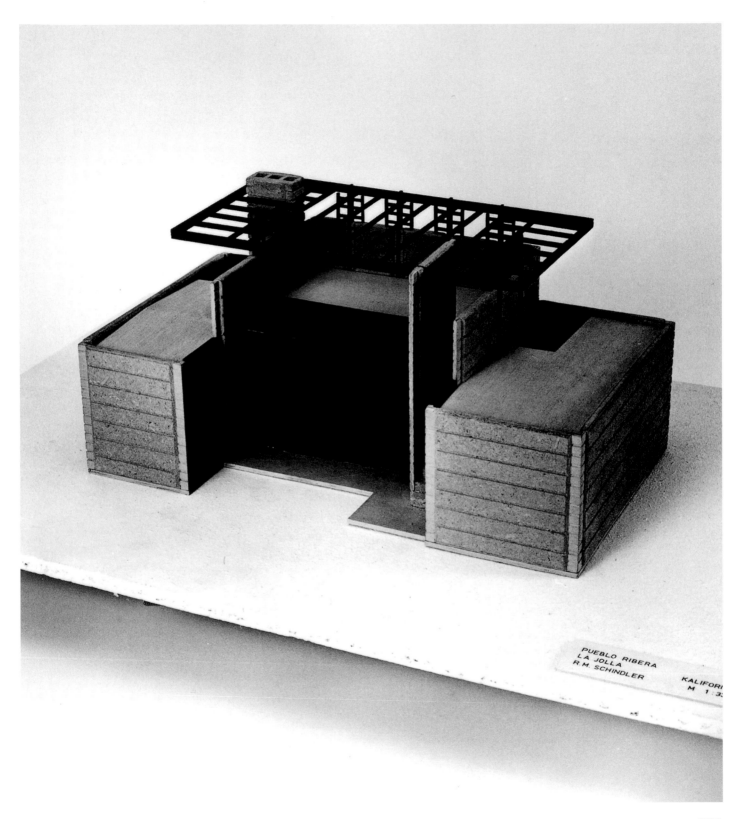

PUEBLO RIBERA
LA JOLLA
R.M. SCHINDLER

KALIFORNI
M 1:33

279

Rudolph M. Schindler
1887–1953

**Packard house
South Pasadena
1924**

Scale model 1 : 33 ⅓
Peter Gossner
Hans Sandmeier

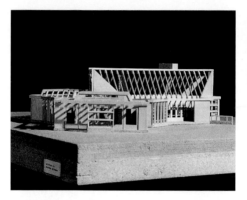

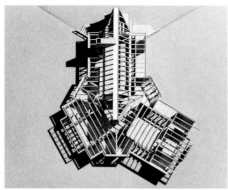

The three-winged ground plan for this single-storey building centred on the kitchen is reminiscent of ground plan configurations designed by Frank Lloyd Wright.

The outer shell of the building is not so much the "façade of a convex mass, as the inner wall of an exterior room (patio)" (Schindler). Thus the building and the surrounding gardens form six different open areas.

Building regulations forced Schindler to use a saddleback roof. The result was a combination of flat roofs and steep roofs with flattened ridge and bevelled gables. The interior – as David Gebhard pointed out – shows similarities with houses designed by Bernard Maybeck in Berkeley.

M. K.

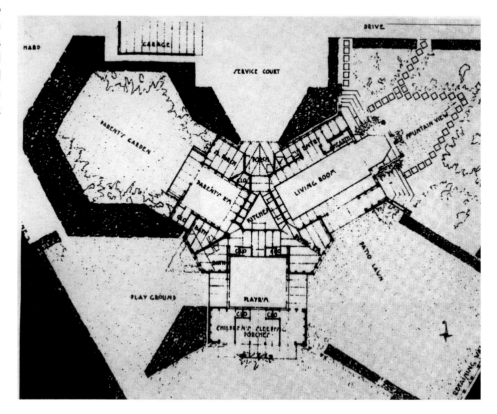

Rudolph M. Schindler
1887–1953

**Lovell beach house
Newport Beach
1925/26**

*Scale model 1 : 33 ¹/₃
Harald Moertl
Albrecht Thalmann*

The Lovell beach house stands right beside the promenade along the Pacific. The architectural leitmotiv of raising the house on five ferroconcrete frames was suggested by the traditional form of building on wooden piles. Wooden beams at right angles to the frames support the floors. Both the ground plan and the façades were designed using a grid, in order to guarantee the uniformity of the measurements. For the same reason, all the woodwork, including the concrete shuttering and the furniture are made from eight-inch planks. The furniture was made on the site, from the same wood that was used for the construction of the house.

Because the building is raised, the greater part of the site is retained as playground and car park. Access to the house is by two opposite staircases, one of which leads to the balcony in front of the two-storey living-room; the steeper one leads to the kitchen, dining-area and housekeeper's room, and on to an internal bridge. This gives access to the bedrooms, which serve merely as dressing-rooms, since the beds are on the verandas in front.
T. B.

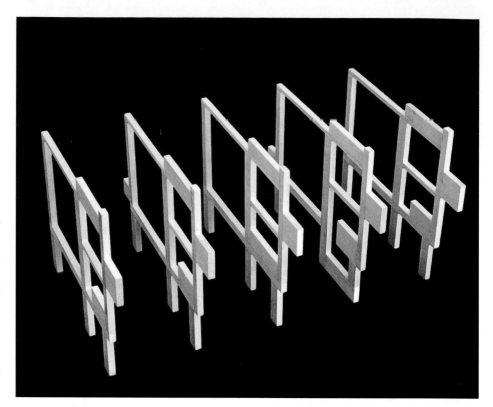

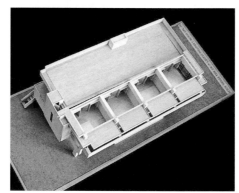

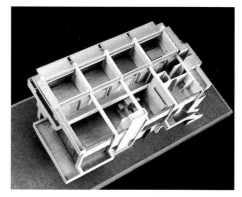

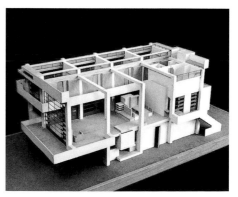

Rudolph M. Schindler
1887–1953

Wolfe summerhouse
Avalon
1928

Scale model 1 : 33 ¹/₃
Klaus Greilich
Andreas Meck

Schindler's design for this "house on tiptoe" makes it seem to hover above the 45° slope. The site is tiny. Three sides of the house have only small openings; only the façade facing down towards the Bay of Avalon is entirely glazed. Three living-areas of different sizes with balconies in front, together with a roof terrace constitute the four levels of the building. Access to the house is by outside staircases; a narrow exterior ramp, behind the slim wooden bars of the street façade, leads to the top level. The vertical construction consists of 2 × 4-inch and 2 × 6-inch wooden supports; the ceiling construction is of corrugated iron with a thin layer of concrete, over 2 × 10-inch beams. The terrace railings are water-pipes with sprinkler perforations, to water the flower boxes below.
M. K.

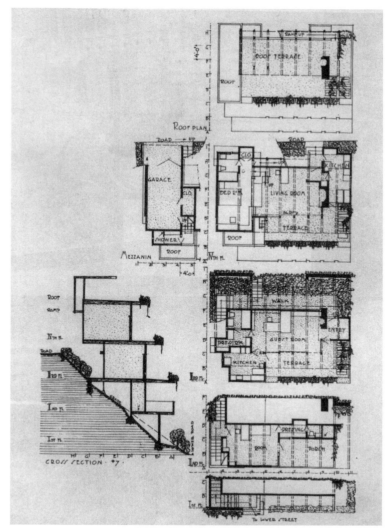

Rudolph M. Schindler
1887–1953

Oliver house
Los Angeles
1933

Scale model 1 : 33 ¹/₃
Dietmar Dölling
Wolfgang Vogl

The diagonal positioning of its L-shaped structure allows this house, built on a narrow site at the top of a hill, to take full advantage of the magnificent view over Silver Lake and as far as the San Gabriel Mountains, as well as that over western Los Angeles to the Pacific. Only the garage below is parallel to the road. The angled building encloses the principal open area, which is formed by the garden into a courtyard. The interior rooms are distributed so that the "public" rooms, such as living-room, dining-room and kitchen are on the entrance side of the angle, while the bedrooms are on the other side. Building regulations forced Schindler to plan a saddleback roof; the elegant ambiguity of his compliance with this is demonstrated by his treatment of sloping and flat roof sections, which allows him to plan different heights and configurations for the rooms underneath, according to their importance. The house appears to the observer, according to where he is standing, as a cuboid structure or as a house "protected" by a saddle roof.
M. K.

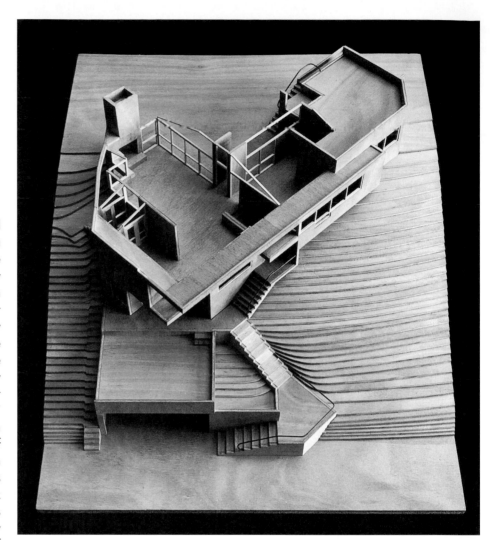

Rudolph M. Schindler
1887–1953

**Walker house
Los Angeles
1935/36**

*Scale model 1 : 33 ¹/₃
Andreas Hlawaczek
Babette Pernice*

Seen from the street side, the architectural appearance of the Walker house with its simple cuboid forms and strip windows under the eaves, might be ascribed more to the International Style. The composition of the lower side, however, with the eight supporting ferroconcrete pillars, the horizontal trellises, terraces and roof, is quite in keeping with Schindler's De Stijl conception. The particular quality of the interior lies in the volumetric shaping of the living-area and the resultant link with the floor below. Exterior and interior colours harmonise with the surrounding trees, the green of the garden and the blue-green of Silver Lake.
T. B.

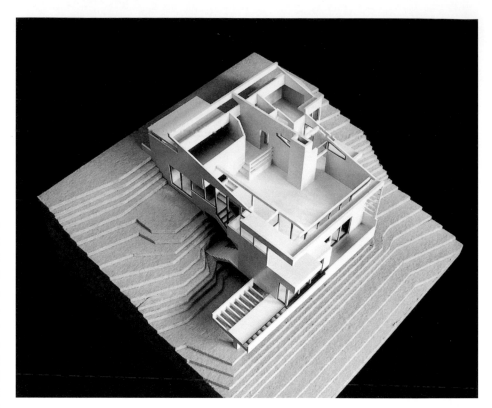

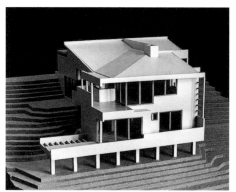

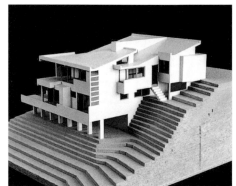

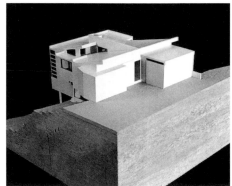

Rudolph M. Schindler
1887–1953

**Warshaw house project
1936**

Scale model 1 : 33 ¹/₃
Maren Betzler
Alexander Pfletscher

The entrance to the Warshaw house is on the entresol, with direct access to the kitchen. By way of a split-level landing, one reaches either the bedrooms on the upper floor or the lower split-level living-area. This continues on to a terrace on two sides, at an angle of 45° to the main structure. Below this is a one-room flat with separate entrance, and below this again are the two garages.

The typical feature of this project is the rounded roof, sloping from the upper edge on one side and curving down on the other to form the exterior wall, which bends horizontally to the downhill end, to form an added quadrant containing the dining-area.

T. B.

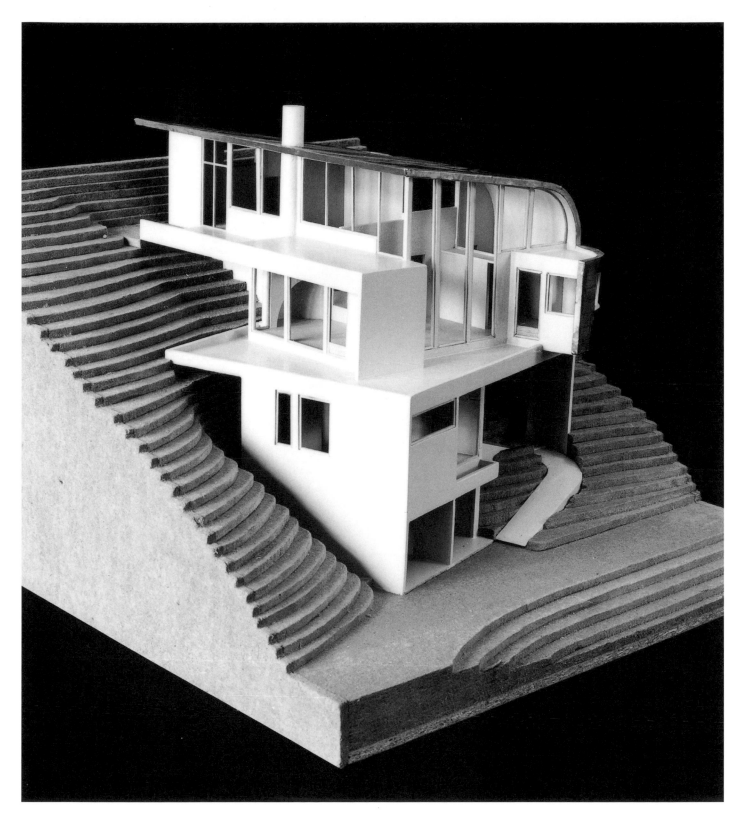

Rudolph M. Schindler
1887–1953

Jacobs house project
1936

Scale model 1 . 33 ¹/₃
Heidi Achtiani
Mathias Gossner

The ground floor of this house is formed by two separate structures, over which the upper storey stretches like a bridge, its main feature being the curved roof. Schindler planned something similar – a combination of cuboid forms and curved roofs – for the Warshaw house. It may be assumed that the architect knew the barrel-roofed Steiner and Horner houses by Adolf Loos, built in Vienna two decades previously.
M. K.

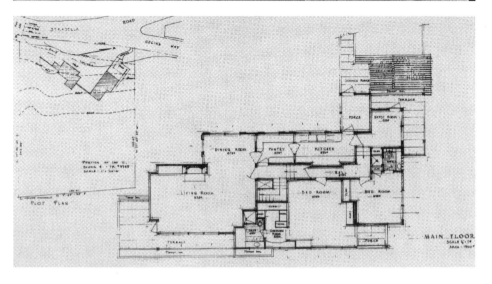

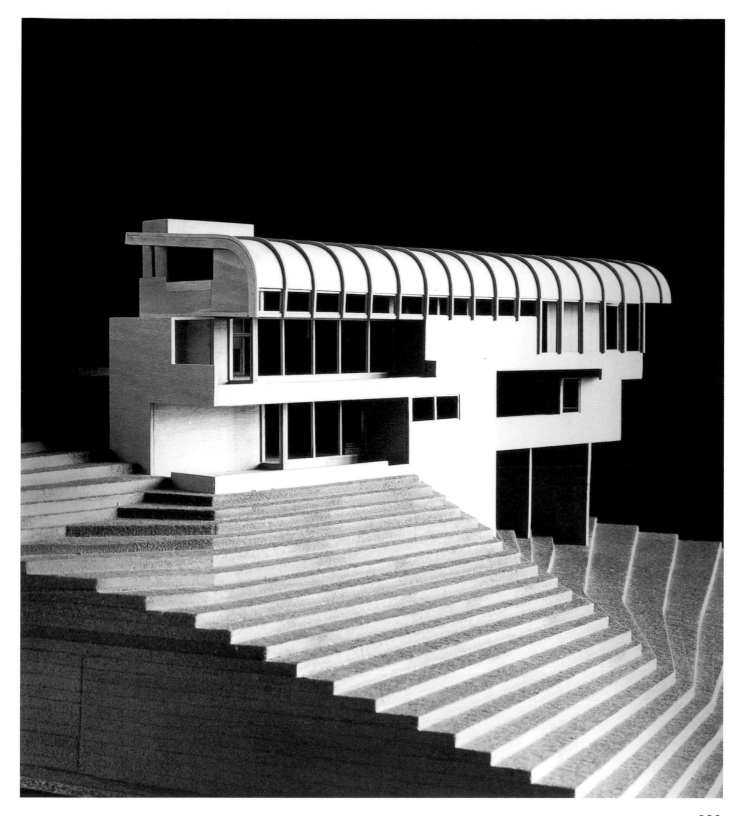

Rudolph M. Schindler
1887–1953

Wilson house
Los Angeles
1938

Scale model 1 : 33 ¹/₃
Elisabeth Daffner
Sandra Grguric
Roland Reisinger

Like many of Schindler's houses, this, too, seems to hover over an almost 40° slope. The wing-like roofs with their tapering edges give the impression that the house is about to take off. The three storeys intended as living-quarters are distributed over five levels. Two outside staircases connect the floors with each other by way of terraces. Their marked plasticity gives the façades a striking quality; they show Schindler's personal Californian answer to De Stijl in Europe. The exterior colours harmonise with the play of colours in the landscape.
M. K.

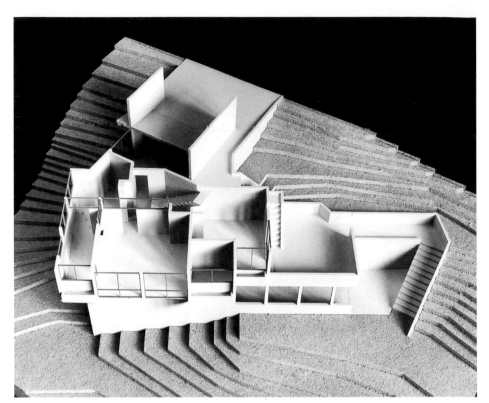

Rudolph M. Schindler
1887–1953

Harris house
Los Angeles
1942

Scale model 1 : 33 ¹/₃
Michaela Durst
Botho von Oheimb

This little house-for-one, built on a slope, includes the natural topography and rock formation of the site as an integral component of the overall design.
The wall facing the road extends beyond the rock and has strip windows with a pergola above, which, together with the body of the house, encloses the patio. Below the building, in the slope, is the garage, from which a partially covered outside staircase leads to the storey with the living-area. The fairly conventional arrangement of rooms is accessible by way of an interior hallway. The living-room, lit from two sides, has an open fireplace on the uphill side of the house. The basic construction consists of a plastered wooden frame.
T. B.

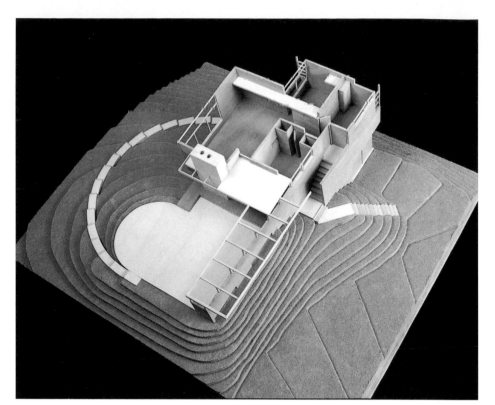

296

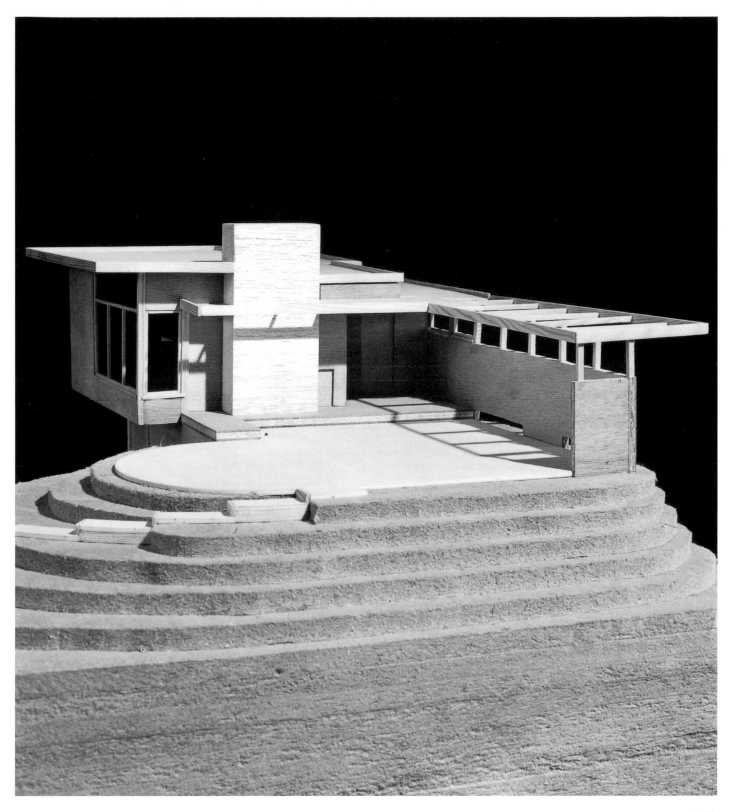

Rudolph M. Schindler
1887–1953

Tischler house
Los Angeles
1949/50

Scale model 1 : 33 ¹/₃
Richard Büchler
Franz Kollmann

This house, situated on a slope in Bel Air, was designed for the family of a silversmith named Tischler.

The appearance of the house is determined by the saddle roof flattened at the ridge, with a translucent blue fibreglass covering over the living area. At street level, instead of a garage there is a semicircular carport. From here, a curved outside staircase leads first to the silversmith's workshop. The main part of the house is on the uppermost level of the site, which was levelled to make a lawn and a badminton court. The entrance and the living- and dining-area are separated by the stove, installed and masked in stainless steel. Kitchen, bedrooms and bathroom are in the section facing the slope, and are accessible through a central corridor.

The building stands on the concrete block walls of the bottom storey, which supports a wooden frame construction with plastered exterior walls. The interior walls do not reach right to the top, but are glazed up to the roof; together with the translucent roof, this results in a living area where interior and exterior merge.
T. B.

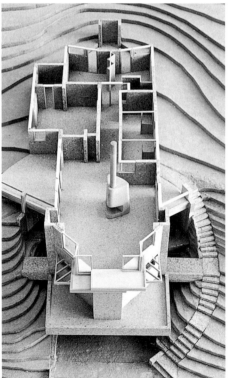

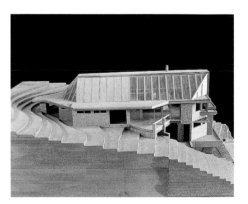

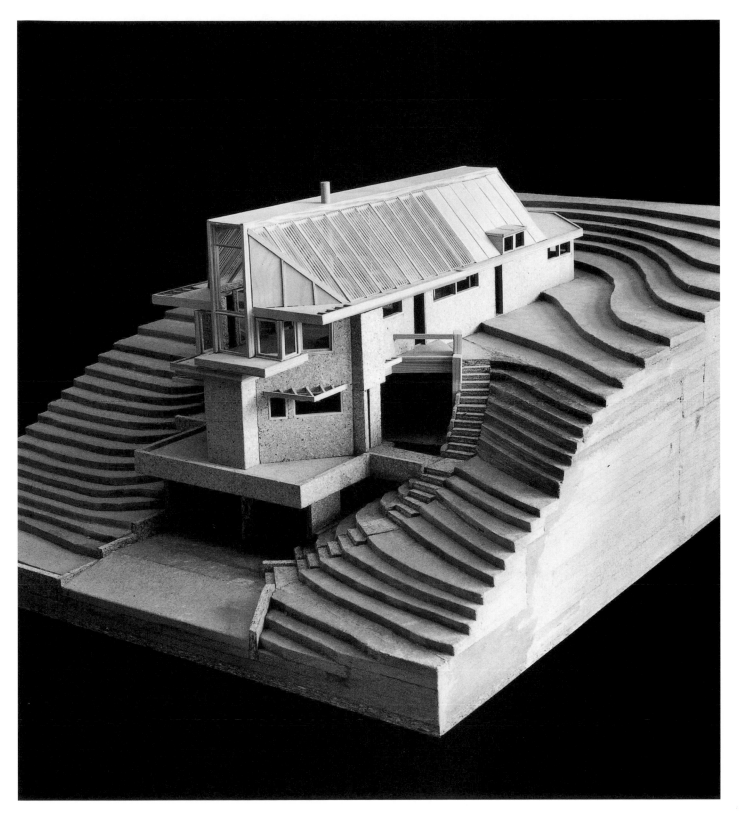

Rudolph M. Schindler
1887–1953

Janson house
1949

Scale model 1 : 33 ¹/₃
Robert Cachado
Bernd Triebel

The small tower-like Janson house stands on a very steep slope in the Hollywood Hills. Like many of Schindler's houses, this one has separate areas for living and working. On the level with the entrance is a small separate studio. Around the central kitchen on the living-area level are grouped the living-room and bedrooms, as well as the dining-area and the bathroom, both accessible from two sides. Typical features of this house are the terraces, projecting far over the slope. As in the Tischler house, Schindler tried here to develop a transparent house, by designing parts of the exterior walls in coloured translucent fibreglass.

T. B.

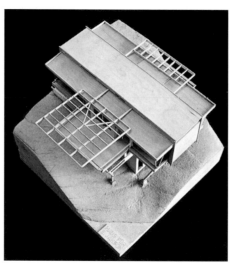
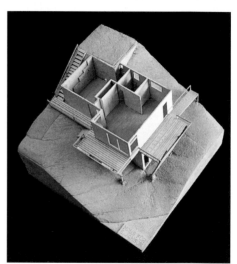
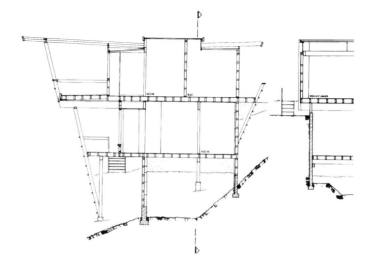

Mart Stam
1899–1986

Weissenhof housing estate, houses 28, 29, 30 Stuttgart 1927

Scale model 1 : 33 ¹/₃
Irina Schillinger
Martin Wich

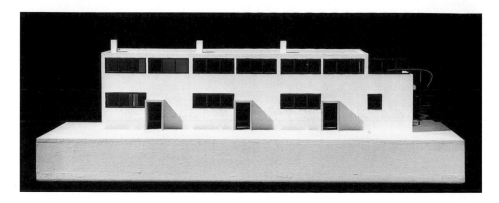

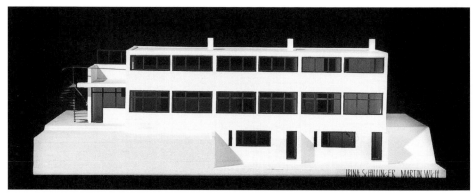

Mies van der Rohe asked Stam to plan a group of three terrace houses for middle-class families with children and a daily help.

On the ground floor of the houses are a cloakroom and WC, and a narrow kitchen with a serving-hatch to the living-room. This is the largest room in the house, open to the staircase, and with a sliding partition of glass elements. In two of the houses, the living-room is linked with a basement room giving on to the garden; in the third one, the hall opens on to a conservatory with a sun terrace above it. On the upper storey are the bathroom with dressing-room and three bedrooms, one of which has no direct light or ventilation.

Mart Stam aimed at the greatest possible economy by using standard constructional elements and choosing suitable materials. The houses were designed to be built as metal skeleton constructions with hollow slab-concrete blocks. He chose white for the façade, grey for the porches and blue for the metal windows.

Stam himself designed the interior furnishings for houses 28 and 29. Here he showed the public the first chairs without back legs – the chair invention of the century – in a form reducing material to the absolute minimum.

B. S.

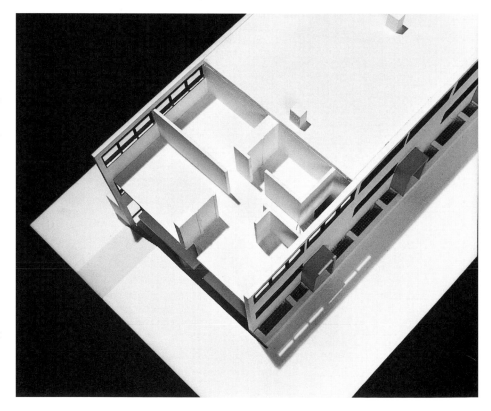

302

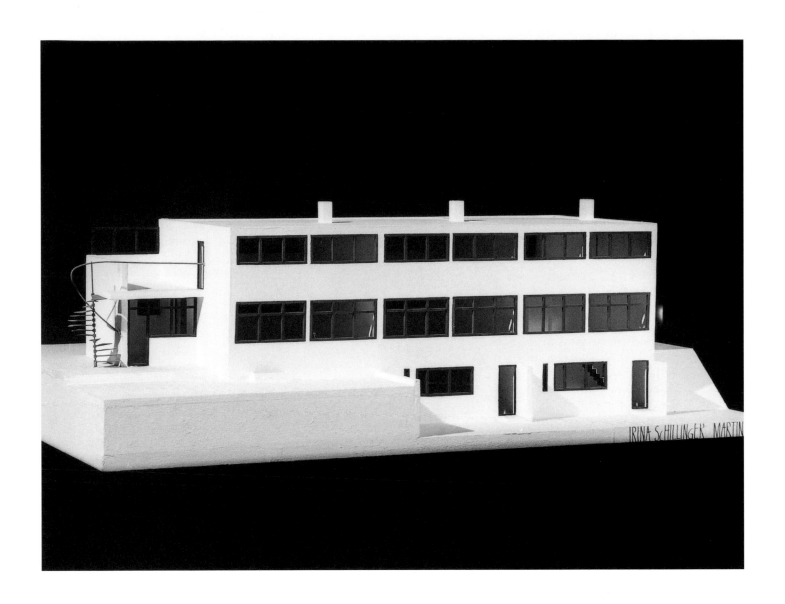

Oskar Strnad
1879–1935

Vienna Werkbund housing estate
1932

Scale model 1 . 33 ¹/₃
Knut Kernchen
Peter Mayer

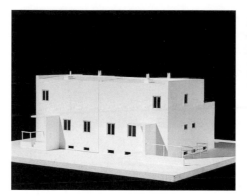

Here Oskar Strnad developed a pair of two-storey semi-detached houses with 77 m² floor space, running north-south and axially symmetrical. The houses are accessible up three steps from the street side to the north, by way of a covered threshold open towards the east.

Through a small porch, the visitor enters a larger hall facing the staircase, and passes the kitchen to reach the centre of the house: the living room.

This is divided into a smaller dining-area lit from the north, and a spacious living-area looking on to the garden in the south; the outer wall curves like a proscenium into the garden, combining with the covered veranda to form an interesting approach to terrace and garden.

In his article "Harmonie in der Baukunst" (Harmony in the art of building), Oskar Strnad wrote: "[...] as the structure reaches towards the sun, resisting wind and weather, as the garden merges into the floor construction, and as the walls of the rooms project into the open. This is the accord between nature and geometric forms that have assumed significance but are rooted in the earth."

These houses were destroyed in 1945.
S. M.

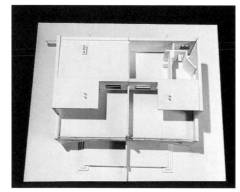

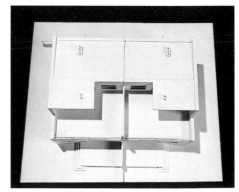

Bruno Taut
1880–1938

The architect's house
Dahlewitz
1926

Scale model 1 : 33 ¹/₃
Günther Baumann

This two-storey structure, with a single-storey utility wing adjoining its north angle, advances with its "prow" from the narrow site into the landscape.

"[...] and yet this is not form in the aesthetic sense. The oblique angle of the ground plan has the advantage that no window has another one directly opposite." The (warm) west side is white, the convex east side facing the street is black (thermal collector). The interior is a three-dimensional colour composition with colourful surfaces and stripes. "The overall shape of the ground plan is that of a sundial." The axis of the entrance opens on to the main room; to the right is the dining-area with kitchen and utility rooms; to the left is the so-called "little room". The staircase leads past a "prism window" to the bathroom, box-room and three bedrooms opening on to a balcony roofed in glass bricks at the west corner. This allows sunlight into the north-west facing room.

"The curve of the ground plan is a space-saving factor [...]; the ground plan shapes, diverging from the dogma of the right angle, offer many useful possibilities for the division and furnishing of the rooms."

(From: Ein Wohnhaus, 1927. Here Taut uses his own house as an example to explain aspects of "new living design".)
B. S.

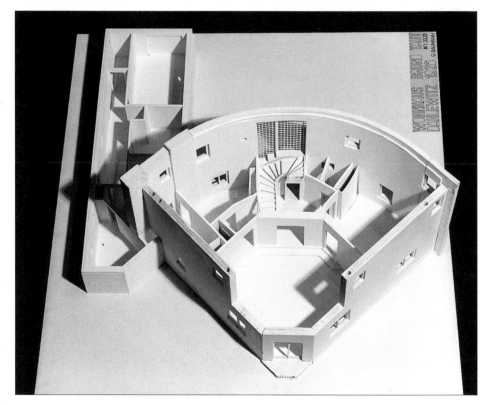

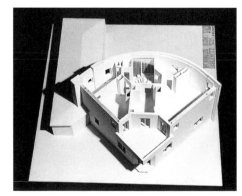

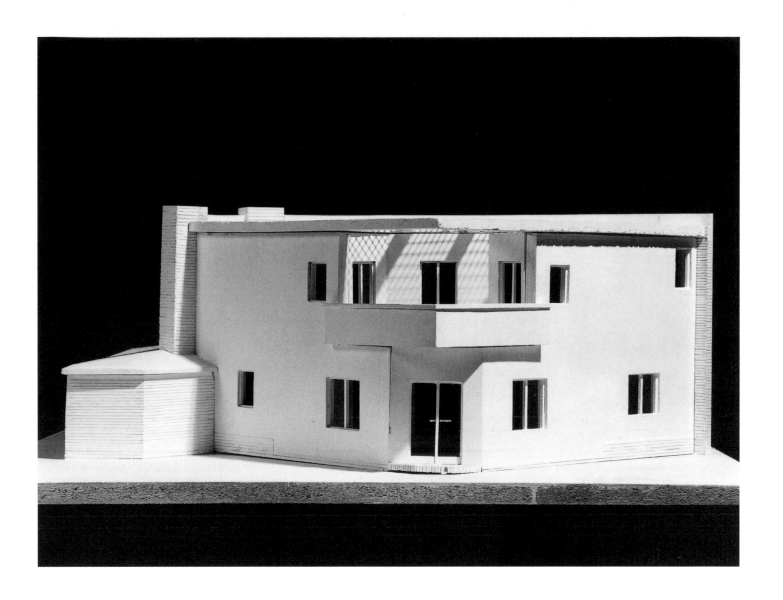

Bruno Taut
1880–1938

**Weissenhof housing estate, house 19
Stuttgart
1927**

*Scale model 1 : 33 $^1/_3$
Franz Putz
Ralf Emmerling*

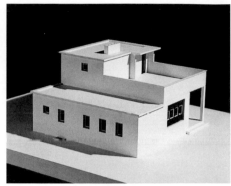

The requirement was for a worker's house fulfilling the needs of a family with four children, to be built on the smallest plot of the estate (317 m²).

The main rooms of the two-storey house are combined on the ground floor, in order to give the impression of a single-storey house. To the west are the entrance, washroom and WC, and the kitchen with sink unit and veranda. The living-room with veranda faces the slope to the east; the bedrooms face south. A straight staircase leads to the upper storey with drying-room and two further small rooms. The large, high living-room is designed as a multi-purpose area. The dining-recess is partitioned off by a folding glass screen so that it can be used independently. The study recess can also be partitioned off. Above the living-area is a sun-terrace with closed parapet and a shower installed under the projecting roof.

All the fixtures are designed as fitted furniture. The walls, ceilings and floors are painted with colourful gloss paint. The strikingly coloured exterior, too, is conspicuous by its contrast to the general off-white prescribed by Mies. "[...] and there is nothing more delightful than brightly coloured houses in the snow." (Bruno Taut)
B. S.

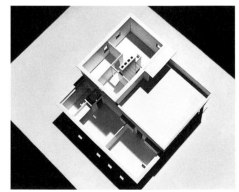

Giuseppe Terragni
1904–1943

Villa sul lago project
1936

Scale model 1 : 33 ¹/₃
Harry Schöpke

In this design, Terragni follows the idea of the free ground plan, similarly to Le Corbusier in the Savoye and Stein villas. A system of pillars supports the ceilings of all the storeys, and the dividing walls can be placed at will, so that each room has the size and shape required for its function. Like the Savoye villa, here a kind of "promenade architecturale" runs through the building, beginning with the large outside staircase leading to the "piano nobile", over further interior and exterior staircases and up to the roof garden. The important independent element of this design, however, is the broad gallery around the storey with the living-quarters, almost completely surrounding the building.

With this "house-within-a-house" concept, Terragni achieves in a simple manner the desired separation of public and private areas.

Similarly to other designs of his around this time, the ground plan shows a marked formal relationship with the paintings of the abstract artist Mario Radice, whose principles of construction inspired Terragni in his work.

S. M.

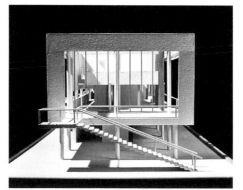

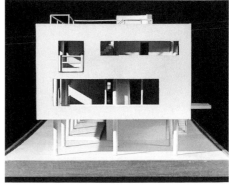

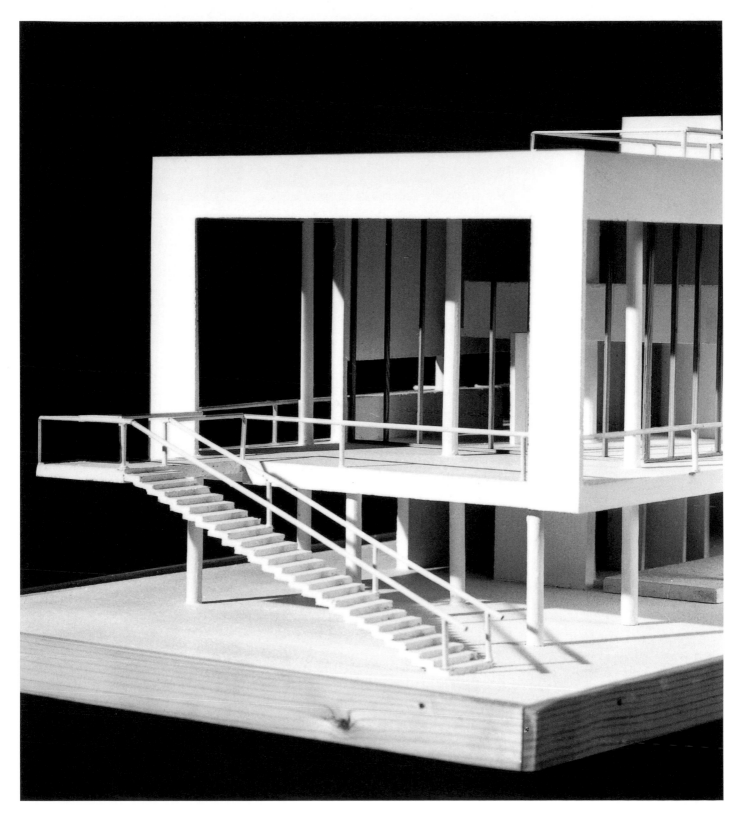

311

Giuseppe Terragni
1904–1943

Danteum project

Scale model 1 : 50

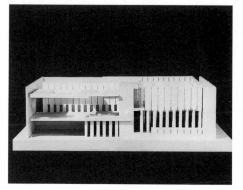
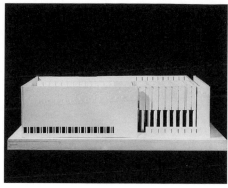
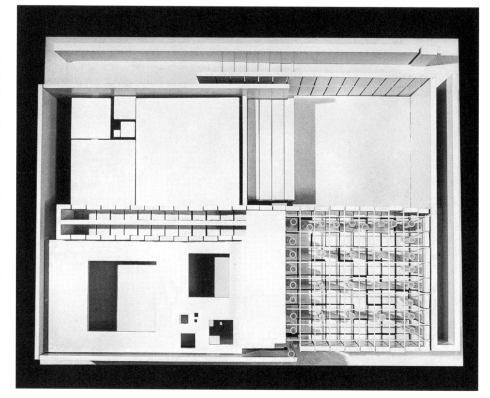

Commissioned in 1938 by the director of the Academy of Art in Brera for the E'42 exhibition, Terragni developed this project in collaboration with P. Lingeri. It was to be sited opposite the Basilica of Maxentius on the via dell'Impero in Rome.

The figuration of the building represents an attempt to render the formal and symbolic structure of Dante's "Divina Commedia" in a geometric architectural order. This is based on the division and combination of the numbers 1, 3, 7 and 10, and the rectangle with proportions according to the Golden Section. The long side, which corresponds to the shorter side of the Basilica of Maxentius, contains an open access courtyard and three large rooms. Hell is symbolised by seven monolithic columns, each bearing seven square stone blocks of different sizes, whose centre of gravity gives a line spiralling to infinity. More hope is offered by Purgatory, with openings in the ceiling following the line of the spiral. A narrow entrance opens on to Paradise, with 33 transparent columns. Terragni: "This is why [...] the building must be first and foremost a temple – not a museum, not a palace, and not a theatre. A temple divided into three rooms, each representing a process on one level and – although differently constructed – mutually integrative, so that they can prepare the visitor gradually for a sublimation of the subject-matter."
S. M.

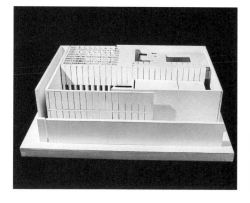
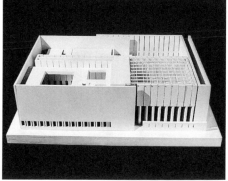

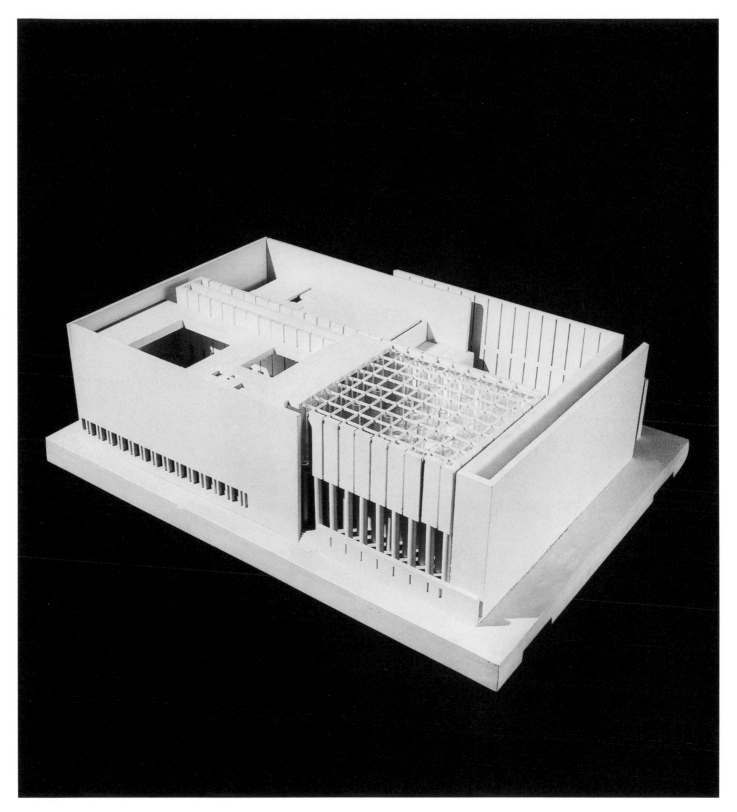

Robert Venturi
1925

**Vanna Venturi house
Chesnut Hill, Philadelphia
1962–64**

*Scale model 1 : 33 ¹/₃
Rolf Gruber*

The two-storey detached house with rectangular ground plan stands across an L-shaped site. The north and south façades, which project beyond the roof and side walls, derive unity from two parallel reglets. The house is spanned by a wide saddle roof, the gable being divided in the middle by a vertical slit.

On the central axis is a square entrance porch with a flat, wide lintel on which a delicate arc is superimposed in relief.

A pent roof with a fanlight is inserted into the ridge of the saddle roof. The chimney, slightly to the left of the central axis, merges with the side of the pent roof. Seen from the south, the impression is that of a hipped roof, stepped back from the façade to form a terrace. Under the hip end, a segmental window extends symmetrically over the axis.

Focal points of the interior are the fireplace, slightly off-centre, and the staircase, reduced by the width of the fireplace so that together they form a nucleus, surrounded by bathroom, guestroom, bedroom, living-room, dining-room and kitchen. The staircase ends blind.

B. H.

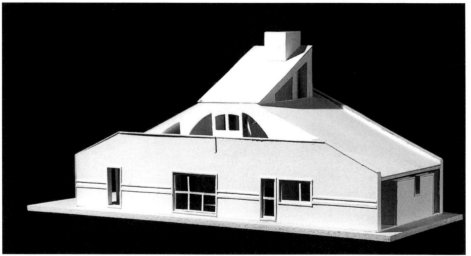

Otto Wagner
1841–1918

**Wagner villa
Vienna
1912**

*Scale model 1 : 33 ¹/₃
Tilman Göhlert*

Wagner built this cuboid, asymmetric summerhouse in neo-Renaissance style adjacent to and a quarter of a century after his first villa (1886), which was of axially symmetrical design, around a central hall with portico. His last house, it establishes him as a modern architect. "The 'style' imported from Munich is at present enjoying a real orgy here. Viennese wit has named it 'Bräustil' [style favoured by wealthy Munich brewers], and we now have the pleasure of seeing an abundance of examples. It is unbelievable but true that in an age when science, industry, invention, etc. show enormous progress, opinions on architecture – and thus the buildings themselves – have sunk, with few exceptions, to a complete lack of feeling and intelligence. […]
The determining factors for the ground plan were: the requirement for well-lit rooms and their effective and individual arrangement; simplicity and durability of the execution; use of those materials that industry has recently provided us with (high-quality plaster, plate glass and marble facing, ferroconcrete, asphalt, asbestos cement, glass mosaic and aluminium, etc.)."
(Otto Wagner, Einige Skizzen, Projekte und ausgeführte Bauwerke, vol IV)
S. M.

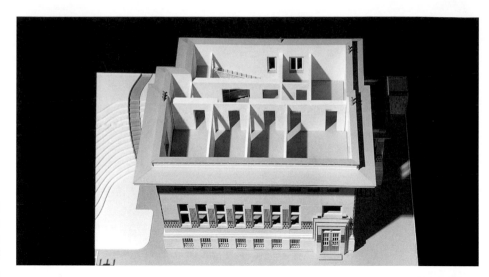

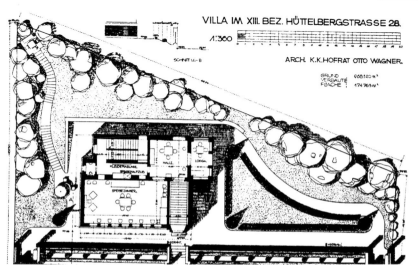

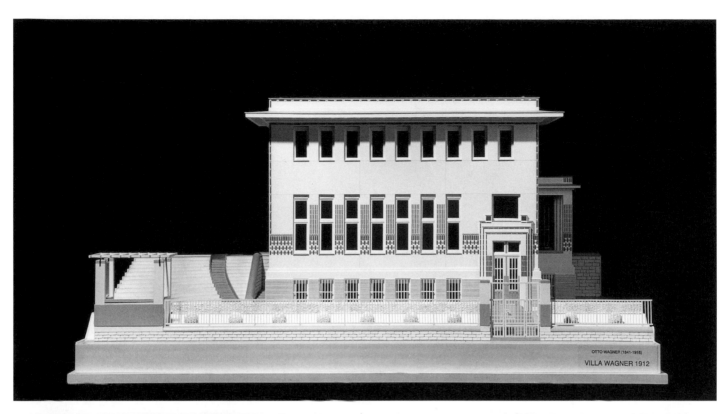

OTTO WAGNER (1841-1918)
VILLA WAGNER 1912

OTTO WAGNER (1841-1918)
VILLA WAGNER 1912

Lois Welzenbacher
1889–1955

Settari house
Bad Dreikirchen near Waidbruck,
South Tirol
1923

Scale model 1 : 33 ¹/₃
Thomas Szyia

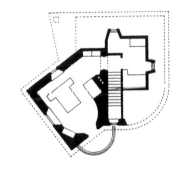

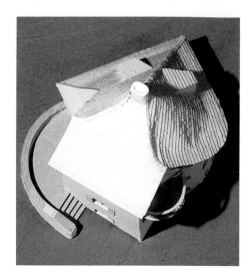

On a small hill above Dreikirchen, at 1200 m altitude, stands one of Welzenbacher's early works, overlooking the Grödner and Eisack Valleys. Here the architect developed his theme for the ensuing years: the house in the landscape.

By turning and swivelling two large squares around the chimney, used as a supporting pillar, he takes into account the view, the topography and the climatic conditions. The sunny semicircular terrace in front of the entrance on the west side, offering a panoramic view from its lofty height, and the sectoral balcony on the west side emphasise the dynamic of interior and exterior movement. The effect of a windbreak is achieved, sheltering this area from the weather.

Thick walls, small openings, a roof of larch shingles and a marked cornice following the lines of the eaves determine the appearance of the vertically developed building, which is really more of a tower-house.

M. J.

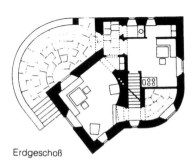

Obergeschoß

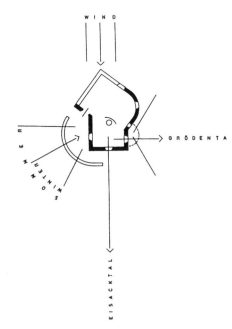

Erdgeschoß

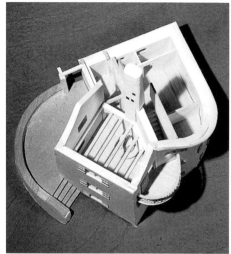

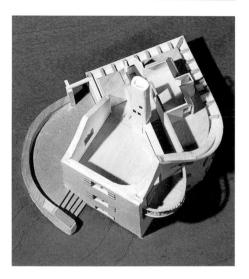

318

Lois Welzenbacher
1889–1955

**Reisch café with dance-hall
Kitzbühel, Tirol
1928**

*Scale model 1 . 33 ¹/₃
Jan Lewerenz*

This café was inserted into an existing building. The sequence of rooms from the entrance to the dance-hall is emphasised by the distribution of light, increasing to distinguish the dance-hall as the focal point and the centre of action. The various seating levels can be extended by means of a folding partition made of white metal and frosted glass. Light-coloured walls, simple walnut furniture, lighting appliances also in white metal, expressionistic openings for air-conditioning – a poetic and formal echo of a technical product – complete the overall picture. This work represents a consistent development from the Odeon Café (1923) in the direction of "New Building".

Today alterations have largely destroyed the original concept. "A building of the highest standard, literally eradicated and replaced by a rustic barn." (F. Achleitner)

M. J.

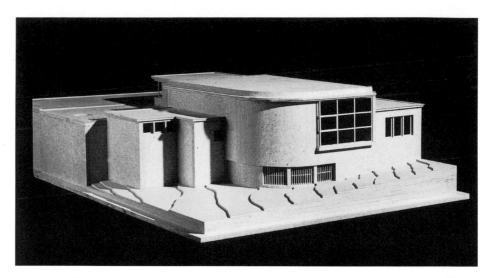

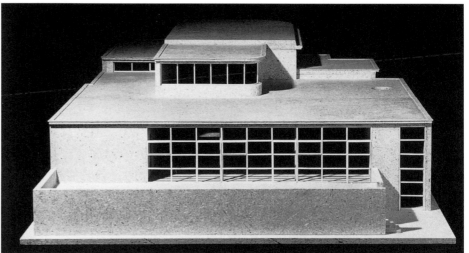

320

Lois Welzenbacher
1889–1955

**Buchroithner house
Schmittengraben, Zell am See,
Salzburg
1928–30**

*Scale model 1 : 33 ¹/₃
Josef Brandstetter
Helmut Menger*

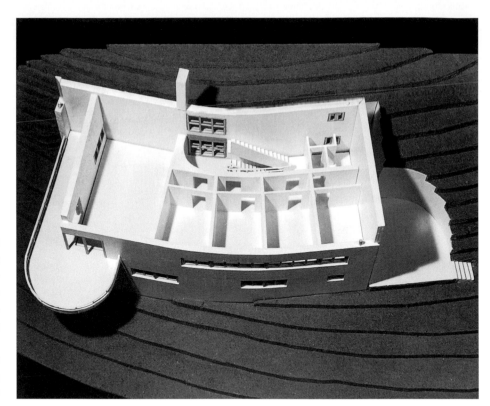

Here is apparent a highly subtle demonstration of Welzenbacher's basic vocabulary, later to become characteristic of his work in the trend of "New Building": his consideration of topography and the orientation of the building to sun and view.

The house itself stands parallel to a south-west/north-east slope, the curve being taken up in the western exterior wall, along which the rooms are oriented towards sun and view, with the slightly curved hall and staircase as the backbone. The objective of the staircase and hall is the living-room, its diagonal dimension emphasised by the right-angled French window, ensuring the view on two sides. When the French windows are pushed back into the reveal, the boundary between interior and exterior space disappears.

The wide roof overhanging on one side and ending in an attic ledge, the verticality of the chimney and the long projecting semicircular balcony are the dominant features of "this still misunderstood building" (F. Achleitner).

M. J.

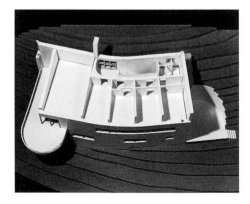
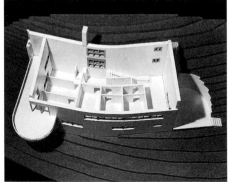
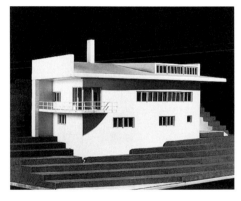
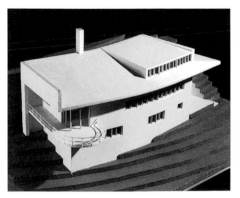

Lois Welzenbacher
1889–1955

**Schulz house
Recklinghausen
1928/29**

*Scale model 1 : 33 ⅓
Winfried Warner*

This work represents Welzenbacher's masterpiece in urban housing: perfectly elaborated detail, and the design of the complete interior furnishing and décor, including the integration of artistic textile works.

Interpenetration of space through an open ground plan and a simple arrangement of rooms stand in mutual contrariety, generating a compositional tension. All proportions are deliberately chosen to maintain this tension in the rooms as well as in the façades.

Thus a dovetailing is achieved, reaching from the living-room (by means of French windows which can be mechanically lowered right into the ground) to the right-angled corner window of the parents' bedroom, and on through the pergola to the swimming-pool and out to the park. This linking of interior and exterior is enhanced by the artificial creation of different levels round the outside.

The exterior walls of the house are built of dark-coloured clinker. At particular points, such as the corners, horizontal and vertical bricks adjoin. The interior walls are of white plaster; the doors and windows are also white. Unfortunately, the house has since undergone considerable alteration.

M. J.

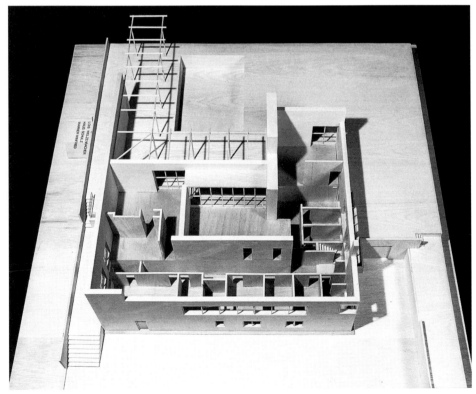

Lois Welzenbacher
1889–1955

Rosenbauer house
Pöstlingberg, Linz
1929/30

Scale model 1 : 33 ¹/₃
Hans G. Schwarz

Set into a south-facing slope, its rooms
following the overall line, this house
develops parallel to the contour lines,
with the chimney as the point of stability.
Here is the entrance to the hall, the
general access to the interior. A few
steps lead to the living-room, where a
large window at right angles over the
corner offers an extensive view over the
Danube Valley. This is surpassed, however, by the view from the bedroom
above, which, borne on a single steel
support, hovers in the air like the bridge
of a ship. The semicircular glazing
continues, like a skin, round the other
bedrooms, ending in the north-facing
wall and opening on to a roofed sun-
terrace.
Here the projection of the east-facing
end of the house is mirrored, enhancing
the overall composition. The principal
materials are white masonry, steel and
glass.
M. J.

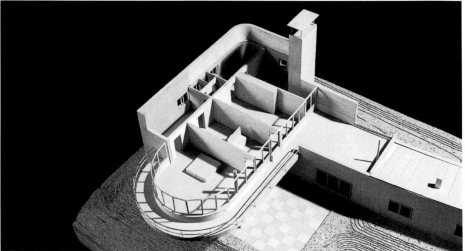

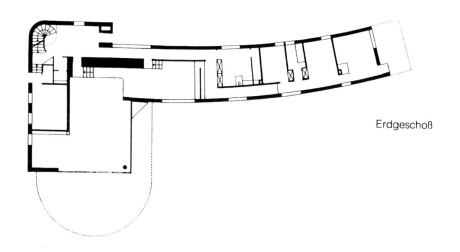

Erdgeschoß

326

Lois Welzenbacher
1889–1955

Ehlert children's home
Hindelang, Bavaria
1931–33

Scale model 1 : 33 ¹/₃
Rainer Pfau

This building was completed in 1933, at the time of the political upheaval in Germany, and the final peak of "New Building" in Welzenbacher's work.

Like a ship with a look-out post, the building stretches from west to east, anchored on the verticality of the tower. Two staircases, staggered in the line of access, lead up to the sun-terrace, which follows the side of the house and projects far out over the eastern end. A flat projecting roof underlines this movement, and offers shelter from sun and weather.

On the lower floor are bedrooms, an office and utility rooms; on the main floor the private quarters of the Ehlert family and a large right-angled corner window overlooking the countryside. The building is crowned by the cubicle-like rooms for the children, with the windows so placed as to give a view into the mountains. The lower and main stories are plastered in white, the remainder is sheathed. After Ehlert's death, the building was demolished in 1976/77 by his heirs. This meant the disappearance of what was perhaps the best example of "New Building" in Bavaria before the Second World War. M. J.

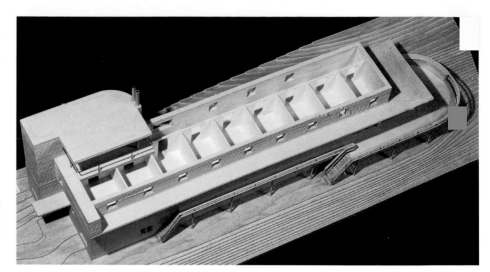

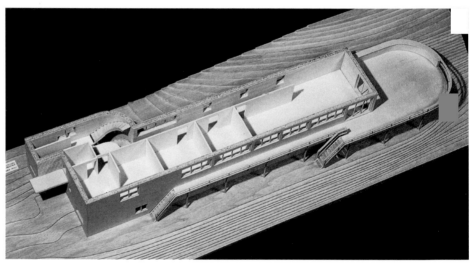

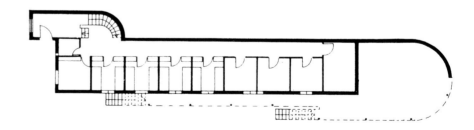

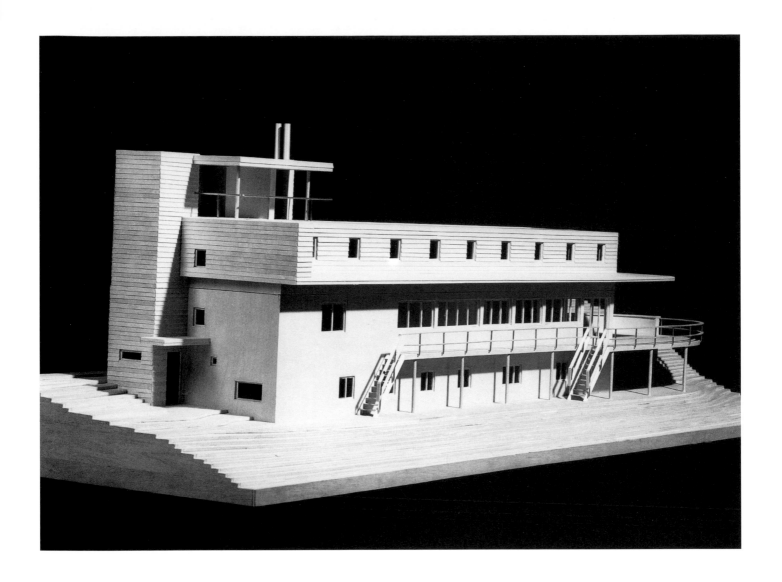

Lois Welzenbacher
1889–1955

**Heyrovsky house
Thumersbach, Zell am See,
Salzburg
1932**

Scale model 1 : 33 ¹/₃
Feliz Altin

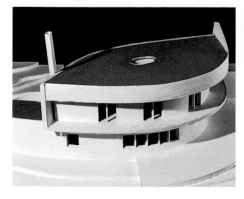
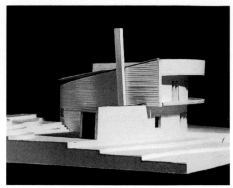

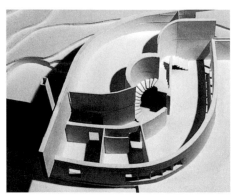

This house represents the absolute peak of Welzenbacher's work in "New Building". It is a masterpiece of building in harmony with the landscape.

The house evolves from the landscape towards view and sun; this results in a curve along which the main rooms are fanned out. In the interior, a circular hall is formed as a focal point; this function is underlined by a round skylight, particularly striking in the dark-coloured ceiling. The staircase, mounting by the shorter route against the "flow", forms an axis of rotation "anchoring the house to the ground". This staircase is joined by a second one via a landing; here the contrary directions of the house dovetail. The inner rotation is reflected in the horizontality of the surrounding balcony. Widely projecting eaves with a broad fascia underline the link with the slope, offering protection from sun and rain. The living-quarters on the lower floor have strip windows allowing a view over the landscape. The family bedrooms are on the upper floor; they have individual windows, showing clearly the intention of privacy. Even the bathroom is treated as a main room. The materials used are plasterwork masonry, white-painted wood and metal.
M. J.

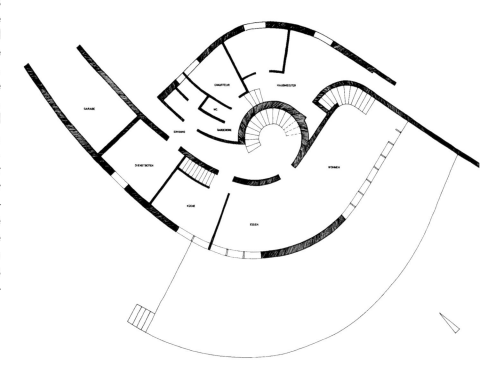

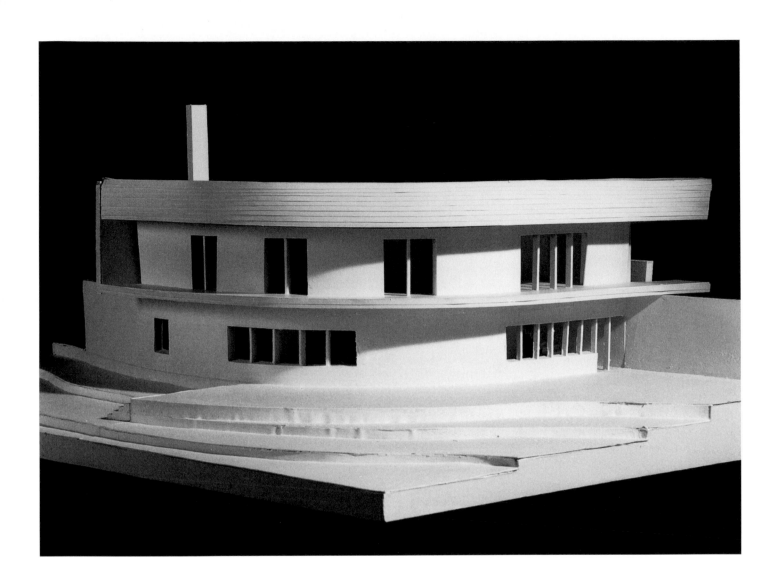

Lois Welzenbacher
1889–1955

**Wex house
Oberjoch, Allgäu
1934**

*Scale model 1 : 33 ⅓
Rudolf Kleeberger*

The ground plan of the Wex house is in the shape of a horseshoe around a central staircase.

The determining element is the staircase, lit by a north-facing dormer-window over the landing, and spiralling to the upper floor against the original direction of flow. A particularly striking feature is the pent roof, sloping down to the north, almost like a driveway. To the south, the sleeping-quarters open on to a suspended balcony. The exterior shows the first signs of a change in design: in the use of wood shingles and in the shutters. Otherwise the walls are plastered in white.

M. J.

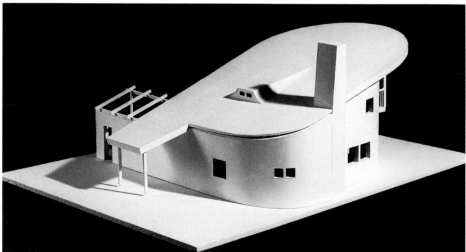

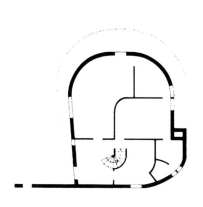

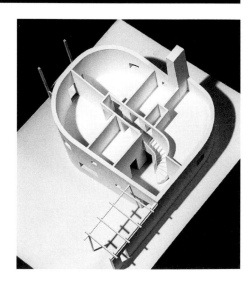

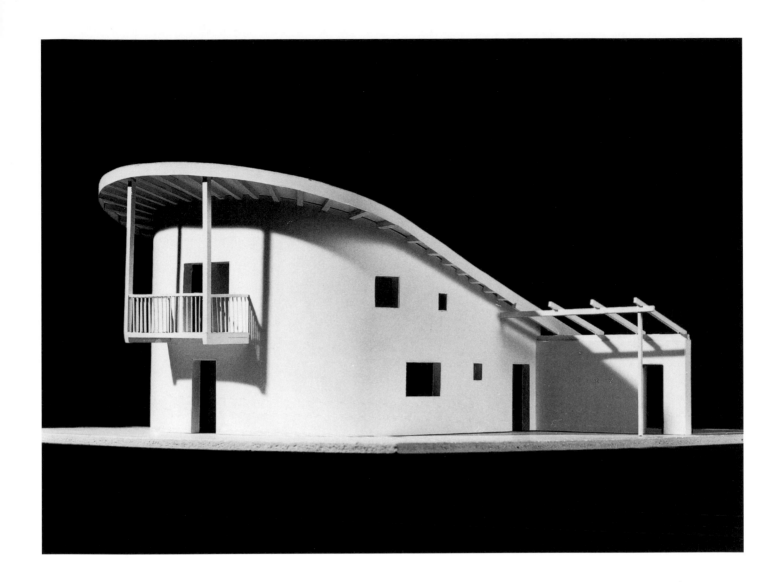

333

Lois Welzenbacher
1889–1955

**Dr. von Borch house
Obergrainau, Upper Bavaria
1934**

*Scale model 1 : 33 ¹/₃
Sabine Oertgen
Hans Mener*

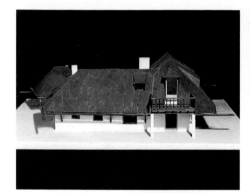
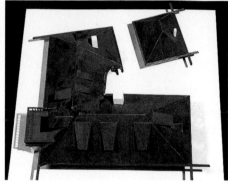
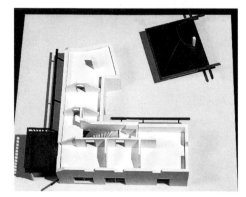
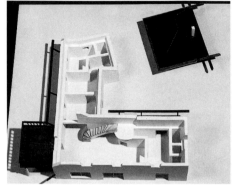

Together with a square outhouse, the main, hook-shaped house forms a U-shaped outward-looking layout. The ground floor of the main building contains the living-room with fireplace and the staircase dividing it from the dining-area and kitchen, beyond which are servants' quarters, hall and WC. On the upper floor, under the roof, are the bathroom and bedrooms, with a terrace on the west side. These rooms are lit by dormer-windows, which also make for extra space. The overall exterior appearance is completed by a wide overlapping shingled roof, window-shutters and white-plastered façades.

Were it not for the diversity of cleverly placed openings and the judicious arrangement of access from north, east and west, one might well imagine the house to be the work of an anonymous architect. It was demolished in the early 1980s.
M. J.

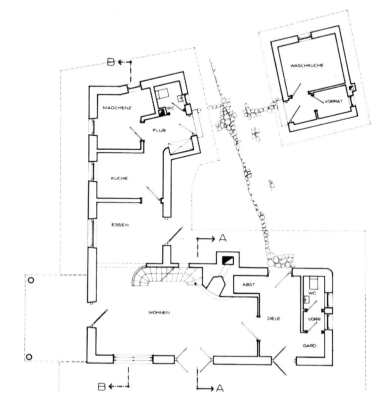

Lois Welzenbacher
1889–1955

Martin house project
Klais, Karwendel
1934/35

Scale model 1 : 33 ¹/₃
F. Krissmayr
A. Wenkl

This house, designed for an artist, dates from the time of Welzenbacher's inner emigration. It was to have been built near the Koppe house in Klais. For the exterior, the architect borrows from the *Heimatstil*, but the interior is designed with all his typical diversity and consideration for landscape, sun and view – a "camouflaged" house.

A striking feature of the interior arrangement is the staircase, which begins outside, under the sloping roof. It extends through the hall into the upper storey, where it divides at a slight angle on the landing, to continue up to the attic. This staircase accords with the flow of the house, which stretches with a slight curve, "like a caterpillar", up the slope towards the sun.

The picture is completed by the wide projecting roof, the prominent chimney, the semicircular balcony, the precisely calculated openings and dormers, and particularly by the large terrace facing the access to the north.

M. J.

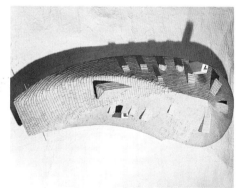

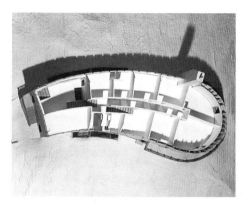
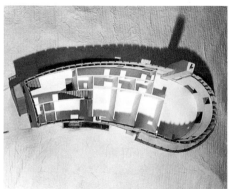

Lois Welzenbacher
1889–1955

Koppe house
Klais, Karwendel
1934

Scale model 1 : 33 ¹/₃
Monika Haessner
Ralph Wawerla

Starting from the cuboid block of the terrace at the lower end of the slope, the house – some 21 m long and 10 m wide – curves slightly into the slope towards the south-west. Behind the terrace is the two-storey living-area with open fireplace. An open-plan wooden staircase leads to the attic storey, giving an impression of spaciousness. A shingled gable roof with dormers, and white plastered walls with a variety of windows and doorways characterise the exterior of the simple cuboid structure. A salient feature is the side of the chimney, which projects on the entrance side.
M. J.

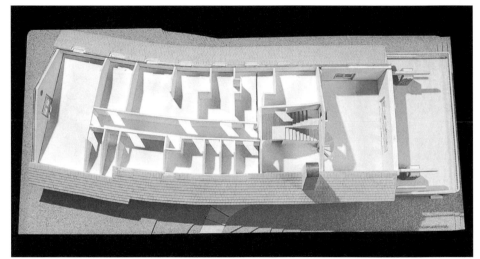

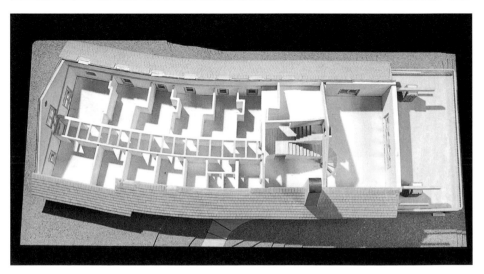

Lois Welzenbacher
1889–1955

Welzenbacher house
Absam, Tirol
1945

Scale model 1 : 33 ¹/₃
Hermann Thurner

According to wartime regulations, this house (planned as a temporary home) was allowed a basic area of only some 6 × 6 metres. With a ground area of about 38 m², however, the interior volume achieved is 400 m³. Besides the rooms necessary for living, the house contains a room for weaving and a studio. The attic under the pavilion roof is converted to form two small bedrooms. The arrangement of the rooms and the staircases, together with the balconies to east and west, combine with the tower-like appearance of this house to lend it charm and character. The pointedly simple execution bears a strong resemblance to the traditional architecture of South Tirol.
M. J.

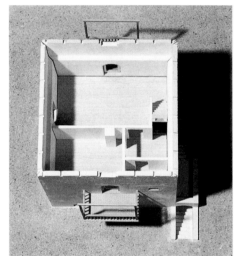

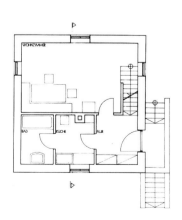
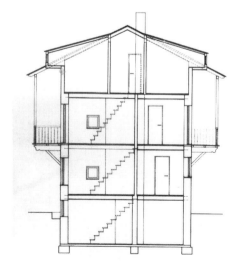

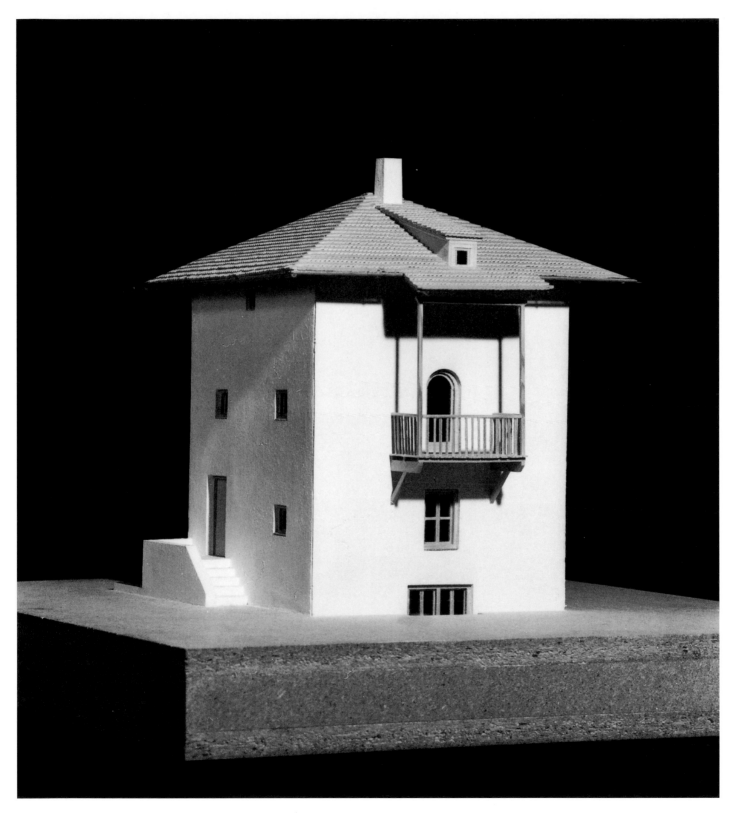

Ludwig Wittgenstein
1889–1951
Paul Engelmann
1891–1965

**Stonborough house
Vienna
1926–28**

Scale model 1 : 33 ¹/₃
Rudi Rollwagen

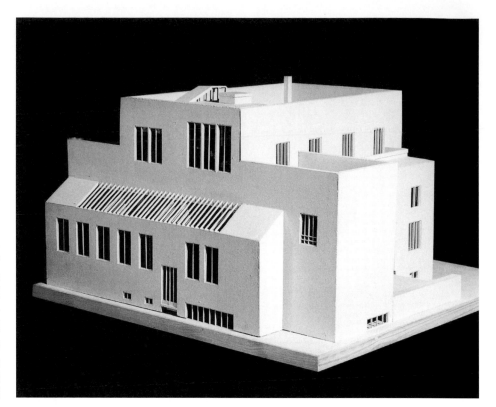

This house in the Third District of Vienna, built for Ludwig Wittgenstein's sister Margaret, was originally planned for a different site, near the palatial paternal villa in the Fourth District. Paul Engelmann, a pupil of Adolf Loos, received the planning commission in 1926; it was not until later that his friend Ludwig became interested in building, and gradually took over the planning and design.

The building itself is the unique and solid testimony of a philosopher who proved one of the most independent thinkers of the 20th century (Tractatus logico-philosophicus, 1921). Although the architecture might be classed as akin to that of Loos and the cubist architecture of the 1920s, it is nevertheless incomparable in the relentless consistency of its proportions, reduction in the use of materials and precision of detail. (Wittgenstein had studied engineering.) The house was rediscovered in 1959, and in the early 1970s there were plans to raze it, to make way for a high-rise building. The concerted efforts of Viennese cultural institutions succeeded in enforcing its preservation, and today it houses the Bulgarian embassy.
F. K.

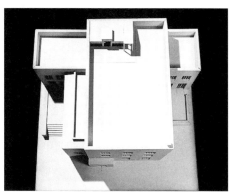
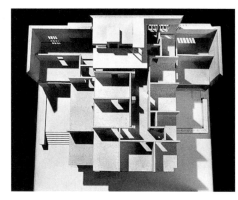
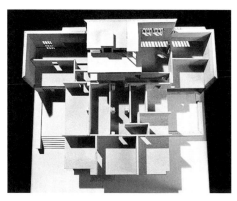
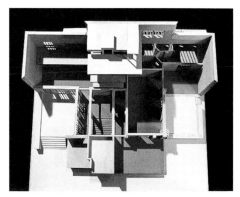

Frank Lloyd Wright
1867–1959

Residence, 1889
Playroom addition, 1893
Studio, 1895
Oak Park, Illinois

Scale model 1 : 33 ¹/₃
Hanspeter Grohs
Alfred Öchslein

This extremely complex structure in Oak Park, Illinois, developed in three separate stages. The house, with its imposing triangular gable, was realised first; its exterior structure is characterised by wood shingles, the surrounding brick wall and the raised terrace. The interior is still dominated by a traditional division of rooms. The surrounding band running under the architrave is an innovation. It is not the walls that enclose the interior rooms, but the level surfaces of the floor and ceiling that determine the spatial form.

The playroom was the first addition. The barrel vault is not apparent from the exterior. An ornamental skylight in the ridge shows the room with its brick chimney-corner to excellent advantage.

The studio, the last part to be built, runs parallel to the road. It is divided into three sections: the longitudinal loggia as a filter to the street, the square design-room surmounted by an octagonal lantern-like superstructure, and the octagon containing the library. All these elements are self-contained, yet linked in harmony with each other. The subtly differentiated lighting through skylight and high fanlights enhance the overall impression.
M. J.

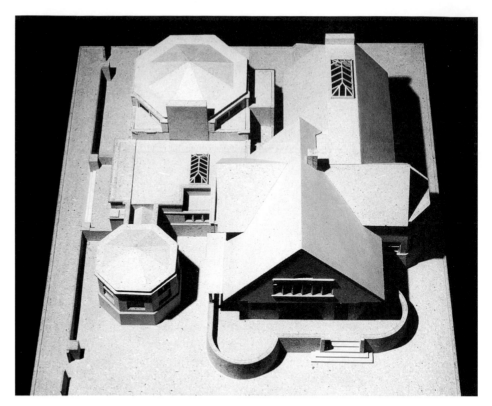

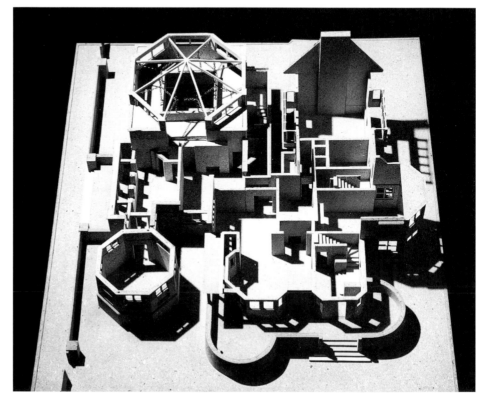

MODELL M 1/33⅓

HANSPETER GROHS   ALFRED OECHSLEIN

345

Frank Lloyd Wright
1867–1959

Jacobs house
West Moreland, Wisconsin
1937

Scale model 1 · 33 ¹/₃
Martin Julinek

The low-cost house, Frank Lloyd Wright maintained, is America's greatest architectural problem; his "Usonian" houses offer a solution. This one, based on an L-shaped ground plan, evolves from the pavement towards the garden. A covered drive leads along a wall to the entrance area. Here are the kitchen, bathroom and utility rooms; these are raised to improve ventilation, and separate the living- and sleeping-quarters, which are also defined by different room heights, and open through full-length French windows on to the garden.

The whole house stands on a concrete foundation mat, under which heating pipes are laid – similarly to modern underfloor heating; this makes for a pleasant and comfortable ambience. The walls are constructed of plywood faced with wide boards alternating with narrower laths. The kitchen and bathroom, the wall of the carport and the corner at the end of the living-room are all of brick.

M. J.

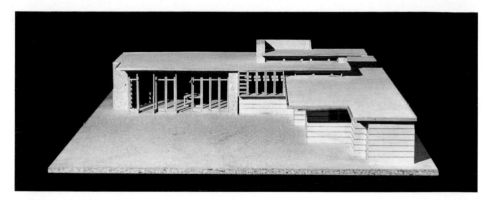

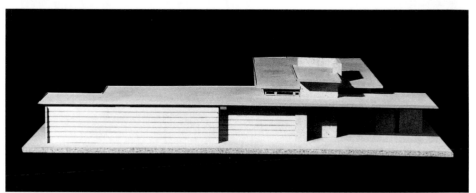

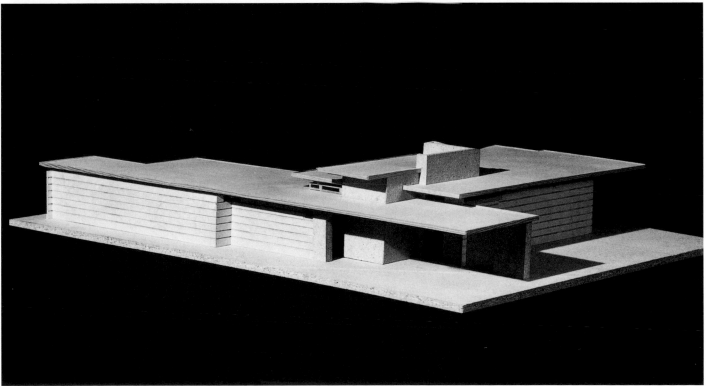

Frank Lloyd Wright
1867–1959

**St. Mark's apartment tower
project
New York
1929**

*Scale model 1 : 33 ¹/₃
Anneliese Göbel
Ortrud Ackermann
Toni Vogt*

This is the design for a group of three high-rise buildings, each containing 4×9 duplex apartments, in The Bowery, New York. It was commissioned by William N. Guthrie, a long-standing personal friend of Wright's.

A basic square is divided into four modules, turned at 30° round a central square and built of concrete. The arms of the cross thus formed contain the kitchens with small balconies, the internal connecting staircases and the two compulsory emergency staircases. The bedrooms, arranged like galleries, are connected with the living-areas below. The central hall gives access to the individual levels branching out from it.

This constructive spatial concept is followed through in the designs for the Suntop Homes, the Grouped Apartment Towers and the Crystal Heights Hotel, and reaches its peak in the office tower block for the Johnson Wax Building. M. J.

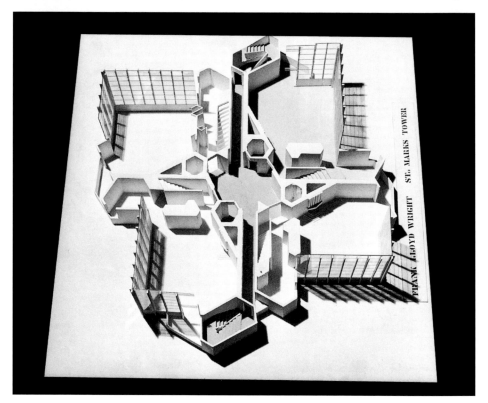

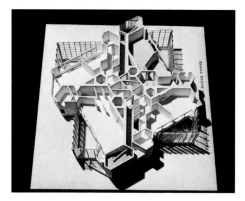

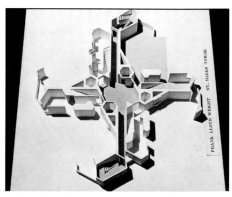

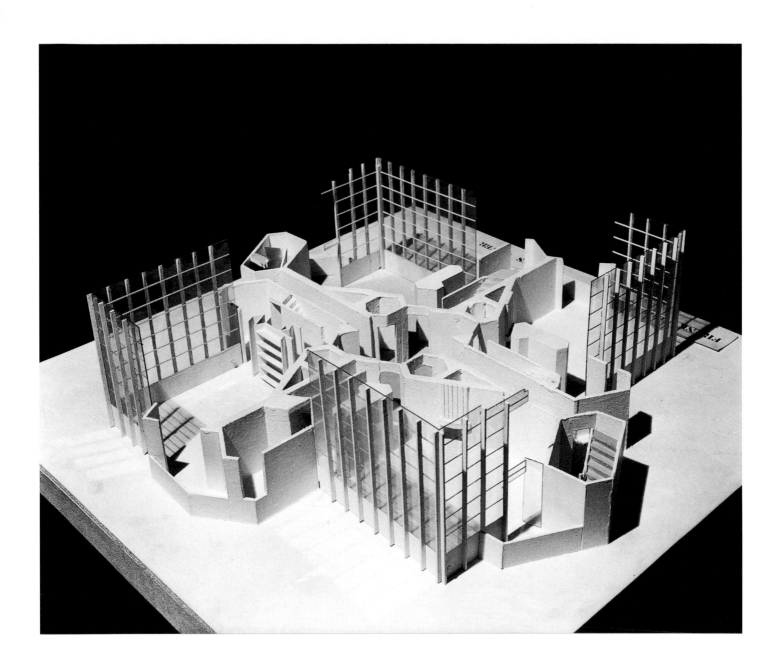

Frank Lloyd Wright
1867–1959

**Sturges house
Brentwood Heights,
Los Angeles, California
1939**

*Scale model 1 : 33 ¹/₃
Robert Brand
Urban Frick*

The house and its surroundings are linked by a chimney-wall running parallel to the slope and separating the public area from the private.

The long projecting pergola construction stretches from the carport to the entrance and on into the living-area, which in turn opens on to a wide projecting terrace overlooking the surrounding country-side. A narrow corridor gives access to kitchen, bathroom and bedrooms, which command the same panorama. A rear staircase leads to the roof terrace, reminiscent of the look-out post on a ship, and a staircase below this, accessible from within, leads directly to the store-room.

This brick and wood house, with its extreme reduction of form, creates a strong field of tension with the surrounding landscape.

M. J.

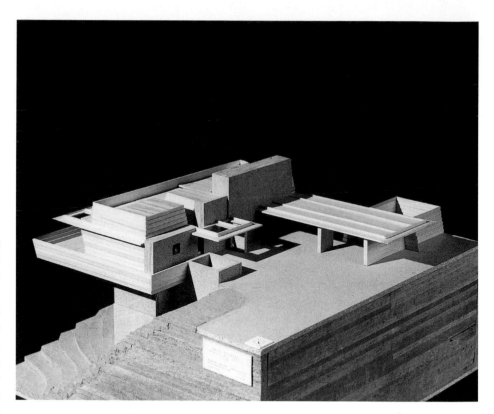

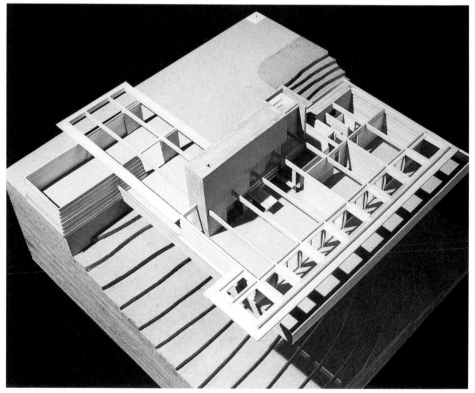

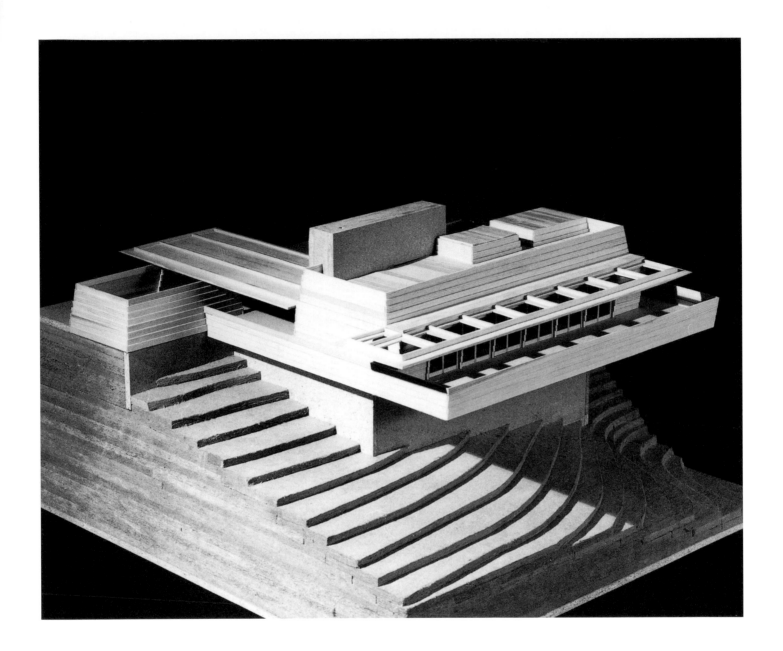

351

Frank Lloyd Wright
1867–1959

Kaufmann house
Fallingwater, Pennsylvania
1936

Scale model 1 : 33 1/3
Mathias Pfeil
Heinz Saalfrank
Gösta Waubke

With this house, the architect achieved a unique symbiosis of nature and constructed form. It is also characterised by an inspired balance between vertical and horizontal elements. The natural route through the house stratifies the space, emphasising the horizontal plane. This movement is stopped by the vertical plane, which diverts it and anchors it in the rock. The opening of the corners breaks away from previous visual convention, lending a dramatic quality to the form.

The main storey with living-room extends to the other sections and to the large terrace. A slender staircase, at the foot of which a landing seems almost to float, leads down to the waterfall. The upper stories contain gallery and bedrooms, which also open on to a terrace.

The materials – natural stone for the vertical and whitewashed concrete for the horizontal – are chosen to emphasise the structural concept.

M. J.

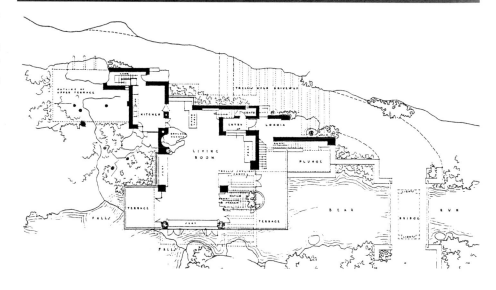

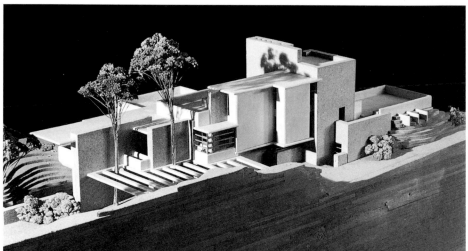

Frank Lloyd Wright
1867–1959

House for John C. Pew
Shorewood Hills, Wisconsin
1905

Scale model 1 : 33 ¹⁄₃
Thomas Fehsenmayr
Robert Zengler

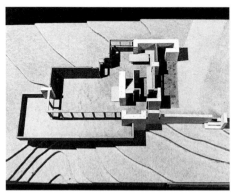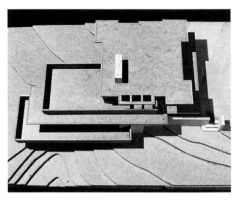

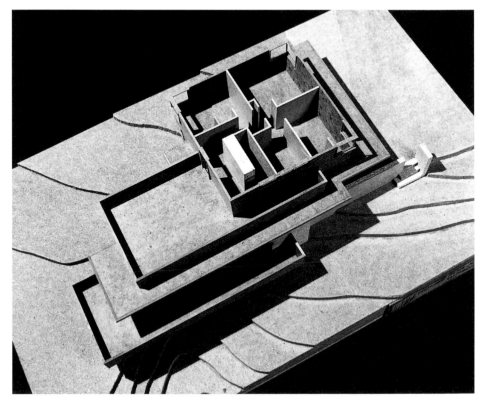

Anchored to the slope by the chimney and hovering with one wing over the hollow, this open structure evolves – taking account of the existing trees – from Mendota Drive down to the lake.

A drive with carport leads to a small entrance hall and on through the kitchen to the dining-room – or along a wide row of windows to the living-room with its large terrace. Living-room and dining-room are linked by an open intermediate zone. The staircase, following the line of the chimney, leads down to the cellar, as well as up to the sleeping-quarters with bathroom and the large canopy-like roof terrace, which shelters the area below.

Each bedroom has a view of the landscape through a right-angled corner window.

Local limestone and cypress wood are the predominant building materials.
M. J.

Frank Lloyd Wright
1867–1959

Lloyd-Lewis house
Libertyville, Illinois
1940

Scale model 1 : 33 ¹/₃
Gerhard Bodenmüller
Wilhelm Längerer

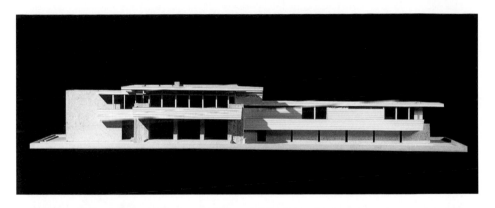

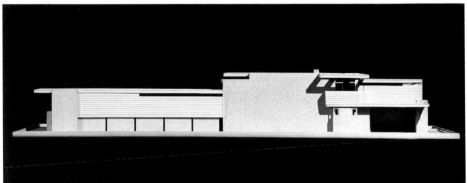

The conditions of building here are prescribed by the marshy site on the banks of Plaines River, near Libertyville. This house, basically single-storey, contains a variety of levels with strong emphasis on the transverse axis. Access is through a loggia with pilotis under the living-room. Here is also the guest-room (or servant's room) and the main and side staircases. Both of these lead to the upper area: the side staircase directly to the utility room and kitchen, the main staircase past the mezzanine bedroom and into the spacious living-room, which opens on to the large glass-roofed terrace overlooking the river to the south. The house is bounded to the rear by a brick chimney-wall. The study with balcony offers additional privacy. The row of bedrooms extends from west to east. Longitudinal slits in the wall allow the necessary ventilation in the cavity wall. This construction and the use of natural materials such as brick and wood give an ecologically flawless atmosphere for living. The place determines the house.
M. J.

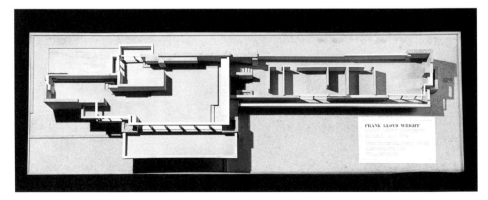

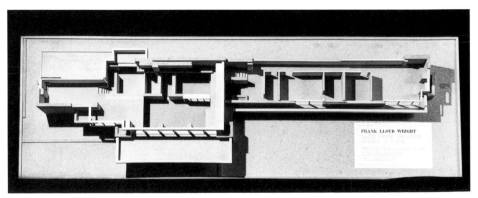

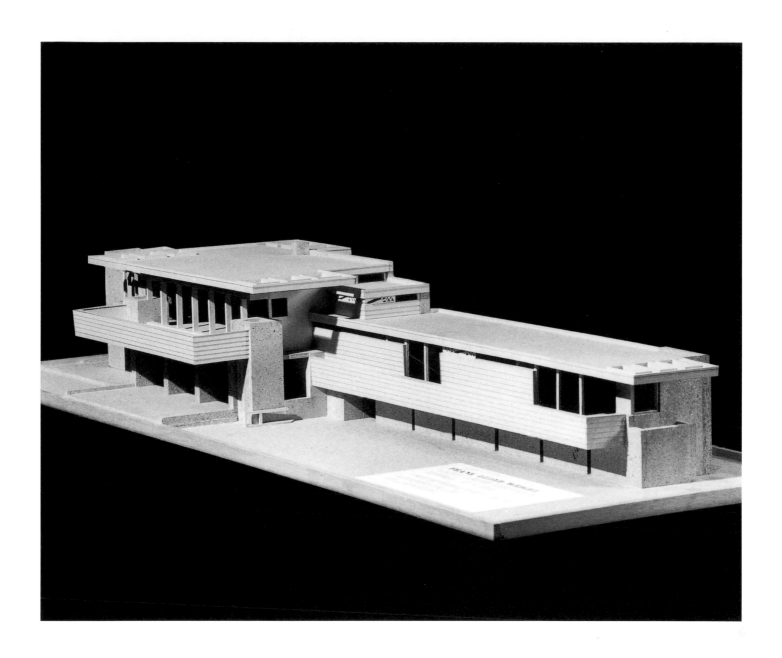

Frank Lloyd Wright
1867–1959

**Jacobs house I,
"Solar Hemicycle"
Wisconsin
1944**

*Scale model 1 : 33 ¹/₃
Frank Bildhauer
Heidi Hoh*

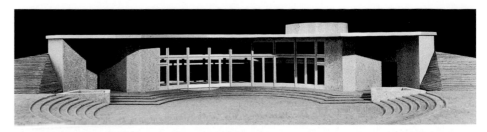

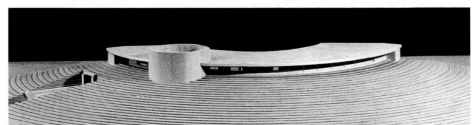

Starting from a circle, or semicircle, and the course of the sun, Wright designed a house open towards the south and closed off to the north by an artificial embankment.

The fixed points in the natural stone semicircle are the circular cylinder containing the offices with the side staircase, anchors and the "obligatory" chimney, as the heart of the house.

A round pond to the south-west links the inner semicircle with the outer circular form, with nature. The ground floor contains the living-area, the upper storey the bedrooms – the whole spanned by a high roof-space, which allows the sun to penetrate deep into the building during the winter, while in summer it is shaded by the overhanging roof.

Thus the interior and the exterior of the house are adapted in a simple, old-fashioned way to the climatic conditions. Long before the invention of so-called solar architecture and the massive technical resources often entailed, this house had already anticipated many of the principles.

M. J.

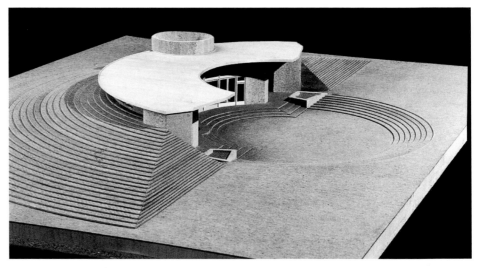

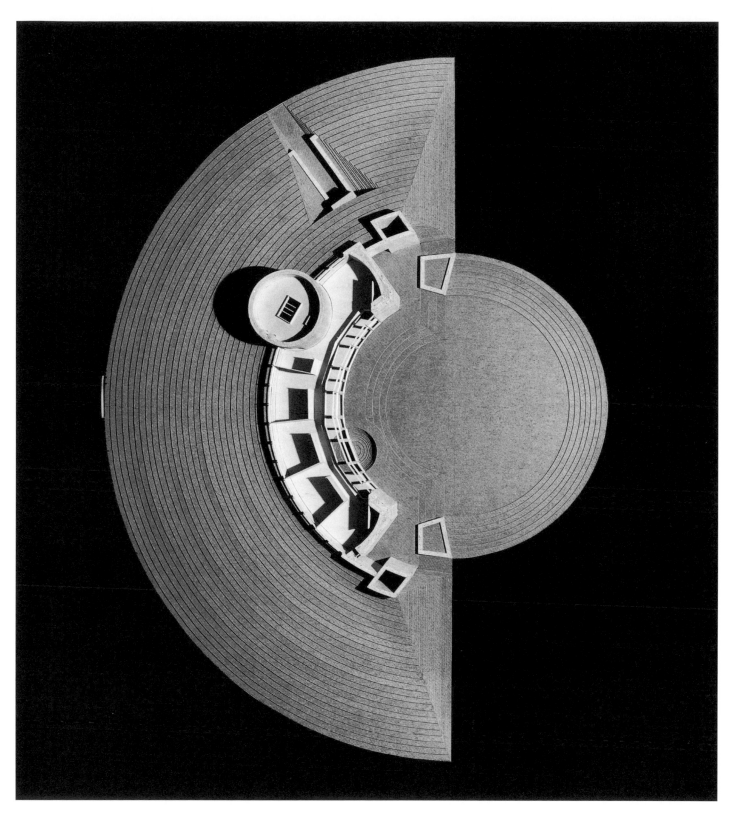

Frank Lloyd Wright
1867–1959

House for V. C. Morris
San Francisco, California
1945

Scale model 1 : 33 ¹/₃
Alexander Böhme
Olaf Langer
Susanne Straub

The architect describes this project as a house on the rock, facing the ocean, with a garden on the roof, built of steel and concrete to resist earthquakes.

A straight, horizontal covered drive leads to carport and entrance, connecting house and cliff like a landing-stage. While the access path is almost completely closed for shelter on one side, on the other it gives a clear view over the ocean. It leads into the ground floor, which contains living-room with dining-area, kitchen and utility room with a small balcony. On two further levels, there are five bedrooms, bathrooms and a study.

A cylindrical air-shaft with a central skylight gives a sense of spaciousness, and the storeys are all connected by a ramp. As a contrast to the predominant circular forms, the roof over the living-room and the terrace on the level of the guest-room both project squarely, producing a strong tension between the linear horizontal and the circular and square elements.
M. J.

361

Frank Lloyd Wright
1867–1959

**House for Kenneth Laurent
Rockford, Illinois
1949**

*Scale model 1 · 33 ¹/₃
Marc Leonhardt
Tobias Kern*

This single-storey house, built in 1949, consists of two flattish arcs facing each other, with rectangular insertions such as carport, living- and dining-area and bedroom.

A large glass wall giving on to garden and pond runs the length of the house, linking interior and exterior. The parallel rear brick wall forms the northern boundary; between roof and wall runs a long strip window. The opposite exterior arc is formed by a breast-high wall which provides the transition between the garden and the natural landscape.

Bare brick walls, white plastered ceiling and natural wood underline the structural concept.

M. J.

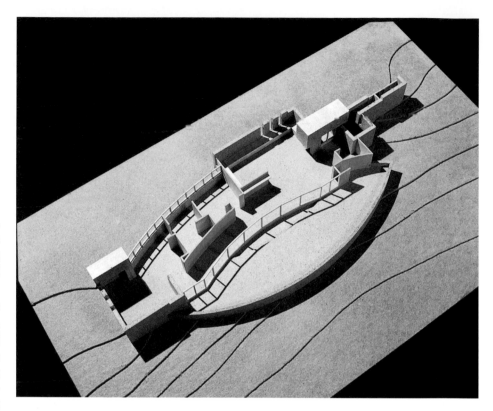

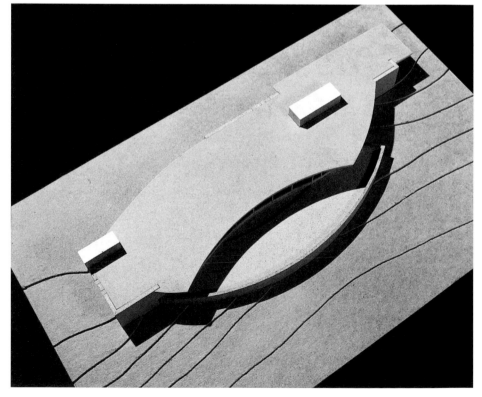

Frank Lloyd Wright
1867–1959

D. Wright house
Phoenix, Arizona
1950

Scale model 1 : 33 ⅓

This house, designed for his son, evolved from a circle.

The building is raised in order to give a clear view over the existing lemon trees, and to allow the wind to provide a cooling effect from below during the hot Arizona summer. The wide spiral ramp leads up to the living-quarters. A structure like a flattened cone, tangential to the circular chimney and containing the utility rooms with the side staircase, anchors the nautilus-like building to the ground. A narrow outside ramp leads up to the roof terrace. The living-room looks on to the round courtyard and the open countryside, and a further stratifying effect is created by the balconies projecting on both sides. The adjoining bedrooms are accessible by means of the inner gallery or the outer balcony. At the end is the large, fully glazed master bedroom, projecting into space and supported only by the vertical wall of the cone-shaped chimney. Here the movement has come full circle.

The "nautilus" is built largely of standard bare concrete blocks. The roof is covered with copper sheeting, the fitted furniture and the curved ceiling panels are made of red Philippine mahogany.
M. J.

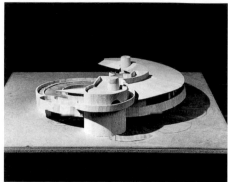
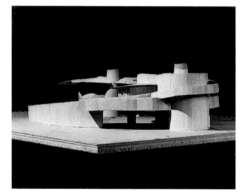
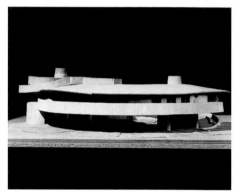
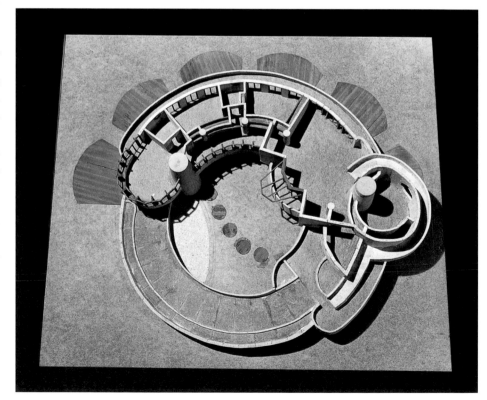

364

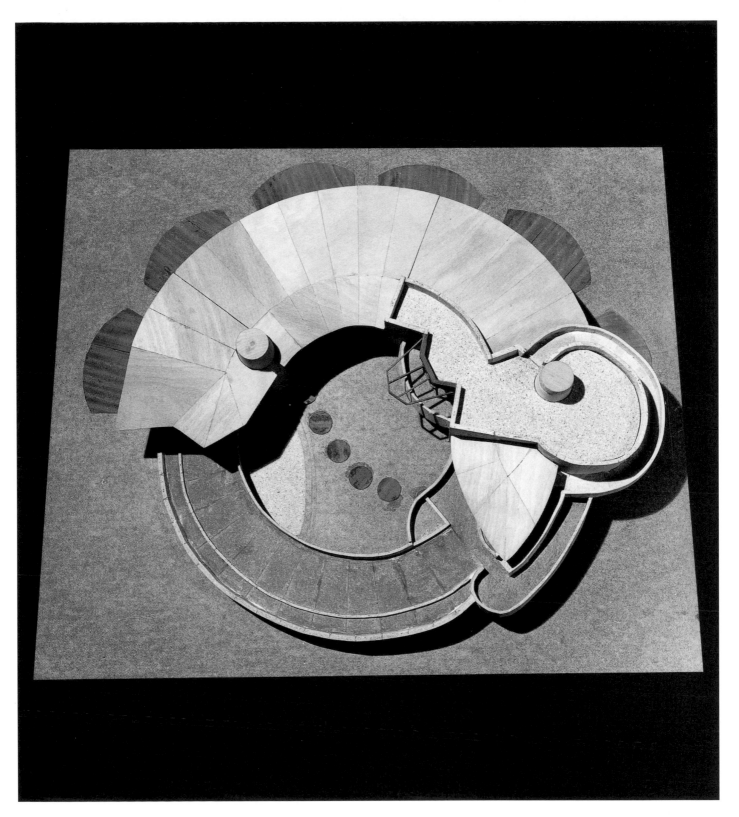

Frank Lloyd Wright
1867–1959

**Boomer house
Phoenix, Arizona
1953**

*Scale model 1 · 33 ¹/₃
Günther Hartmann
Klaus Kast*

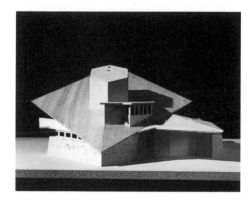

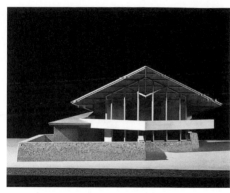

The Boomer house in the Arizona desert, designed for one person, faces north, away from the remorseless sun. The matrix is a rhombus. On the ground floor, a walled courtyard adjoins the living-room. On the same level are a study, a guest-room with bathroom, and the chauffeur's room with shower and WC. Above are the bed-sitting-room with a large balcony, and a further small room.

The striking feature of this house is its roof, which spans the whole building and soars from the stone wall at one end to the large glass front with the balcony. A hipped roof is set against this, providing an unexpected contrast. The massive chimney is both focal point and anchor. The roofs are covered with wood shingles; the masonry consists of stones found in the desert, similarly to Taliesin (Wright's house in Wisconsin). A further striking feature is the horizontal wooden fascia along the large balcony.
M. J.

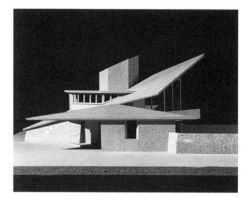

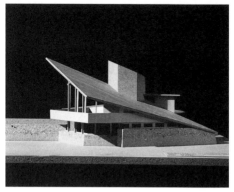

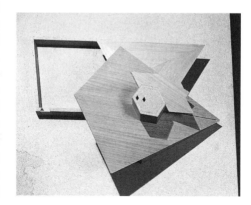

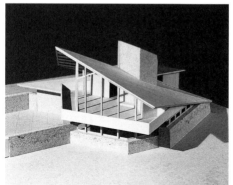

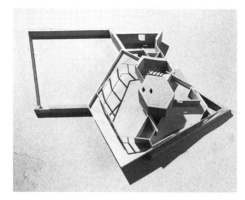

366

Frank Lloyd Wright
1867–1959

Masieri project
Canale Grande, Venice
1953

Scale model 1 : 33 ¹/₃
P. Hanfstingl
D. Ricker

In 1952, the architect Angelo Masieri visited the "master" in America. He wanted to have a house built on the Canale Grande, but died on the way back from Wisconsin. His family then commissioned Wright to plan the house as a students' hostel with a library.

The limitations of the site resulted in a triangular ground plan with the entrance along the left-hand passage. This floor contains the library with fireplace, the refectory and kitchen. On the level above are four student rooms with a bathroom; these are reached via a gallery.

Each of the next floors also contains student rooms, bathroom and a large common-room opening on to a balcony overlooking the canal. At the top is an apartment with a roof garden – in keeping with the Venetian tradition.

The planned building material was concrete faced with marble, with bronze and glass for the vertical window strips. The project provoked fierce criticism. Even Hemingway wrote to the architect, asserting that it would be preferable to see Venice burned down to its foundations, than to have a Frank Lloyd Wright building spoil the look of the famous canal. Wright's cool reply dismissed this comment as "a voice from the jungle".

M. J.

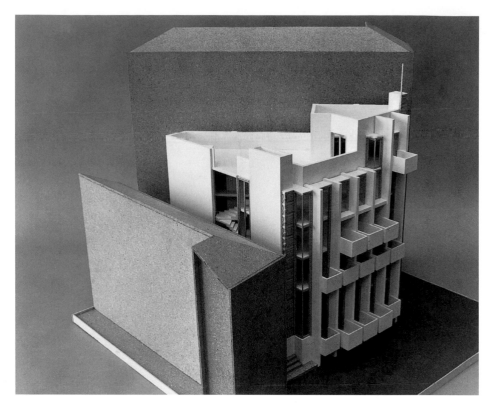

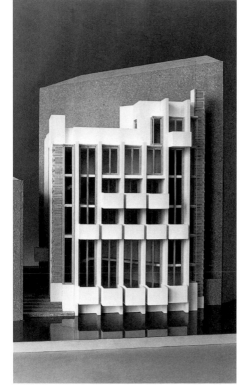

Appendix

Anonymous building

**Hostel
Haidhausen an der Kreppe,
Munich
probably 18th century**

Scale model 1 : 33 ¹/₃
Birgit Diez

Until the Second World War, in places even into the 1960s, hostels determined the character of whole streets in the Munich suburbs of Au, Giesing and Haidhausen. These were properties divided into individually owned living-units. These buildings, some dating back to the Middle Ages, were constantly altered, extended or added to by their various owners. Each hostel had its own entrance. The result was "Romantic" variety in individual houses and whole streets, which attracted hordes of artists around the turn of the century.

Forms of living developed here quite pragmatically – such as split-level and maisonette – long before these were included in architects' plans, and some-times the most modern materials were used quite ingenuously.

The property "An der Kreppe 2a–d" is one of the few that have survived. Until alterations were carried out in 1977, it consisted of four hostels in which, around 1805, there lived some 20 people (giving an area of 7.2 m² per person).

The brick structure and the typical mansard roof indicate that the original building dates from the 18th century.
F. P.

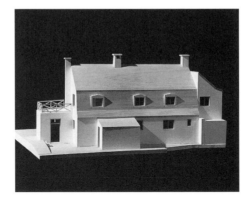
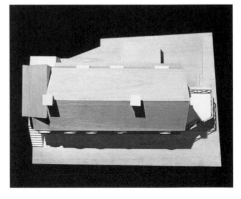
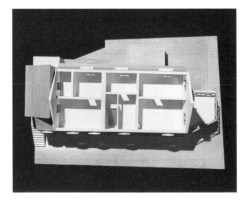
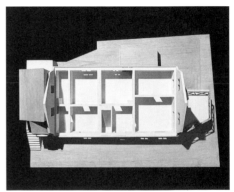

372

Anonymous building

Hostel property
Lohstrasse 23, Giesing, Munich
19th century

Scale model 1 : 33 ¹/₃
Eva Brügel
Ulrich Fritsch

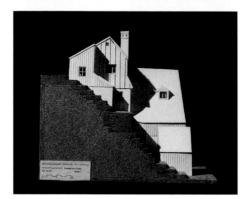
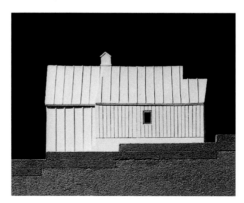
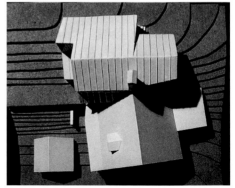
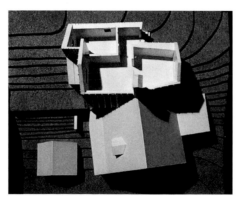
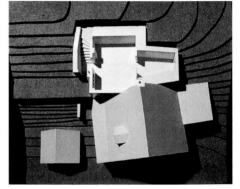

This property, consisting of two sections, was built on the steep slope of the Giesinger Berg. In 1885, the upper section contained two hostels, one of which – with an area totalling 17 m² – included the ground floor and a tiny room on the first floor, the other – on the remainder of the first floor – measuring 15 m²; there were probably at least five people living there. The room heights were 2.2 m on the lower floor, 1.8 m on the upper.

On the slope, the building was supported by a massive wall, to protect it from landslip and water seepage. There were also advantages in the hillside situation: a separate entrance to the upper storey was feasible without an extra staircase. Only the façades of the lower section, with its steep gable roof, are represented, since the arrangement of the ground plan cannot be reconstructed. The entrances and the variety of materials used for the façades are the sole remaining indications of the division of ownership.

The property was demolished in 1933. The complex structure and the intricately interlocking surfaces made it one of the most original houses in Munich.
F. P.

Anonymous building

"Paschihaus" hostel in the Au district, Munich 14th–20th century

Scale model 1 : 33 ¹/₃
Thomas von Ginkel
Schaffmeier

The "Paschihaus" is reputed to have been the oldest house in the Au district, its original part dating back to 1370. The name derives from the 16th and 17th centuries, because the page-boys were accommodated here when the ducal court was in residence at the nearby hunting lodge of Neudeck. In 1700 the house was reconstructed, extended and divided into hostels; by 1907 it contained ten hostels, with a floor area of 450 m² including two storeys and two extended attics, and housing more than 40 people. While the oldest part was built of brick, later extensions and additions were made of wood. Two of the hostels were maisonette flats. The hostels on the first floor were reached by way of a porch.

The "Paschihaus" belonged to one of the largest hostel districts in Munich west of the Mariahilfplatz. Together with the neighbouring houses, it can be seen on many photographs and paintings. The apparent idyll was deceptive, however, since by 1900 the living conditions were appalling. During the Second World War, the Au hostel district was largely destroyed, and even surviving buildings such as the "Paschihaus" had to make way for new building in the early 1950s. Its demolition meant an irrevocable loss for the history of building in Munich.

F. P.

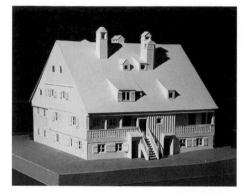

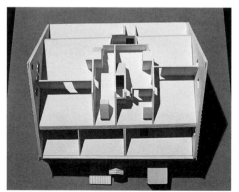
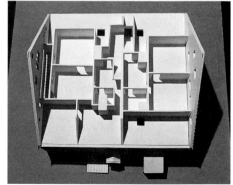
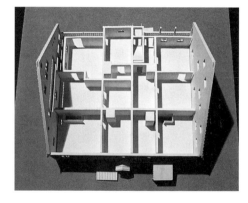
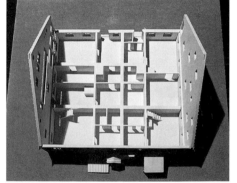

Anonymous building

Turkish house
Alanya
18th century

Scale model 1 : 33 ¹/₃
Eva Maria Ulm

From a courtyard (avlu) adjoined on the ground floor by utility and working quarters, a single staircase leads to the open covered hall (hayat), the family's main living-area on the first floor. This gives access to all the living-quarters, which are divided into two areas: one supported by a massive wall at the rear, parallel to the slope, offering protection from the cold north wind during the winter months, and at right angles to this a light wooden structure on stilts, with ample windows, allowing good ventilation in summer. The focus is the "divan", the reception room reserved for the master of the house; this offers on three sides a view over courtyard, street and surrounding terrain. Forming a structural unit with this is a second room, reached by an extra outside staircase, thus allowing the master to accommodate primarily male guests without intruding upon family privacy.

This house is a splendid example of how to adapt to the climatic conditions, as well as taking into account religious and cultural tradition ("harem" = the forbidden, private women's quarters; "selamik" = the reception-area, the public, male province).

S. M.

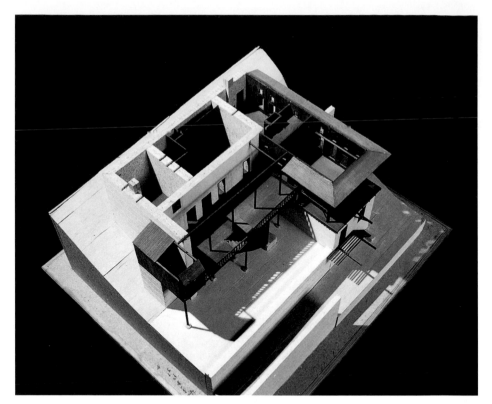

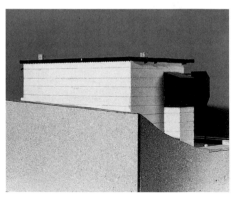

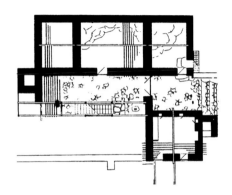

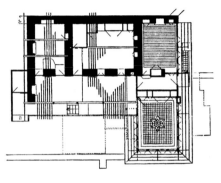

Anonymous building

Turkish house
Halepli Tanaş house
Fener, Istanbul
19th century

Scale model 1 : 33 ⅓
Alfons Breindl
Rolf Rupp

The complex consists of the two-storey house, a walled garden and a small two-storey reception pavilion with a view over the street from the first floor. Under the pavilion is the entrance to the garden; a few steps lead up to the house, the main rooms of which project on the first floor over the garden. From the two-storey glazed entrance hall, a single-flight staircase with a landing giving on to a separate living-room leads to a gallery running the length of the hall. A further (double-flight) staircase, with a landing offering a view of the street, leads to the upper floor. Here a central elongated octagonal hall gives access at two corners to the two main rooms. For the sake of symmetry, the other two corners form fitted cupboards. On the garden side, the hall opens on to a "sofa", a raised platform. On the lower/ground floor are the side-rooms and utility rooms, including (on the lowest level) a cistern, on the roof of which a pergola forms the transition between house and garden.
S. M.

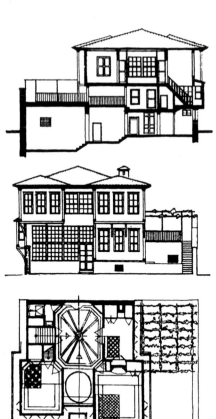

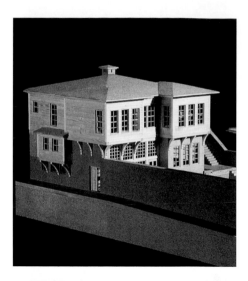

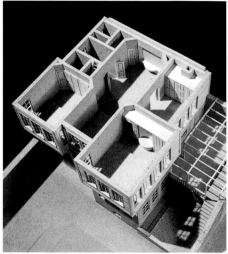

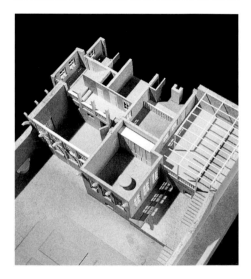

Anonymous building

Japanese house

Scale model 1 : 33 ¹/₃
Thomas Molnar
Rainer Schoder

The Japanese house is the model of a "natural house". It is built of wood, it has clay walls, paper windows and straw floors, wide areas can be opened to the outside, and a garden is an integral part of it. The use of natural materials is partly due to their ready availability, but also to the particular local conditions, such as protection against earthquakes, which has led in Japan to the wooden skeleton frame's being preferred to masonry walls. The structure of the traditional Japanese room is formed by supports, several layers of movable partitions (paper or wooden sliding doors) and floors and ceilings of various heights, but clearly separate, so that as the movable elements are opened or closed, a wide variety of combinations can be achieved, both between the individual sections and between interior and exterior.

The space is divided according to the various flooring materials: earth floors for heavy work in house and courtyard, wooden flooring (to be walked on only with slippers) for interior or exterior passages, and tatami (rice stalks) flooring in the living-quarters. These compressed straw mats, measuring about 90×180 cm, determine the basic framework and thus the size and function of all the rooms, such as tea-, living-, bed- and guest-rooms, and thus the dimensions of the entire Japanese house.

V. H.

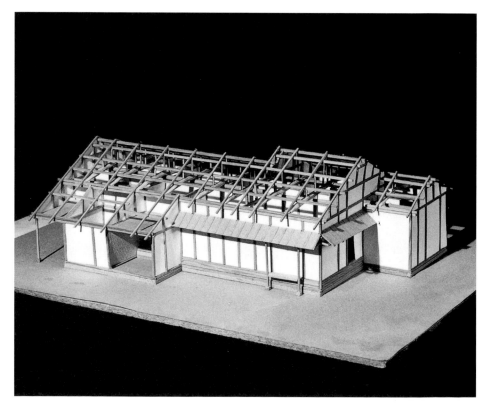

Dominikus Zimmermann
1685–1766

Wieskirche
1745

Scale model 1 : 50
Klaus Jürgen Probst
Hans Peter Wörndl

Even apart from its iconography, the volumetric form and the distribution of light in this gem of late baroque religious building give it relevance today.

The oval interior, extended by a portico at one end and the apse at the other, is doubly surrounded: by the amply fenestrated outer wall, and by the inner framework of pillars. The "vaulting" is not masonried, but consists of concave wooden structures fixed to the roof truss. The lighter weight allows the widest possible placing of the walls and supporting elements – an advantage for the incomparable lighting concept. The changing light bathes the colourful interior in different atmospheres, according to the time of day.

F. K.

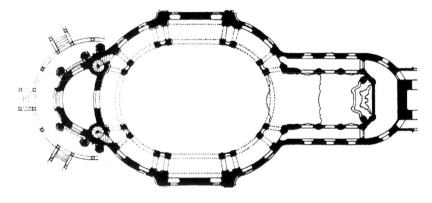

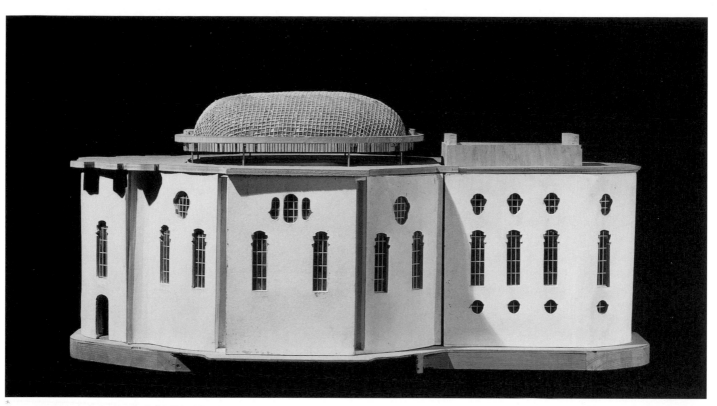

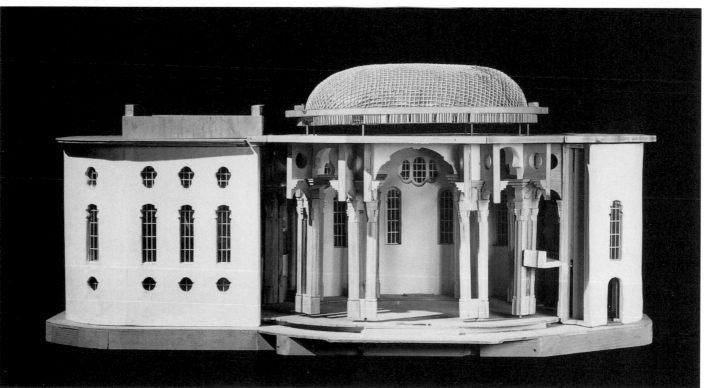

Cosmas Damian Asam
1686–1739

Monastery church of Weltenburg
1716–24

Scale model 1 : 50
Irene Ring
Karl Schnieringer
Manfred Schuller

In the concept of form and lighting, this church – built within the existing monastery grounds – represents a unique example of baroque religious building. Within the basic cuboid form, the structure is divided into various sections. A canopy-like vestibule leads to the oval main section and on, along the longitudinal axis, to the well-lit apse, with St. George "riding into" it. The dome over the main section is false, being in fact only a brim screening twelve windows which bathe in bright light the fresco on the horizontal ceiling under the roof truss. The two side windows of the apse are not in the direct line of vision. The measurements are mostly based on whole-number proportions.
F. K.

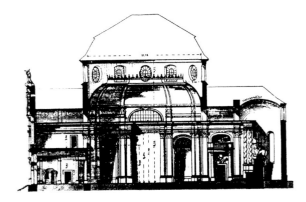

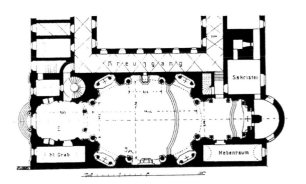

386

Johann Michael Fischer
1692–1766

Church of St. Augustine
Ingolstadt
1735–39

Scale model 1 · 50
Werner Frick
Manfred Grüner
Hubert Koukol

The Church of St. Augustine is one of Fischer's principal works, in which his design for a monastery church reaches full maturity for the first time. He distinguishes the function of the "lower church" for the congregation from that of the "upper church" for the monks, which encircles the nave with passages and galleries.

In the centre is the large octagon, open to all sides between curved pilasters spanned by arches. The outer walls are subordinate in comparison. The effect of spaciousness is enhanced by the subtly differentiated lighting; the radiant light in the diagonal oratories contrasts vividly with the uniform illumination of the main octagon and the muted indirect lighting of the chancel.

In 1945, the church suffered serious damage in two bomb attacks. After years of debate, the remaining torso was demolished, although Elfinger, an Ingolstadt architect, had submitted detailed and realistic suggestions for its restoration.
F. P.

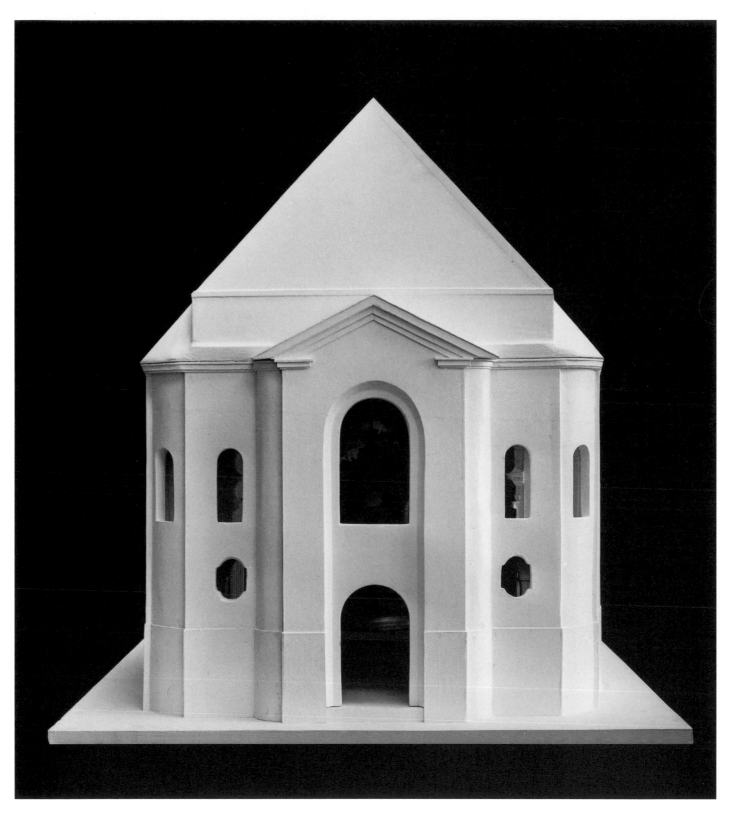

Jože Plečnik
1872–1957

Church in Bogoijna
1925–27

Scale model 1 : 50
Christian Vogt
Nicole Gänzler
Michael Hoche

This church, near Murska Sobota in north-west Slovenia, was built to include as a vestibule a baroque-style church that had become too small. The width of the new church takes in the length of the old one, of which the structural form can be followed within the new building.

Plečnik planned the new building with naves of differing widths, in keeping with the structure of the baroque vaulting. Spanning the naves are semi-circular transverse arches of different sizes, and ceilings with wooden beams. Despite the rural character of the village, costly materials are used, such as finely polished grey marble for the pillars. The local artisans commissioned by Plečnik supplied colourful ceramic vessels (symbols for bread and wine); Plečnik fixed the plates to the ceiling and hung the jugs on the altar.

At the side of the compound building under its saddle roof, Plečnik placed a cylindrical bell-tower, visible from far and wide, and topped by a small baroque roof similar to that over the sacristy.

F. K.

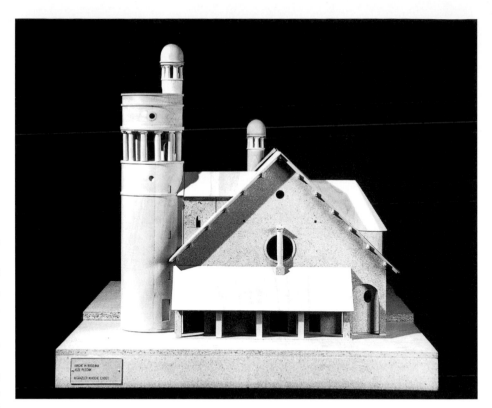

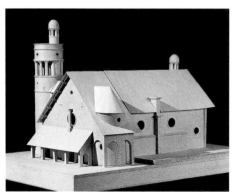

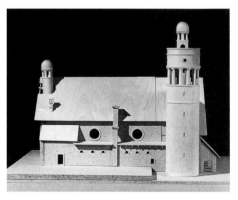

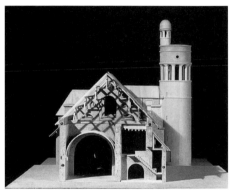

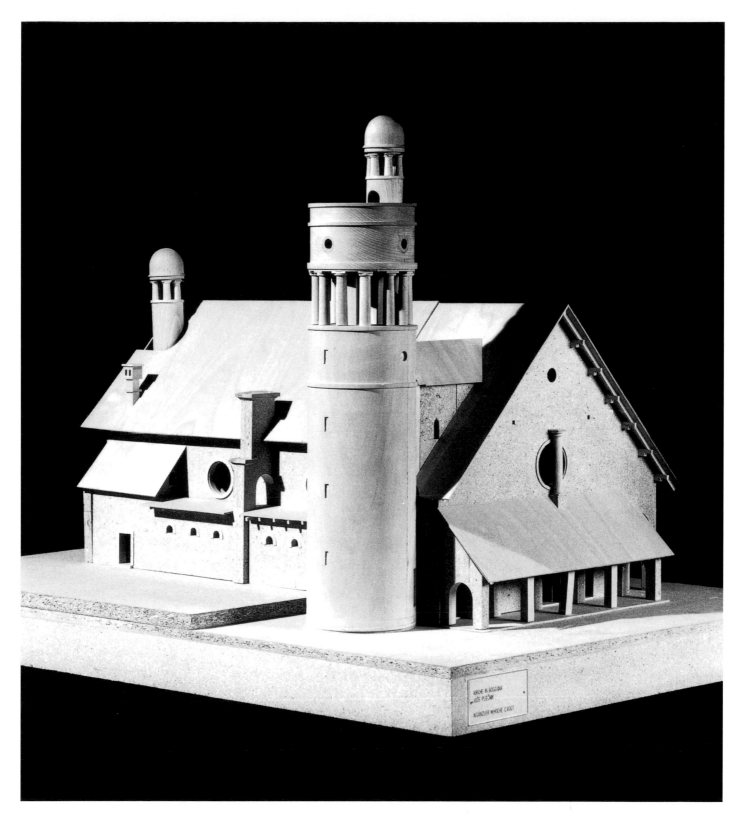

Jože Plečnik
1872–1957

Church of St. Mary of Lourdes
Zagreb
1936/37

Scale model 1 : 50
Karlheinz Beer
Gerhard Hess
Bernd Krause

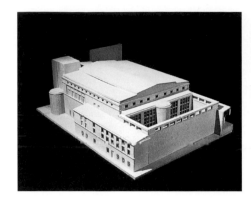
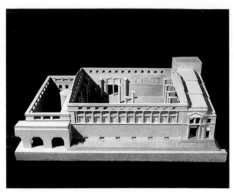

The first design for this building was made in 1934; in fact only the crypt was built.

The entrance to the church was to have been by way of a transverse narthex, similar to that in Bogoijna. An innovation would have been the irregular placing of pillars in the interior – apparently arbitrary and unsystematic, but nevertheless planned precisely according to points of view, since in the five-aisle flat-ceilinged hall they obstruct the view of the altar less than conventional placing would.

An apse was planned behind the main altar, with full-length glass walls on the right and left looking on to a "sacred garden" (inner courtyard).

The spatial effect would have been like the view through a fairly sparse forest.

F. K.

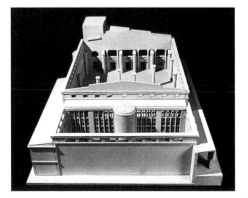
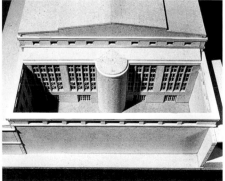

392

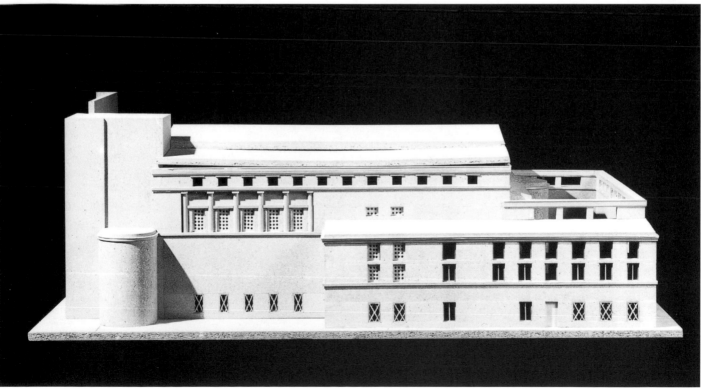

Jože Plečnik
1872–1957

**Church of St. Michael
Barje
1937/38**

*Scale model 1 : 50
Barbara Lindner
Susanne Heindl*

This small church on the moorland near Ljubljana has a transverse rectangular interior entered through a slim bell-tower by a free-standing open staircase. The materials are bare stone and brick masonry with wood fillings divided by round pillars made of concrete pipes from the municipal sewage system.

An invention of Plečnik's is the fenced-in area in the middle, in front of the apse, designed for children taking their first communion (according to Damjan Prelovšek). The interior, including the transversely placed roof, is completely of wood.

Because of the poor quality of the land, the church is on a raised level, with a lower storey at ground level.

F. K.

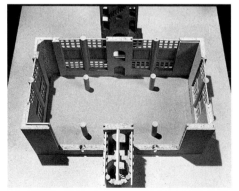

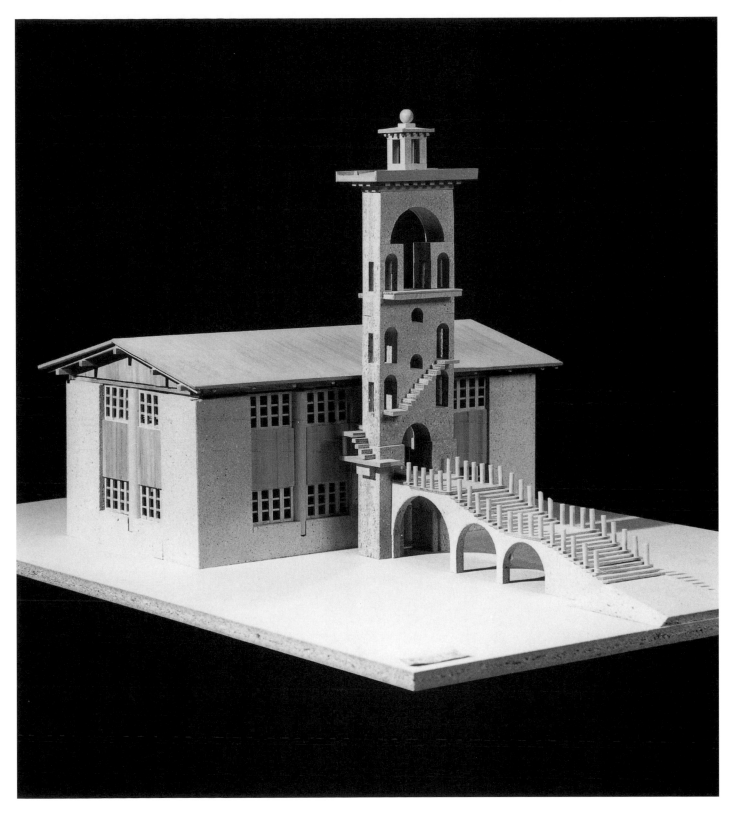

Frank Lloyd Wright
1867–1959

Unity Temple
Oak Park, Illinois
1906

Scale model 1 : 50
Abel Schönthaler

Unity Temple, built at the same time as Otto Wagner's church on the Steinhof, is the result of dividing and fitting together. An entrance hall lies between the most important parts of the building – the auditorium and the Sunday school – separating and linking them. Each area retains its own focal point.

The corners are conspicuous as independent volumetric forms, carefully separated from the main body. While in the auditorium they contain important elements such as the staircases, in the Sunday school they are simply side-rooms. The interior of the auditorium is based on the form of a cross with arms of equal length – that is, on the spatial relation of the areas above and below the galleries with the central cubic form. The strong demarcation of the supporting structures by the glazed coffered ceiling and the high side windows of the annexes heightens the impression of convergence and interpenetration.

"Here the Cubism of the Larkin Building (1904/05) is further structured, to complete an avant-garde ferroconcrete construction" (Manfredo Tafuri, Francesco Dal Co, Architektur der Gegenwart). M. J.

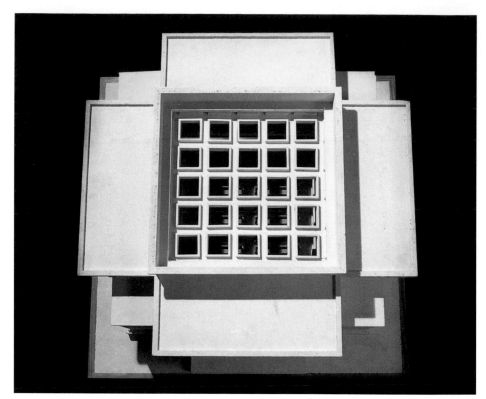

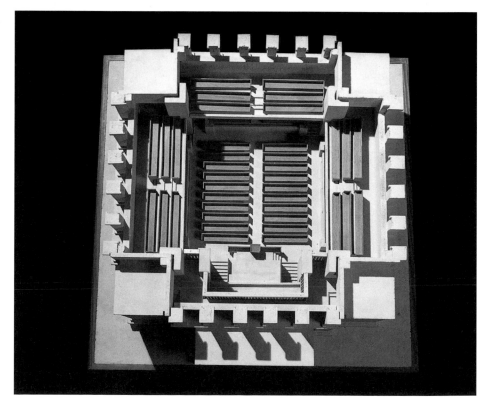

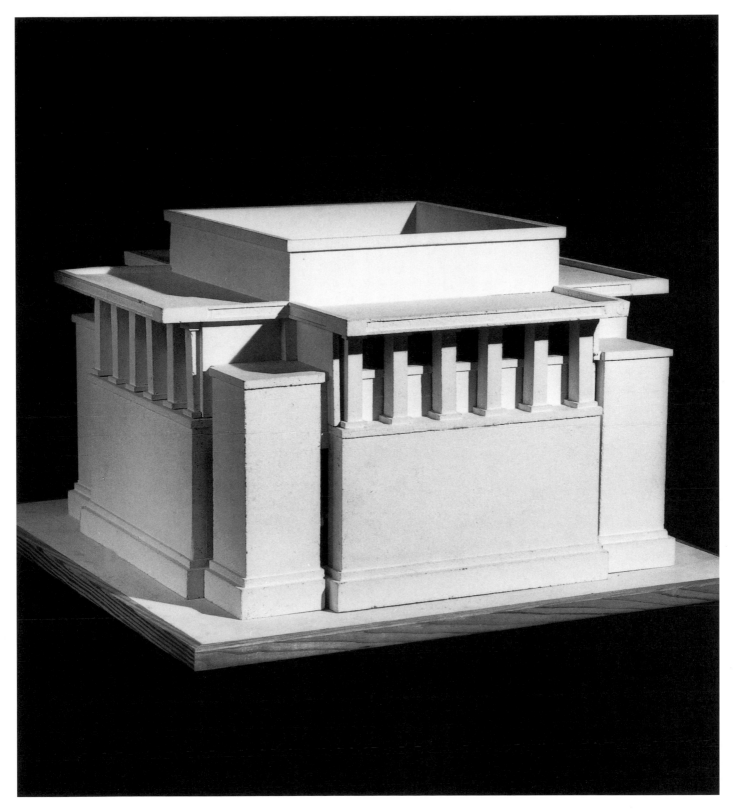

Theodor Fischer
1862–1938

Protestant church project Pilgersheimerstrasse, Munich 1914/15

Scale model 1 : 50
Harald Nigl
Christoph von Negelein

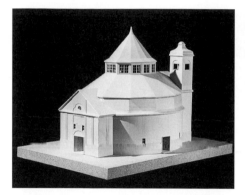

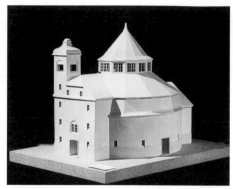

In this unrealised design for a church in Munich-Giesing, Fischer harks back to the type with oval central structure.

The layout is based on a main oval with annexes at each end of the longitudinal axis for the entrance, the staircases and the sacristy. The tower rises asymmetrically from one side of an annexe.

The middle of the oval, which is lit only by the windows surrounding a central superstructure, is kept free for the altar, placed slightly off-centre. With this innovation in the liturgical order, Fischer follows the idea of the centralised building through to its logical consequence.

The raised interior is reached by three stairways, starting from a surrounding gallery. From the central area, the tiered seating rises on all sides, as in an amphitheatre, interrupted only by the access stairs, the raised pulpit behind the altar, and the twelve pillars supporting galleries and roof.

T. B.

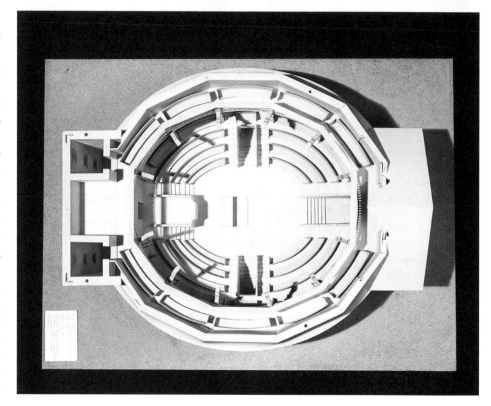

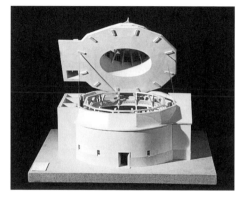

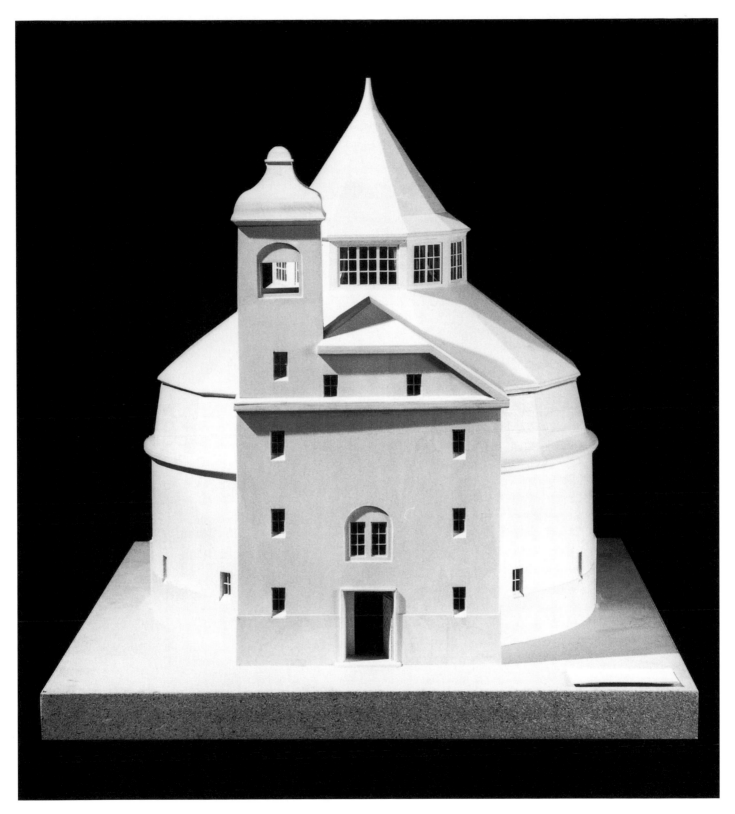

Theodor Fischer
1862–1938

Forest church
Planegg, Munich
1924–26

Scale model 1 : 50
Regina Stein
Tim Brengelmann
Nikolaus Zieske

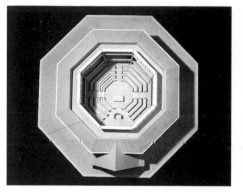

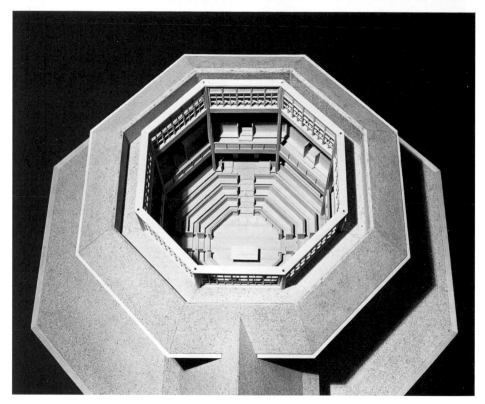

This little Protestant church is Fischer's last realised church building. The layout is based on an octagon with a broach roof and an annexe topped by a tower. The interior rises over an equilateral octagonal ground plan, each side measuring 7.46 m. Eight wood-clad concrete pillars support the surrounding gallery and the coffered ceiling panelled with larchwood. There are three entrances, two of which lead to the galleries. At the lowest point of the room is the altar, placed slightly off-centre, and behind it the pulpit. The tiered seating rises on all sides, with a sector left free behind the preacher. Here the church hall adjoins at ground level, as a link with the tower; on the upper floor is the choir and organ gallery.

The church is lit through windows in the outer walls and dormers in the roof.

T. B.

Otto Bartning
1883–1959

Church project
Constance
1923

Scale model 1 : 50
Ute Meinhardt
Heinz Thum

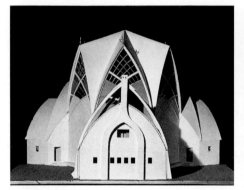
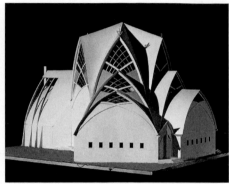

In a competition for church architecture, held in 1923, Otto Bartning took up and modified his ideal design for a "Stern-kirche" (star-shaped church), first conceived in the years following the First World War.

In this version, he planned one area as an auditorium for sermons, centred on the pulpit, and a raised area for the celebration of the mass, centred on the altar, seating altogether 588, and spanned by a dome-like structure.

The main central area consists of a hexagon with three adjoining aisles containing the galleries, and a longer aisle behind the ceremonial area, with choir and organ gallery, under which is a community functions room. The main and side access passages are positioned at the junctions of these aisles.

The preaching area, with auditorium seating (three out of six segments – five out of seven in the "Sternkirche") is separate from the slightly raised ceremonial area around the altar (three out of six segments – two out of seven in the "Sternkirche"), the whole arrangement rising by degrees towards the centre. Light enters the church between the tiered roof elements.

V. H.

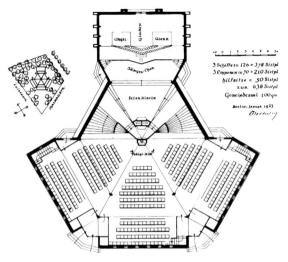

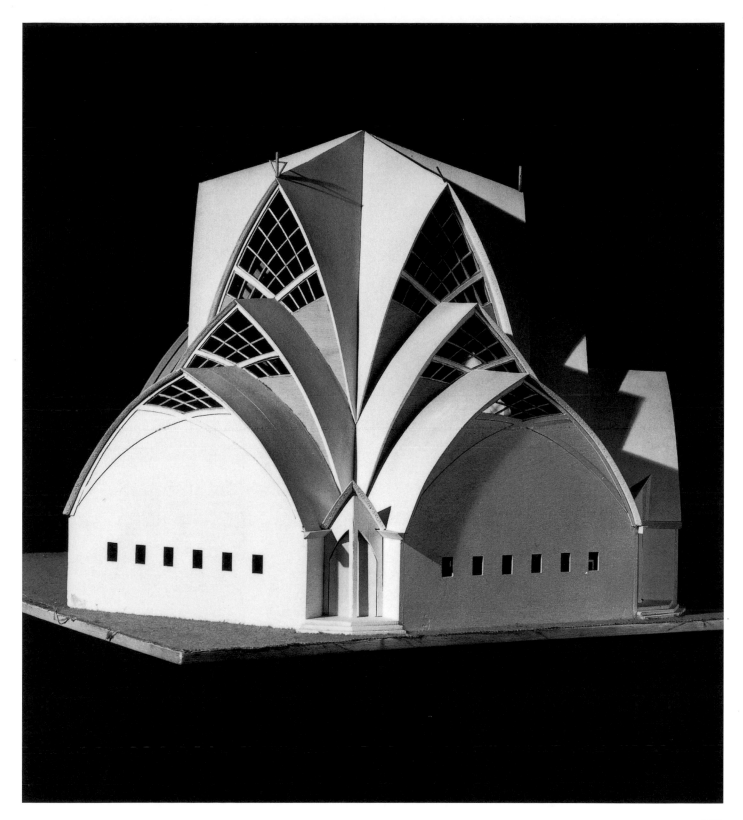

Hans Döllgast
1891–1974

St. Boniface church project
Munich
1966

Scale model 1 : 33 ⅓
Martin Harald
Bertram Pressl

Immediately after the end of the war, Döllgast, using the simplest resources, had taken the surviving torso of the St. Boniface basilica (built in 1835–50 by Georg Ziebland and bombed between 1943 and 1945) and made it into a dignified and functional church. Together with the Alte Pinakothek and the old south cemetery building, this church – unfortunately much altered since – belonged to the outstanding examples of creative reconstruction.

When alterations and extensions to the post-war substance were under consideration, Döllgast submitted several designs.

In this project, the only feature remaining of Ziebland's original is the vestibule. Adjoining this, Döllgast planned in the southern third of the former nave, an open atrium, and in the middle and northern thirds, the nave of a new basilica, the aisles of which would correspond to the five inner aisles of the previous building, while in place of the former outer aisles, rooms for the presbytery were to be built.

Döllgast wished to adopt the form, height and axis measurements of Ziebland's building, but to reinterpret them in construction, material and reduction of form.

F. P.

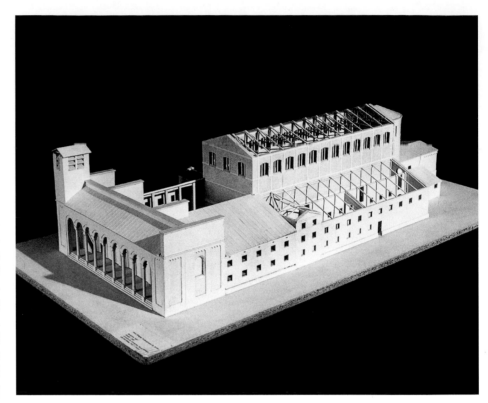

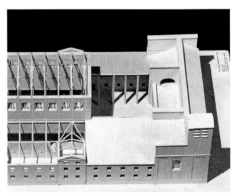

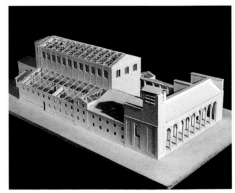

404

Hans Döllgast
1891–1974

**St. Boniface basilica project
Munich
1967**

Scale model 1 : 33 ¹/₃

Whereas in the 1966 project Döllgast was ready to sacrifice his own post-war church to a new order, here he treats the old building substance with considerably more sensitivity, retaining the existing substance and adding new features while observing the old order.

The liturgical area remains in the shortened basilica; to the north of this, community rooms were to replace the aisles that had been destroyed, and between them, in the former nave, would be a garden. In contrast to the old aisles, Döllgast planned the new buildings with pent roofs sloping inwards, thus creating an interesting tension between old and new fabric. The wall of the former apse would be retained to form a chapel for the convent.

Döllgast's 1967 project would have given Munich a unique ensemble of creative reconstruction and independent reinterpretation, but unfortunately it was not realised.

F. P.

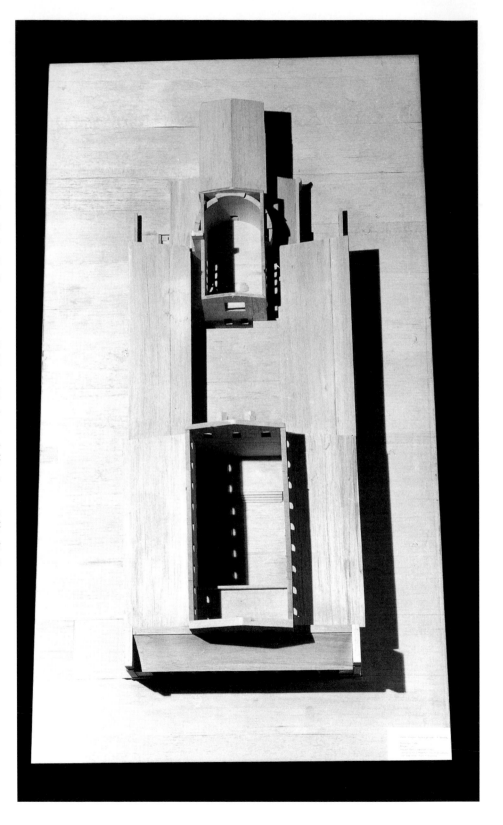

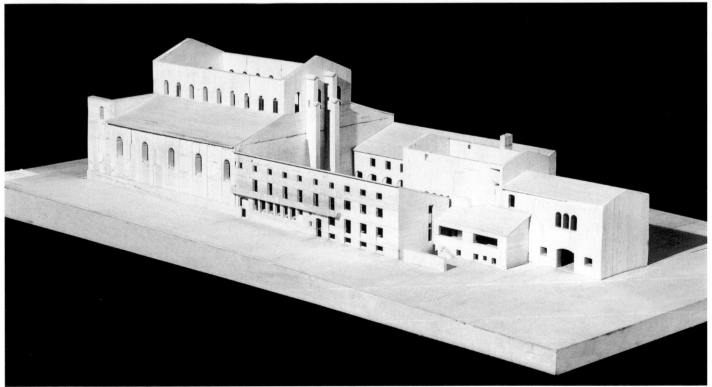

Hans Döllgast
1891–1974

Church of the Redeemer
Traunreut
1953–64

Scale model 1 : 33 ⅓
Monika Janka
Wolfgang Kirchberger
Bärbel Thiel

The first church Döllgast built after the war shows how far his further stylistic development was influenced by his long involvement with the St. Boniface project. In 1953/54, for a newly-founded refugee housing estate in Traunreut, he built a simple, compact cuboid, 30 m long and 15 m wide, with a close-fitting gable roof, the ridge height being 15 m. All the exterior walls are of bare brick masonry, divided by two bare concrete peripheral tie beams. As in the north gable of St.Boniface's, the entrance side is enhanced by two massive buttresses. A delicate wooden ridge turret crowns the gable.

The simple interior achieves a splendid accord of form and construction. Supporting the roof are two longitudinal beams, lying across pilasters on the gable walls and four free-standing pillars, which mark the apse to the east and the entrance to the west. The wooden roof truss, the whitewashed brick walls and the natural stone floor give an impression of spacious austerity. In 1964, Döllgast added a north aisle, a south transept and a free-standing bell-tower in front of the church.
F. P.

408

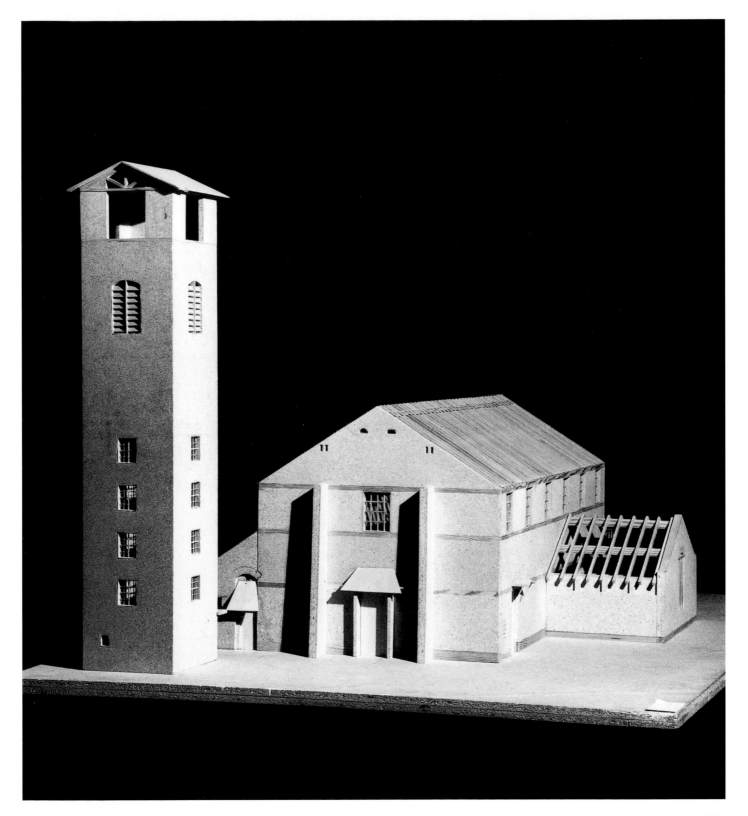

Hans Döllgast
1891–1974

**Church project
Pfändhausen
1964**

Scale model 1 : 50
Otto Hartmann

In 1964, Döllgast designed for a small village in Upper Franconia a Roman Catholic parish church, which was to be built at the edge of an old cemetery and next to a small baroque church with no tower. Here again, Döllgast starts with a simple cuboid structure, this time with a steep saddle roof in keeping with the surroundings. Beside it was planned a free-standing square tower, with a sloping roof inserted between high pillars.

More than in all Döllgast's other church buildings, this interior is determined by the open wooden roof truss lined with wood-wool slabs, measuring more than half the height to the ridge.

The lighting gives an interesting effect; four round-gabled pedimental windows, one in each wall, admit light in the form of a cross, the perpendicular following the central aisle and the transverse running in front of the communion rail. The windows in the side walls extend upwards to form dormers, giving an extra lighting zone from the roof level and lending the exterior two interesting features.

This church was built in 1965/66, to a revised plan without the dormers and with many details simplified, so that the building does not match the quality of the 1964 project.

F. P.

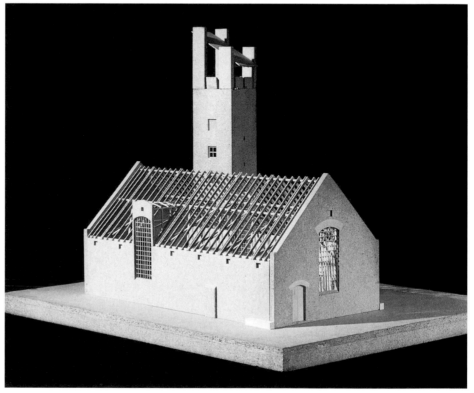

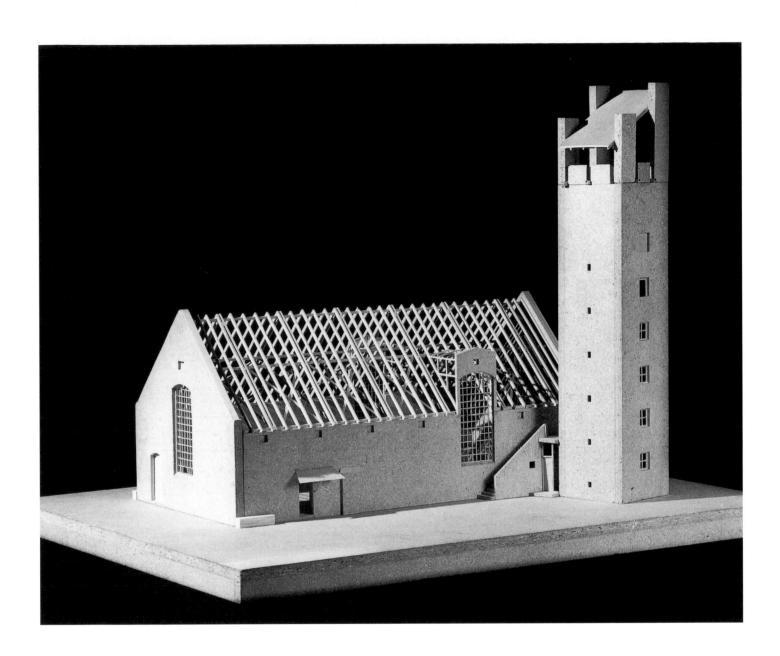

411

Hans Döllgast
1891–1974

Building for the municipal cleansing department
Old North Cemetery, Munich
1957

Scale model 1 : 33 ¹/₃
Joakimidou Soultana

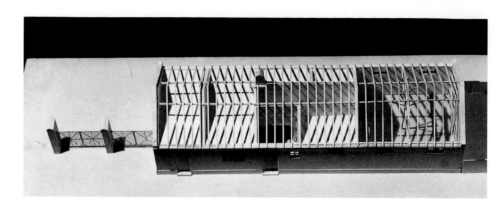

Besides the Alte Pinakothek and the church of St. Boniface, the reconstructions in the Munich cemeteries are amongst Döllgast's outstanding post-war works. Here, too, he repaired the bomb damage with bricks from the rubble, retaining the former proportions, but in a new form. He integrated into the wall of the Old North Cemetery along the Arcisstrasse a new building for the municipal cleansing department, with the dimensions of the former building (Arnold von Zenetti, 1868), which had been destroyed.

The ground plan, access routes, and distribution of openings for windows and ventilation follow strictly functional requirements. The construction uses the simplest of materials, but in all its details, including the adjoining wrought-iron gates, it bears Döllgast's unmistakable signature. An original feature is the tree-like central support of the vehicle shed.
F. P.

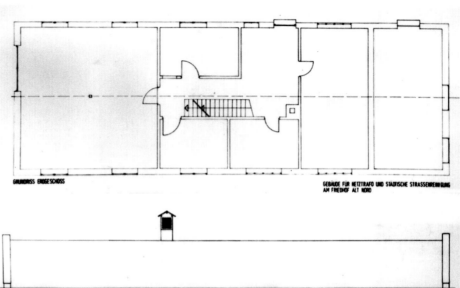

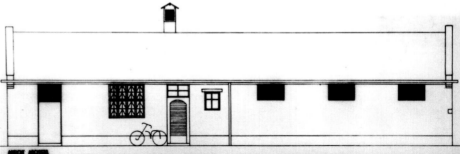

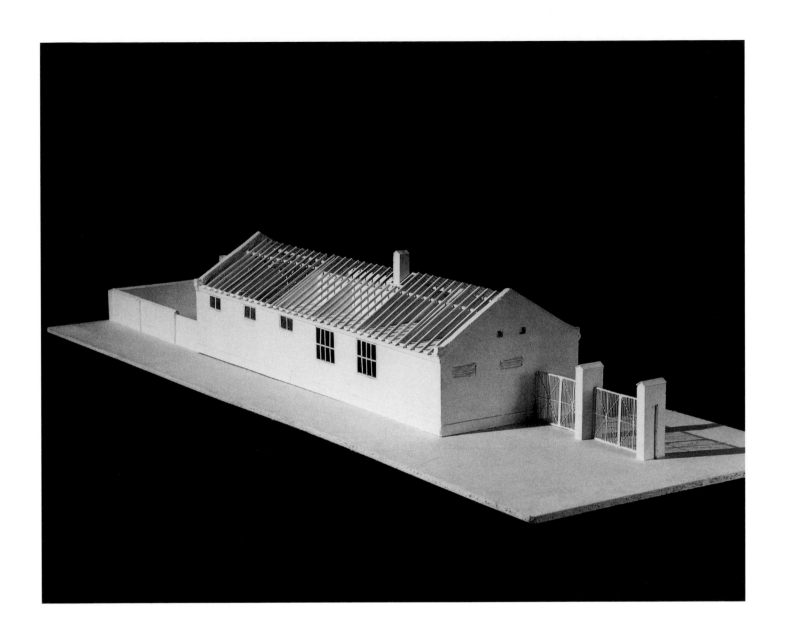

Hans Döllgast
1891–1974

Mortuary
Hohenfeld
1951–61

Scale model 1 · 20
Wolfgang Fischer

This small house on a basic square of 6 × 6 m was designed for a cemetery with a Gothic church on a hill overlooking Kitzingen (Lower Franconia). Built of undressed stone, like the cemetery walls of which it forms part, it marks the eastern corner of the site. The distinguishing feature is a steep broach roof, covered in slate and held by diagonal ties halfway up. This protecting roof spans an open forecourt, the mortuary chamber and the secluded shed for the gravedigger's implements.
The adjoining gate and well were also designed by the architect. This layout on Hohenfeld Hill focuses on Döllgast's art of cemetery design on the smallest possible scale.
F. P.

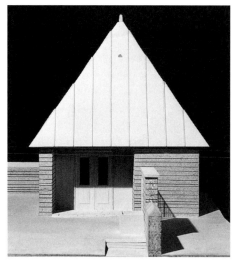

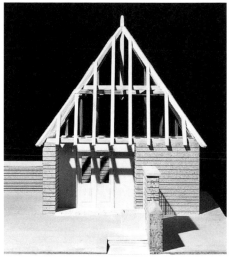

415

Rudolph M. Schindler
1887–1953

Bethlehem Baptist church
Los Angeles
1944

Scale model 1 : 33 ¹/₃
Ralph Bauer
Peter Korinski

Schindler's Bethlehem church stands on
the south side of Los Angeles, and has to
be seen in the context of the surrounding
one- or two-storey buildings, which look
as though they came from a world of
cardboard boxes. He uses a horizontally
structured "De Stijl" façade, rather like a
hoarding, which was at once sufficiently
simple and striking to attract the attention of passing motorists. The open
tower in the form of a cross shows the
purpose of the building, and stands as a
Christian "advertising sign", which
Schindler placed behind the façade, as
the spatial arrangement demanded.
The angled interior contrasts with the
simple exterior, the two wings merging
in the altar and tower area. The inter-
stices in the tower are glazed, thus
integrating it into the interior.
T. B.

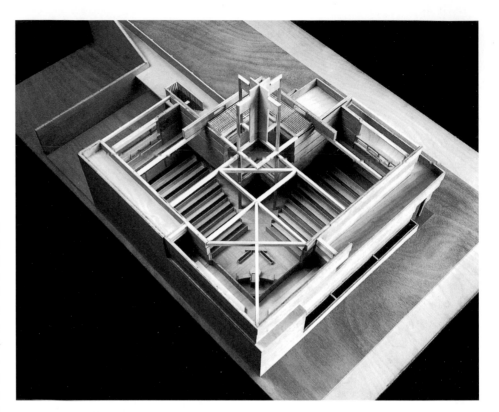

Martin Correa
Gabriel Guarda

**Benedictine monastery church
"De las Condes"
Santiago, Chile
1963/64**

Scale model 1 : 50
Andrea Buchner
Stefan Mayerhofer
Oliver Stuke
Ulrike Wietzorrek

The model shows the church building of a monastery complex built during the years 1959–80 under the patronage of the high abbey of Beuron in Las Condes (Santiago).

The overall concept of the monastery emerged from a competition held in 1953. The architectural ensemble has since been declared a national monument.

The church itself, which certainly owes much to classic modern European architecture and the influence of Le Corbusier, is nevertheless – in view of the specific liturgical requirements and of its relation to the topography – an absolutely independent building.

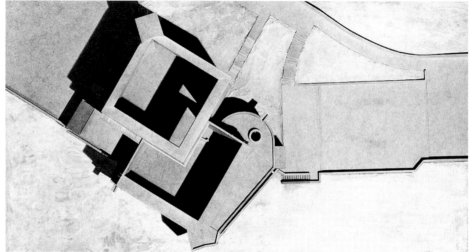

In the ground plan, two squares overlap diagonally, resulting basically in three areas which also emerge formally and volumetrically.

The altar is placed where the surfaces overlap. This leaves a section for the 50 or so members of the holy order, seated in a semicircle around the altar, to celebrate daily mass.

The other, larger section houses a congregation of some 180, for Sunday mass.

F. W.

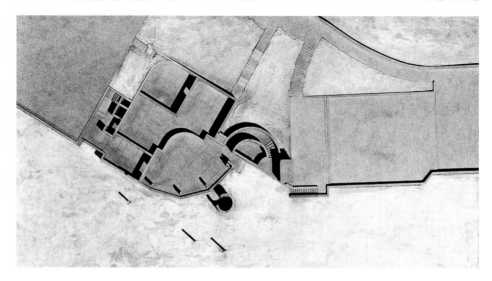

Alvar Aalto
1898–1976

was born in Kuortane, central Finland, and studied architecture at the Technical University in Helsinki. In 1927 he opened his own office in Turku, and moved it to Helsinki in 1934. He established the firm of ARTEK, which produced and sold his furniture. His work includes houses, civic centres, libraries, university buildings, hospitals and factories.

Principal buildings include:
Paimo Sanatorium 1929–33; Viipuri library 1930–35; World Fair pavilion, Paris 1936/37; "Mairea" villa, Noormarkku 1937; World Fair pavilion, New York (1939–40); Otaniemi University, from 1949; Helsinki cultural centre, 1955; Aalborg Museum, Denmark 1958; Wolfsburg cultural centre, 1958; church in Riola, Italy 1966.

Cosmas Damian Asam
1686–1739

son of the painter Georg Asam, was born in Benediktbeurn. He spent the years 1711–13 in Rome. In collaboration with his brother, Egid Quirin (1692–1750), sculptor, painter and stuccoer, he designed the following churches:
Ensdorf 1714; Rohr 1717–23; Aldersbach 1720; Weltenburg 1716–24; Freising cathedral 1723/24; Fürstenfeld 1722–37; Einsiedeln 1724–26; Bruchsal court chapel 1728/29; Osterhofen 1729–35; St. Emmeran, Regensburg 1731–33; Johann Nepomuk church, Munich, from 1733, known as "Asam's church" beside which he built a house for himself, where he died in 1739.

Gunnar Asplund
1885–1940

was born in Stockholm, where he trained at the Royal Technical University and the private Klara School. He made study-trips to Germany, France, Italy and the USA. In his day, Asplund was the outstanding figure amongst Swedish architects.

Buildings include:
Göteborg town hall, from 1913; Snellman villa, Djursholm 1917/18; workers' housing estate 1918; chapel in Stockholm 1918–20; Stockholm municipal library 1920–28; Skandia cinema, Stockholm 1922/23; Stockholm exhibition centre 1928–30; Stockholm crematorium 1935–40.

Otto Bartning
1883–1959

was born in Karlsruhe. From 1904 to
1908 he studied architecture in Berlin
and Karlsruhe. He designed the Protestant Friedenskirche in Peggau/Styria
(1906), "Sternkirche" model 1922, the
"Stahlkirche" on the "Pressa" in Cologne
(1928), and the Gustav-Adolf church in
Berlin/ Charlottenburg (1931–34).
From 1926 to 1930, he was director of
the College of Architecture in Weimar,
and in 1946 he was chairman of the
re-established Deutscher Werkbund
(German Crafts Alliance). In the post-
war period, he built 48 temporary
churches in both parts of Germany. He
was president of the Association of
German Architects from 1950 to 1959.
Together with Otto Dörzbach he
established an office in 1950. From
1955, he was adviser for urban planning in Berlin, and chairman of the
steering committee of the "Interbau".

Anton Brenner
1898–1957

was born in Vienna, where he studied
with Oskar Strnad and Josef Frank at the
School of Arts and Crafts, and with Peter
Behrens and Clemens Holzmeister at the
Academy of Fine Arts. He built houses in
Vienna and particularly in Frankfurt am
Main, as part of the housing programme
organised by Ernst May of the Frankfurt
urban planning department. In 1929 he
directed the department of architecture
at the Bauhaus in Dessau. From 1951 to
1953, he was professor of Architecture
and Urban Planning at the Technical
University of Kharagpur, near Calcutta.

Le Corbusier
1887–1965

was born in La Chaux-de-Fonds/Switzer-
land, as Charles-Édouard Jeanneret (he
adopted the pseudonym in the 1920s).
He trained as an engraver at the École
des Arts Décoratifs in his home town,
and later worked with Auguste Perret in
Paris and Peter Behrens in Berlin. He
travelled in Italy, Germany and south-
eastern Europe.
Buildings and projects include:
Schwob villa, La Chaux-de-Fonds 1916;
"Citrohan" house-type from 1920; La
Roche/Jeanneret house, Paris 1923;
Stein villa, Garches 1927; two houses
on the Weissenhof housing estate, Stuttgart 1927; Savoye villa, Poissy 1928;
development of the Modulor, from
1941; Unité d'habitation, Marseille
1947; buildings for Chandigarh, from
1951; church in Ronchamp 1955.

Hans Döllgast
1891–1974

was born in Bergheim on the Danube. From 1910 to 1914 he studied architecture with Friedrich von Thiersch and Carl Hocheder in Munich. He worked 1919–22 in Richard Riemerschmidt's office, 1922–26 in the studios of Peter Behrens in Vienna, Berlin and Frankfurt, and from 1927 independently in Munich and Augsburg. From 1929 he held a teaching post at the Technical University in Munich, and became professor of architectural drawing in 1939. Döllgast was known as a brilliant draughtsman and a charismatic teacher, but his importance as a building architect was underestimated. Many first-class reconstructions, such as the Alte Pinakothek, the St. Boniface basilica and the old north and south cemeteries (all in Munich) have played a significant role in German post-war architecture.

Theo van Doesburg
1883–1931

was born in Utrecht, as Emil Maria Küppers. He attended drama school, and started writing art criticism in 1912. In 1917 he founded the periodical "De Stijl". He collaborated with the architects Oud, Wils, Rietveld, van Eesteren (De-Lange house, Alkmaar 1917; Spangen housing estate 1919–21; model for the Rosenberg house 1923; Maison Particulier 1923). He went to Berlin in 1921, held a "Stijl" course in Weimar in 1922, and met El Lissitzky at the Constructivist Congress. In 1923 he moved to Paris. He held exhibitions, some with Mondrian, and created his first projects for houses with studio. The "Stijl Architecture Manifesto" was published in 1924, followed in 1926 by the "Manifesto of Elementarism". From 1926 to 1928 he worked on the "Aubette", with H. Arp and S. Taeuber-Arp. 1929/30 he built his own house with studio in Meudon.

Theodor Fischer
1862–1938

was born in Schweinfurt. From 1880 he studied architecture at the Technical University in Munich, with Friedrich von Thiersch, but he left the university before completing his diploma, in order to study with Paul Wallot in Berlin. From 1889 he worked in Dresden as an independent architect, returning to Munich in 1893 to work in Gabriel von Seidl's office. In 1901, he became professor of building design in Stuttgart, and in 1907 he was appointed First Chairman of the German Crafts Alliance (Deutscher Werkbund).
Principal buildings and projects:
Church in Gaggstatt 1901–05; garrison church, Ulm 1906–10; art building, Stuttgart 1909–13; single men's hostel, Munich 1925/26.

Johann Michael Fischer
1692–1766

learned bricklaying, first with his father, then journeying through Bohemia and Moravia. From 1718 he lived in Munich, and was soon known as "the most successful architect of his generation in southern Germany" (Pevsner).

He specialised in church building, and his main works (Ingolstadt, Aufhausen, Ottobeuren, Rott am Inn, Altomünster) are amongst the supreme works of 18th-century European architecture. Fischer focuses on the octagonal central hall with all its possibilities for development. In his best works, he achieves an accord between construction, functionality and form that presages the modern age.

Josef Frank
1885–1967

was born in Baden near Vienna. He studied at the Technical University of Vienna from 1903, writing for his doctorate a thesis on "The original form of the church buildings of Leon Battista Alberti". From 1919 to 1925, he was professor of building construction at the Vienna School of Arts and Crafts, and in 1925 he established the furnishing firm of "Haus & Garten". He was a founder-member of CIAM.

From 1929 to 1932, he was initiator and director of the Vienna Werkbund housing estate. In 1934 he emigrated to Sweden, where he built five houses in Falsterbo. For the next 33 years, until 1967, he was employed by the furnishing firm of "Svenskt Tenn", designing furniture, textiles and objects for everyday use. 1942/43 he was guest lecturer at the New School of Social Research.

Bohuslav Fuchs
1895–1972

was born in Vsechovice/Moravia. He studied engineering in Brno, then architecture in Prague. From 1919 to 1921, he worked in Jan Kotěra's studio. There followed study-trips to England, Holland, Germany and France. He worked for the urban planning department in Brno 1923–29, and had his own office from 1923. He was CIAM representative for Czechoslovakia in 1935, and professor at the Technical University in Brno 1945–58.

Buildings and projects include:

Hydroelectric power station, Haje 1921/22; Café Zeman 1925; Fuchs house 1927; Avion Hotel 1927/28; Moravian bank 1928 (all Brno); houses for the "Novy dum" (new house) exhibition 1928; Vesna technical college 1929; Eliska Machova hostel 1931; open-air swimming-pool 1931/32 (all Brno); Teplice thermal bath 1935/36.

Johann Wolfgang Goethe
1749–1832

was born in Frankfurt am Main, and studied jurisprudence in Leipzig and Strasbourg from 1765. In Frankfurt, between 1772 and 1775, he wrote 'Götz von Berlichingen', 'Clavigo', 'Die Leiden des jungen Werther' and the first version of 'Faust'. In 1775 he was invited to live and work at the court in Weimar, where he became a friend of the writer Wieland and of Charlotte von Stein, and was appointed privy councillor in 1779. His works 'Iphigenie auf Tauris' and 'Egmont' date from his first sojourn in Italy (1786–88). In 1791 he assumed directorship of the ducal theatre in Weimar; the following year he made major alterations to the house in the Frauenplan, which he had rented from 1782 to 1789, and was now given as a present. Christiane Vulpius had been living there with him since 1788, and he married her in 1806.

Eileen Gray
1878–1976

was born in Brownswood/Ireland. From 1898 she studied at the Slade School of Art in London, and learnt from P. Charles the technique of Asiatic lacquerwork. In 1902 she went to Paris to continue her studies at the Académie Colarossi and the Académie Julian, and extended her knowledge of lacquerwork techniques. In the early 1920s she became successful as a designer of furniture and interiors, but it was not until 1926 that she turned her attention to houses.
Principal buildings and projects:
Furniture, including Bibendum, "Transat" chair, Nonconformist 1925–28; E-1027, Cap-Martin 1926–29; her own house, "Tempe à Pailla", Castelar 1932–34; sculptor's house 1934; holiday centre 1937; barn conversion "Lou Perou", St.-Tropez 1958.

Hugo Häring
1882–1958

was born in Biberach/Riss. From 1899 to 1903 he studied in Stuttgart with Theodor Fischer and in Dresden with Wallot, Hartung, Gurlitt and Schuhmacher. 1904–14 he worked in Hamburg, and in 1921 he set up on his own in Berlin. When the CIAM was established, Häring represented the "Ring" (Mies, Poelzig, Mendelsohn, Hilberseimer, Behrendt, the Taut brothers, Gropius, Bartning). He withdrew from collaboration on the Weissenhof housing estate. Under Hitler's dictatorship he assumed directorship of the school "Kunst und Werk"; after this was destroyed he moved back to Biberach.
Principal buildings and projects:
Gurkau estate 1922/23; apartment house, Berlin/Zehlendorf 1926; apartment house, Siemensstadt 1928–31; "flat roof estate" 1930/31; "the growing house" 1931.

Josef Hoffmann
1870–1956

was born in Pirnitz/Moravia. He studied at the state trade school in Brno, and from 1892 to 1895 at the Academy of Fine Arts in Vienna with Karl von Hasenauer and Otto Wagner, in whose studio he later worked. 1899–1936 he was professor at the School of Arts and Crafts in Vienna, and in 1897 co-initiator of the Vienna Secession, which he left, along with the Klimt group, in 1905. In 1903, with Koloman Moser, he founded the Wiener Werkstätte, for which he designed many items of furniture and objects for everyday use. In 1912 he co-founded the Austrian Arts and Crafts Alliance.
Principal buildings include:
Moser, Moll, Henneberg and Spitzer houses, Vienna, around 1900; sanatorium, Pukersdorf 1904–06; Palais Stoclet, Brussels 1905–11; exhibition pavilion for Venice, 1934.

Clemens Holzmeister
1886–1982

was born in Fulpmes/Tirol, as an Austrian with Brazilian nationality. He studied architecture in Vienna, taught in Innsbruck, Düsseldorf and, from 1924, at the Academy of Fine Arts in Vienna. He emigrated to Turkey in 1938, then travelled to Brazil. He was professor at the Technical University in Istanbul from 1940 to 1950, when he returned to Vienna.
Buildings and projects include:
Crematorium, Vienna 1921/22; Klösterlegrund estate, Bolzano 1925; Festival precinct, Salzburg, from 1926; Eichmann house, Seewalchen 1928; Schlageter monument, Düsseldorf 1929; government district, Ankara 1928–52; palace for King Faisal, Baghdad 1931; Werkbund housing estate, Vienna 1932; Kanzlerkirche, Vienna 1932/34; broadcasting centre (RAVAG), Vienna 1935–39; Kosmogral, since 1975; Belo Horizonte cathedral 1939.

Louis Isidore Kahn
1901–1974

was born on the island of Osel in Estonia. His family emigrated to the USA in 1905, and he attended the Central High School and the Academy of Fine Arts in Pennsylvania (1912–20). 1920–24 he studied at the University of Pennsylvania. He worked in the offices of John Molitor (1925/26) and Paul Philippe Cret (1930), and set up on his own as an architect in 1935. In 1941 he opened an office together with George Howe and Oscar Stonorov. 1947–57 he was professor at the University of Yale, from 1956 professor at the A. F. Bennis Foundation at the M. I. T., and 1957–71 he held the Paul Philippe Cret Chair at the University of Pennsylvania.

Adolf Loos
1870–1933

was born in Brno, son of a stonemason and sculptor. He studied from 1893 to 1896 at the Technical University in Dresden, and spent some time in the USA. He suffered from hardness of hearing. From 1897, in Vienna, he wrote many articles, collected in the two volumes "Ins Leere gesprochen" and "Trotzdem".
1922–27 he was chief architect of the municipal housing department of Vienna. 1922–27 Loos lived in France – in Paris and on the Riviera. He died in Kalksburg, near Vienna, on 23 August 1933.
Buildings and projects include:
"Café Museum", Vienna 1899; house on the Michaelerplatz, Vienna 1910 (his only large-scale work); fittings and furnishings for business and private houses; houses in Vienna, Paris and Prague.

Hans Luckhardt
1890–1954

was born in Berlin. He collaborated with W. Luckhardt from 1921 and with A. Anker from 1924. In 1927 he began experiments with cantilevered chairs. In 1952 he was appointed professor at the Academy of Fine Arts in Berlin/Charlottenburg. He died in Bad Wiessee on 8 October 1954.
Buildings and projects in collaboration with W. Luckhardt include:
Exhibition house at the building exhibition in Berlin 1933; design for Jena University 1946; Berlin pavilion and terrace house at the Constructa Exhibition in Hanover 1951; terrace house at the Constructa Exhibition in Hanover 1951; group of apartment blocks at the Kottbuser Gate, Berlin 1956; department of public utilities for Bavaria and Munich, Munich 1957; multi-storey apartment house (with Hubert Hoffmann) at the "Interbau", Berlin 1958.

Wassili Luckhardt
1889–1972

was born in Berlin, where he completed his 'Abitur' in 1907. He studied architecture at the Technical University of Charlottenburg from 1908, in Dresden 1912–14, and attended evening courses with August Endell. In 1956 he became a member of the Berlin Academy of Arts, and in 1958 he was awarded the Art Prize of the City of Berlin.
Buildings and projects in collaboration with H. Luckhardt include:
design for a glass festival hall; design for a cinema; utopian design "An die Freude" (Ode to Joy) – all 1919; architect's house design 1920; theatre design 1921; experimental housing estate, Berlin/Dahlem, Schorlemer Allee 1925; terrace houses, Berlin/Dahlem 1928; three detached houses, Am Rupenhorn, Berlin 1928.

André Lurçat
1894–1970

was born in Bruyères/Vosges. From 1913 to 1923 he studied at the Ecole des Beaux-Arts in Paris. Together with Auguste Perret, Robert Mallet-Stevens and Gabriel Guevrekian, he belongs, apart from Le Corbusier, to the principal representatives of functionalism in France. He was a founder-member of the CIAM. From 1934 to 1937 he taught in Moscow.

Principal buildings:

detached houses, Paris 1924–27; Cité Seurat, Paris 1924/25; Calvi Hotel, Corsica 1930; Ecole Karl Marx, Villejuif 1931–33; Werkbund housing estate, Vienna 1932; residential estates, detached houses, schools.

Ernst May
1886–1970

was born in Frankfurt am Main. From 1908 he studied architecture at University College, London, and in Darmstadt, and was on Raimond Unwin's staff for urban development in London. He continued his studies with Friedrich von Thiersch and Theodor Fischer in Munich, where he graduated. In 1913 he set up on his own as an architect, and in 1925 he became chief town architect in Frankfurt and director of the department of construction and development. After working in urban planning in the USSR, he emigrated in 1934 to Tanzania, where he lived as a farmer and architect, establishing his firm of Dr. Ernst May & Partners in Nairobi in 1942.

In 1954, Ernst May became director of the planning department of the "Neue Heimat Hamburg mbH", and from 1957 he once more set up as an independent architect and urban planner.

Richard Meier
1934

was born in Newark/New Jersey, and graduated in architecture at Cornell University, NY. In 1960 he worked in the office of Skidmore, Owings and Merrill, and moved the following year to the office of Marcel Breuer. He opened his own office in 1963. During the ensuing years, Meier was guest professor at various universities.

Principal buildings and projects:

Smith house, Connecticut 1965–67; Saltzman house, New York 1967–69; Atheneum, Indiana 1975; Arts and Crafts Museum, Frankfurt 1979–84; exhibition and assembly buildings, Ulm 1986–92.

Konstantin Melnikov
1890–1974

was born in Moscow, and is one of the principal representatives of the 1920s avant-garde. During the Stalin era he had no opportunity of realising his projects.
Buildings and projects include:
"Makhorka pavilion" at the agricultural exhibition, Moscow 1923; sarcophagus for Lenin in the mausoleum, 1924; Soviet pavilion at the International Exhibition of Decorative Art, Paris 1925, and project for a garage over the Seine; several club buildings in Moscow (Rusakov, Zuev, Frunze, Kautschuk, Burevestnik) 1927–29; "green town" project 1930; his own house with studio (double cylinder), 1927, in the Arbat district of Moscow, where he died.

Ludwig Mies van der Rohe
1886–1969

was born in Aachen. From 1905 to 1912 he worked first with Bruno Paul, then with Peter Behrens. In 1913 he set up on his own, and in 1924 founded the "Ring". He was director of the Bauhaus 1930–33, until it was closed. In 1938 he emigrated to the USA, where he became director of the Illinois Institute of Technology. He died in Chicago.
Principal buildings and projects:
monument for Karl Liebknecht and Rosa Luxemburg, Berlin 1926; German pavilion, Barcelona 1929; overall plan for the Illinois Institute of Chicago 1940/41; Farnsworth house, Illinois 1945–50; New National Gallery, Berlin 1962–68.

Richard Josef Neutra
1892–1970

was born in Vienna, where he studied (1911–17) at the Technical University with R. Salinger, K. Mayreder and M. Fabiani, as well as attending Adolf Loos's school of architecture. 1921/22 he worked for E. Mendelsohn in Berlin, before emigrating in 1923 to the USA, where he worked first for W. Holabird and M. Roche in Chicago, and later for Frank Lloyd Wright in Taliesin. Subsequently, he and Rudolph Schindler ran their own office, and in 1926 he opened his own studio in Los Angeles. His particular interest was in prefabricated detached houses such as the Lovell Health House. He founded the Academy of Modern Art in Los Angeles, where he lectured in architecture. From 1949 to 1959 he collaborated with R. E. Alexander on large-scale public projects.

**Robert Örley
1876–1945**

**Jacobus Johannes Pieter Oud
1890–1963**

**Jože Plečnik
1872–1957**

was born in Vienna, where he served a joiner's apprenticeship before studying architecture, painting and graphic arts at the School of Arts and Crafts. He made study-trips to Italy, France, Germany, England and Holland. He taught at the Academy of Fine Arts in Istanbul from 1928 to 1932.

Buildings include:

Kaiser villa, Vienna 1904/05; house in the Lannerstrasse, Vienna 1904/05; block of rented flats in the Vegagasse, Vienna 1905/06; Luithlen sanatorium, Vienna 1907/08; Wittgenstein tomb, Vienna 1914; Wustl house, Vienna-Hietzing, Flötzersteig 1916/17; "George Washington Court" residential estate of the municipality of Vienna 1927–30.

was born in Purmerend/Holland. He trained at the Quellinus School of Arts and Crafts and the College of Draughtsmanship in Amsterdam, before studying at the Technical University in Delft. He worked with Cuypers and Stuyt in Amsterdam, and with Theodor Fischer in Munich, spent some time in Stuttgart, worked for Dudok in Leyden, and opened his own office in Purmerend. In 1916 he met Theo van Doesburg and became an active member of De Stijl the following year. He was city architect for Rotterdam from 1918 to 1933. In 1926/27, he designed and built five terrace houses in the Stuttgart Weissenhof housing estate, even designing some of the furniture. He was a foreign member of the November group. He died in Wassenaar.

born in Ljubljana as son of a joiner. He trained in his father's workshop and attended the School of Arts and Crafts in Graz. From 1892 he worked as a draughtsman and joiner in a Viennese furniture factory, and from 1894 in Otto Wagner's studio. 1895–98 he studied at the Academy of Fine Arts in Vienna, before returning to work with Otto Wagner. From 1901 to 1911 he ran his own architecture office, and in 1912 the teaching committee of the Academy of Fine Arts proposed him as successor to Otto Wagner. Plečnik was professor at the School of Arts and Crafts in Prague (1911–21) and in Ljubljana (1921–56), where he died.

Principal buildings:

Zacherl house, 1903–05, Heiliggeistkirche, 1910–13 (all Vienna); alterations in Hradčany, Prague 1921–35; national and university library, Ljubljana 1936.

Ernst Anton Plischke
1903–1992

was born in Klosterneuburg, Lower Austria. He studied with Oscar Strnad at the School of Arts and Crafts in Vienna (1921/22), then with Peter Behrens at the Academy of Fine Arts. After working in Behrens' office, he became Josef Frank's sole collaborator from 1927. In 1929 he went to New York to work the construction office of E. Kahn. He was awarded the Austrian State Prize in 1935. In 1939 he emigrated to New Zealand, returning to Vienna in 1963 to take up an appointment as professor at the Academy of Fine Arts, succeeding C. Holzmeister.

Important buildings include:
Rie apartment, 1928; Liesing employment exchange, 1930; Werkbund housing estate, 1932; Mühlbauer house, 1932 (all Vienna); Gamerith house, Attersee 1933/34; Wellington apartment houses 1941; houses Koller and Frey, 1972.

Gerrit Rietveld
1888–1964

was born in Utrecht, where he trained in his father's joinery. From 1906 to 1911 he made drawings for a jeweller, attending evening classes in architecture held by P. J. C. Klaarhamer, an architect from Berlage's circle whose collaborator he later became. In 1917 he set up on his own as a joiner. Robert van't Hoff brought him to the "De Stijl" movement, to which he belonged until it was disbanded in 1931. He was a founder-member of the CIAM (together with H. P. Berlage and Mart Stam, both Dutch). From 1944 to 1955 he taught at the Academy of Architecture in Amsterdam.

Principal buildings and projects:
furniture, including the red-blue chair, 1918; Schröder house, 1924; Werkbund housing estate, Vienna 1932; Vreeburg Cinema, Utrecht 1936; exhibition pavilion for Venice, 1954; Academy of Art, Arnhem 1958–63.

Hans Scharoun
1893–1972

was born in Bremen. He studied architecture at the Technical University in Berlin. From 1914 to 1918 he held advisory posts in planning departments in East Prussia; from 1919 he was an independent architect. In 1925, he was appointed professor at the Academy of Art in Breslau, and was a member of the "Ring". 1945/46 he was chief architect in Berlin, 1946 professor at Berlin Technical University. He taught at the Institute of Building and Construction and the Academy of Sciences (1947–50) and was president of the Berlin Academy of Art (1955–68).

Buildings and projects include:
Weissenhof housing estate, 1927; hostel, Werkbund Breslau 1929; Siemensstadt housing estate, Berlin 1930; Philharmonic Hall, Berlin 1957–63; state library, Berlin 1966–78; Institute of Architecture, TU Berlin 1962–70.

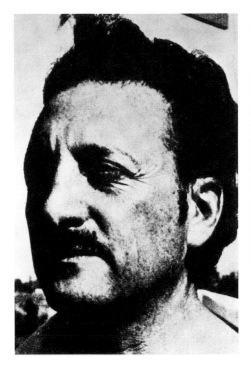

Rudolph M. Schindler
1887–1953

was born in Vienna, where he was a pupil of Otto Wagner at the Academy of Fine Arts. 1917–20 he worked in Frank Lloyd Wright's office, and in 1921 he started working in Los Angeles. After 1925 he collaborated briefly with Richard Neutra. In 30 years of work, he produced more than 200 projects. He died in Los Angeles at the age of 65.

Important buildings:
Schindler house, Los Angeles 1921/22; Packard house, South Pasadena 1924; Lovell beach house; Newport Beach 1925/26; Wolfe summerhouse, Avalon 1928.

Mart Stam
1899–1986

was born in Purmerend/Holland. He studied architecture and worked with Taut and Poelzig in Berlin, where he met El Lissitzky. In the twenties he worked with Moser, Itten, Brinkman and van der Vlugt. He was a founder-member of CIAM and taught at the Bauhaus from 1928 to 1930. Between 1930 and 1934, he was part of Ernst May's team for projects in the USSR. He taught at the School of Arts and Crafts in Amsterdam (1935–48), in 1948 at the Academy of Fine Arts in Dresden, and from 1950 to 1953 at the Academy of Art in Berlin-Weissensee. He opened his own office Amsterdam in 1952, and from 1965 he lived in Switzerland.

Buildings and projects include:
chair without back legs, 1926; Weissenhof housing estate 1926/27; Baba Werkbund housing estate, Prague 1928; Hellerhof estate, Frankfurt 1928–32; terrace houses, Amsterdam 1936.

Oskar Strnad
1879–1935

was born in Vienna, where he studied at the Technical University with Mayreder and König, and gained his doctorate on the subject of Early Christian art. From 1909 he taught theory of form at the School of Arts and Crafts in Vienna, and in 1914 he took over Tessenov's architecture class. From 1919 he worked primarily in stage-set design.

Principal buildings and projects:
house in the Cobenzlgasse, 1910 (with O. Wlach); Wassermann house, Vienna 1914 (with J. Frank and O. Wlach); furniture and objects for everyday use; three-stage theatre 1917; festival hall with circular stage 1918–20; Schallerbach spa building, 1925; Poyaards Theatre, Amsterdam 1925; Theatre for Max Reinhardt, Salzburg 1930; residential estate of the municipality of Vienna, Holochergasse 1932; Werkbund housing estate, Vienna 1932.

**Bruno Taut
1880–1938**

**Giuseppe Terragni
1904–1943**

**Robert Venturi
1925**

was born in Königsberg, where he attended the school of building and construction. He worked in Möhring's office in Berlin, and for Theodor Fischer in Stuttgart (1906–08). From 1909 he had his own office, with Max Taut and Franz Hoffmann. He published articles, was chief architect in Magdeburg (1921–24), and from 1930 professor at the Technical University in Berlin. He moved to Moscow in 1932, emigrated to Japan (1933–36) and became professor at the Academy of Fine Arts in Istanbul in 1936.

Principal buildings and projects:
"Glass house", Werkbund Cologne 1914; mineworkers' housing estate, Katowice 1917; cattle market, Magdeburg 1921; housing developments in Berlin; Dammweg school, Berlin 1927; Hyuga villa, Japan 1935; school in Trabzon, Turkey 1937–39.

was born in Medea/Italy. After graduating in physics and mathematics from the Technical Institute in Como, he studied at the Milan Polytechnic, gaining his doctorate in architecture. In 1927, together with his brother Attilio, he opened an office in Como. With Figini, Pollini, Frette, Larco, Rava and Libera, he founded the "Gruppo 7", which supported Italian "Razionalismo".

Principal buildings and projects:
Novocomum, Como 1927/28; Casa del Fascio, Como 1932–36; five houses in Milan 1933–35; kindergarten Sant' Elia, Como 1936; various villas 1936/37; Palazzo Littorio, Rome 1937; Danteum, Rome 1938; Casa del Fascio, Lissone 1938; Frigerio house, Como 1939/40; total theatre, cathedral (projects) 1943.

was born in Philadelphia. He gained his BA and Master of Fine Arts at Princeton University. He spent the years 1954–56 on an American Academy architecture scholarship in Rome, where he returned in 1966 as "architect in residence". He worked first for Louis Kahn, then for Eero Saarinen, and taught at Pennsylvania and Yale universities. From 1964 he collaborated with John Rauch, and from 1967 with Denise Scott Brown. In 1985, the office of Venturi, Rauch and Scott Brown received the "Firm of the Year" award of the American Institute of Architects.

Research courses and publications:
"Complexity and Contradiction in Architecture" (1966, re. ed. 1977); "Learning from Las Vegas" (with Denise Scott Brown and Steven Izenour, 1972); "A View from the Campidoglio" (with Scott Brown, 1985).

Otto Wagner
1841–1918

was born in Vienna, where he studied from 1857 at the Technical University. He attended the Royal Academy of Building in Berlin (1860/61) and continued his training with Siccardsburg and van der Nüll at the Academy of Fine Arts in Vienna (1861–63), where he succeeded Carl von Hasenauer as professor in 1894. In 1890 he was commissioned to renovate urban planning in Vienna, and supervised the building of the city railway.

Principal buildings and projects:
synagogue, Budapest 1868; house on the Graben, Vienna 1894; blocks of rented flats, Vienna (linke Wienzeile) 1898/99; buildings for the Stadtbahn, Vienna 1894–97; church on the Steinhof, Vienna 1902–07; post office savings bank, Vienna 1903–06; Ministry of War 1908; university library 1910–14; Wagner villa 1912.

Lois Welzenbacher
1889–1955

was born in Munich. He served a bricklayer's apprenticeship, learned technical drawing and attended the Vienna School of Arts and Crafts. From 1912 he studied architecture with Friedrich von Thiersch and Theodor Fischer in Munich. In 1918 he opened a studio in Innsbruck. In 1929 he was appointed director of town planning in Plauen. His house in the Blütenstrasse, Munich, was destroyed in 1943, and he moved to Absam, in Tirol. In 1947 he succeeded Peter Behrens as professor at the Academy of Fine Arts in Vienna.

Further important buildings:
administrative buildings of the electricity board, Innsbruck; Adam brewery, Innsbruck (all 1920–28); Oberjoch terrace hotel, Allgäu (1930–32); Schmucker house, Ruhpolding 1938: Siebel hangar, Halle an der Saale 1939–45.

Ludwig Wittgenstein
1889–1951

was born in Vienna, son of the prominent industrialist Karl Wittgenstein. He studied engineering in Berlin and Manchester, then philosophy at Cambridge. In 1913 he inherited a huge fortune, which he later (anonymously) gave away to needy writers and artists such as Trakl, Rilke and Kokoschka. In 1914 he built a wooden house in Skjolden/ Norway, to which he withdrew to live in total solitude. He took part in the First World War. By 1918, his main work, 'Tractatus logico-philosophicus' was completed, but it was not published until 1921. In 1920 he trained as a primary school teacher, and in 1925 published a dictionary for primary schools. Together with Paul Engelmann, he built a house in Vienna for his sister, Margaret Stonborough, in 1926. From 1929 he taught philosophy at Cambridge.

Frank Lloyd Wright
1867–1959

was born in Richland/Wisconsin. In
1885 he went to study at the University
of Madison. He worked as a draughtsman for the engineer A. Conover,
entered the office of Adler and Sullivan
in 1887–93. He built the Winslow
house, and in 1901 started his "prairie
houses". In 1909 he left his family and
went to Europe, returning to the USA in
1911, to begin building his house,
Taliesin I, which burned down in 1914,
to be replaced by Taliesin II. He spent
the years 1915–21 in Japan, and built
the Imperial Hotel in Tokyo. In 1925,
Taliesin II was destroyed by fire, and he
built Taliesin III. In 1932, he converted
his office into Taliesin College. His best-
known works date from 1936: Falling-
water (Kaufmann house), Johnson Wax
Company offices, start of the "Usonian"
houses. The Guggenheim Museum was
built in 1956–59.

Dominikus Zimmermann
1685–1766

was born in Wessobrunn. A stuccoer by
trade, he spent the years 1708–16 in
Füssen am Lech, and 1716–53 in Landsberg am Lech, always remaining a
"country master-builder". He worked
together with his brother Johann Baptist
Zimmermann, a fresco-painter.
Principal works:
Maria Medingen, near Dillingen on the
Danube 1718–25; St. John's church in
Landsberg am Lech; Liebfrauenkirche,
Günzburg on the Danube 1736; Stein-
hausen 1727–31; pilgrimage church
"Die Wies", 1745–54 – his main work;
beside the church he built his own
house, where he lived from 1753 until
his death.

Sources

Abbreviations of contributors' names

T. B. for Tim Brengelmann
W. G. for Winfried Glasmann
V. H. for Volker Heid
B. H. for Birgitta Heid
M. J. for Martin Jobst
R. K. for Robert Kammergruber
M. K. for Manfred Kovatsch
F. K. for Friedrich Kurrent
S. M. for Scarlet Munding
F. P. for Franz Peter
B. S. for Barbara Schelle
A. S. for Andreas Sternecker
F. W. for Franz Wimmer

During the years 1973–1996, the construction of the scale models was supervised by the following assistants of Professor Friedrich Kurrent in the Department of Interior Design and Religious Building at the Technical University in Munich:
Peter Weise, Michael Gaenssler, Rüdiger Möller, Franz Putschögl, Boris Podrecca, Klaus Wabnitz, Walter Voss, Horst Hambrusch, Nikolaus Schuster, Sepp Horn, Andreas Kampik, Franz Peter, Johannes Zeininger, Reinhard Engelbrecht, Martin Jobst, Manfred Felix, Ulrich Jonas, Franz Wimmer, Volker Heid, Scarlet Mundig, Winfried Glasmann, Tim Brengelmann, Barbara Schelle.
The models of the houses by Rudolph Schindler were supervised by Manfred Kovatsch.

Secretariat: Helag Becker
Workshop supervisor: Wolfgang Wannieck

Photographs for the catalogue:
Photography archives, Architecture Museum, Munich: Barbara Schulze, Gabi Winter
Photography archives, Technical University, Munich: Ulrich Benz, Albert Scharger

Photographs of the models: Franz Wimmer

In addition, plans and illustrations were taken from:

Gunnar Asplund (Holmdahl, Lind, Ödeen) Stockholm 1950; Hans Döllgast, "Häuser zeichnen", Ravensburg 1957; plan of Theodor Fischer's house, Architecture Museum, Munich; Josef Frank, catalogue, Academy of Applied Arts, Vienna 1981; E.A. Plischke, "Vom Menschlichen im Neuen Bauen", Vienna 1969; Rudolf Schindler, catalogue Villa Stuck, M. Kovatsch, Munich 1986; Otto Wagner, "Das Werk des Architekten", O. A. Graf, Vienna 1985; Lois Welzenbacher, "Architekturmodelle der TU München und der Universität Innsbruck", Innsbruck 1990; F. L. Wright, "Falling Water", New York 1978; Türk Evi, Sedad Hakki Eldem, 1984; Rölöve 1, Istanbul 1968; Le Corbusier, "Œuvre complète", Willy Boesinger, Zurich 1937; "De Stijl en de Europese Architectuur", The Hague 1986, Adolf Feulner, "Bayerisches Rokoko", Munich 1923; Robert Örley, catalogue, Architektur Zentrum Vienna; Peter Nigst 1996, model photographs, Lannerstraße Kilian Mattltsch, Vienna.

The portraits of the architects were taken from:

"Möbeldesign", Sembach, Leuthäuser, Gössel, Cologne 1990; "Architektur des 20. Jahrhunderts", Leuthäuser, Gössel, Cologne 1990; "Barockkirchen zwischen Donau und Alpen", Norbert Lieb, Munich, 1953; "Bauhaus", H. M. Wingler, Bramsche 1975; "Hans Döllgast", catalogue TU Munich 1987; "Theodor Fischer", Rudolf Pfister, Munich 1968; "Josef Frank", catalogue, Academy of Applied Arts, Vienna 1981; "C. Holzmeister", catalogue, Academy of Applied Arts, Vienna 1982; "Adolf Loos", Rukschcio, Schachel, Salzburg 1982; "K. Melnikov", F. Starr, New Jersey 1978; "D. Zimmermann", Carl Lamb, Die Wies 1964; "Asplund", Caldenby, Hultin, Stockholm 1985; "A. Lurçat", Œuvres récents, Paris 1961; "Otto Bartning", Bredow, Lerch, Darmstadt 1983.

Illustration credits